Healing
Narratives

Healing Narratives

Women Writers Curing Cultural Dis-Ease

Gay Wilentz

Rutgers University Press

New Brunswick, New Jersey, and London

Library of Congress Cataloging-in-Publication Data

Wilentz, Gay Alden, 1950–
    Healing narratives : women writers curing cultural dis-ease
/ Gay Wilentz.
        p. cm.
    Includes bibliographical references (p.) and index.
    ISBN 0–8135–2865–8 (cloth : alk.) — ISBN 0–8135–2866–6
(pbk : alk.)
        1. American fiction—Women authors—History and criticism.
    2. Literature and mental illness—United States—History—20th
    century. 3. Women and literature—United States—History—20th
    century. 4. American fiction—20th century—History and criticism.
    5. Brodber, Erna. Jane and Louisa will soon come home. 6. Sinclair,
    Jo., 1913–. Wasteland. 7. Silko, Leslie, 1948–. Ceremony. 8. Bambara,
    Toni Cade. Salt eaters. 9. Hulme, Keri. Bone people. 10. Mentally ill
    in literature. 11. Ethnicity in literature. 12. Healing in literature.
    13. Narration (Rhetoric) I. Title.
    PS374.M44 W55 2000
    813'.509353—dc21

                                                            00–028252

British Cataloging-in-Publication data for this book is available from the
British Library

Manufactured in the United States of America

Dedication

This book is dedicated to the stories we tell to keep us healthy and sane, to a potential blending of tales from traditional cultures and the contemporary world, and to the collective memory of my people.

Finally, this book is dedicated to the memory of Toni Cade Bambara and Flora Nwapa and to my female ancestors, especially my grandmothers, Lena and Pearl, and my mother, Stevie Sheresky.

Contents

Acknowledgments   ix

Introduction: Women Writers and Wellness Narratives   *1*

Part One
African-Based Healings
---

1 Reclaiming Residual Culture: African Heritage as
   Caribbean Cures in Erna Brodber's *Jane and Louisa
   Will Soon Come Home*   *27*

2 A Laying on of Hands: African American Healing
   Strategies in Toni Cade Bambara's *The Salt Eaters*   *53*

Part Two
Indigenous Curative Methods
---

3 The Novel as Chant: Leslie Marmon Silko's
   Ceremony as Ceremonial Healing   *81*

4 Becoming the Instruments of Change: Maori
   Healing Visions in Keri Hulme's *the bone people*   *109*

Part Three
Cultural Linkages

5 When the Psychiatrist Is Part of the Cure:
   Healing the "Sick Jewish Soul" in Jo Sinclair/Ruth
   Seid's *Wasteland*   *141*

   Conclusion: Toward (W)Holistic Healing   *169*

                    Notes   173
                References   185
                    Index   197

Acknowledgments

My first acknowledgment is to various places I have lived, the people I have met, the unique cultures that I have been a part of, from West and Southern Africa to South and Central America, and to their "cosmovisión" that has informed the writing of this book. Second, I want to thank my husband and traveling partner, John Sabella, who has always managed to include me in his work throughout the world.

In writing a book of this scope, there are many people to thank who have influenced my thinking and opened me up to other ways of knowing. I thank my friend René Ozaeta for our many discussions and for his major contribution to the inception of this book, but I would also like to thank the curanderas I met in Uxactun, Guatemala, as well as Barbara Hernandez and other traditional healers in Belize. Moreover, conversations with friends and colleagues at conferences, in Flores, Guatemala, throughout Belize, and in Eastern North Carolina, where memories remain of the Igbos who flew back and of African traditions, helped shape the design of this book. A very special thanks goes to Erna Brodber, who spent time with me speaking about her work and mine and invited me to her beautiful African Diaspora Center in the hills of Jamaica, and to Mervyn Alleyne, who showed me his roots of Jamaican culture.

Because this work called for expertise in so many different areas, I have many people to thank at East Carolina University, University College of Belize, and other academic venues. At ECU, I'd like to thank Peter Lichstein and Dona Harris at the Medical School; Ellen Arnold, Sandy Tawake, Holly Matthews, Seodial Deena, Heidi Jacobs, Bob Segal and David Gabbard for their comments and thoughts; and both the English Department and the School of Arts and Science for time off to write. At UCB, I'd like to thank Dorian Barrow, Eve Aird, Javier Reyes, Wawat Napatha, Alex Vega, and Joann Griffin for their input and thoughts on healing, as well as Kevin Geban for just being there. Special thanks also to

Joseph Palacio and Zee Edgell for our conversations. There are many others, but I'd like to also mention some colleagues and friends at other institutions that have helped formulate my thought on this work: Karla Holloway, Joyce Pettis, Myriam Chancy, Jane Marcus, Lemuel Johnson, Pat Powell, Suzanne Poirier, Ann Folwell Stanford, Paula Morgan, Paul Lauter, Angeletta Reyes, Danny Dawson Naana Banyiwa-Horne, Arlene Elder, Marie Umeh, and Ada Azodo. Most valuable are my students, past and present, whose discussions inside and out of class helped me tease out these ideas. A particular thank-you goes to my fall 1999 Ethnic Studies class. Thanks also to my former students and now colleagues Karen Jones, Kermit Leggett, Mark Ferri, Wendy Rountree, Reginald Watson, Sharon Raynor, Todd Lovett, Joe Campbell, Doug Smith, Clay Deanhardt, as well as graduate assistants and friends: Cathy Crooks, Gabrielle Brant, Mel de Jesus, Danielle Lewis, Washella Turner, Jenee Hulin, Beth Harmon, Shau-Ann Longsworth, Janine Roverol, Ana Cowo, Noel Novelo, Carla Pastor, Jenny Vickers, and Melissa Edwards.

Special thanks go to my friends who have helped me along the way, both intellectually and emotionally: Kathleen Cusick, Michael Bassman, Bucky Whaley and Marie Farr, Irline François, Maureen Shea, Robin Martin, Lillian Robinson, Judy Lucas, Julie Fay, Janice Periquet, Carl Campbell, Jonathan Landeck, Kathy Mintz, Bill Roberts, Lori Munch, Selden Durgun, Carol Castellano, Ana Sisnett, Sandy Shattuck, and particulary to Alan Wald for his constant support and encouragement as well as to Gloria Chance for our discussions about the possibility of moving this healing project forward. Finally, thanks to all of my extended families, the Wilentzes, the Royces, and the Sabellas, particularly my aunt Norma Hess, my father, Warren Wilentz, and my father-in-law, Ed Sabella; my brothers, Wayne and Michael; sisters-in-law, Connie, Lisa, and Beronica; brothers-in-law, Jack and Ray; cousins Jimmy, Amy, Sankey, and Connie, and to the next generations: Charley and the Sabella girls, baby Rubén, Betsy and Jennie, Peter and Maggie, Jason and Derrick, Samantha and the Baime boys, Amy, Serena and John, Emma and Tyler, Zoë, Ellen and Alice, Andrew and Adam, and my most wonderful niece, Dana.

A final thanks goes to Leslie Mitchner, who saw what this book could be, Adaya Henis, and all the rest of the helpful people at Rutgers University Press, bringing me back to a Wilentz family tradition of involvement with the Old Raritan.

Gay Wilentz
Belize City, Belize

Healing
Narratives

Introduction

Women Writers
and Wellness
Narratives

A few years ago, I took time off from teaching for a stay in Guatemala, where I began the book that I am presenting now. In some of the works I was reading and teaching I had noticed a trope that appeared to challenge conventional notions of ethnicity and health. At this time, I also met René Ozaeta, an artist of the Mayan world, who noted, in connection with the disappearance of the Maya, that cultures themselves can be ill. Ozaeta's insight is uncannily reinforced by a cryptic but telling comment made by Sigmund Freud in a 1915 paper, "Some Character-Types Met with in Psychoanalytic Work." In examining what one type, "the Exception," perceives as "unjust injury inflicted on them in childhood," he notes that this injury can come from many sources, one being a protracted illness (320). Then, almost as an afterthought, he adds that he does not "propose to go into the obvious analogy between deformities of character resulting in protracted sickliness in childhood and the behavior of whole nations whose past history has been full of suffering" (321). What Freud alludes to here, but does not expand upon, is Ozaeta's notion that one can be culturally ill—in other words, that there is a relationship between individual psychosis and ethnicity, particularly in a despised group whose "history is full of suffering."

Western medicine has only recently addressed this relationship of culture to health, beyond notions of diet and genes. Focus has been primarily on a somatic, biotechnical model—the treat-

1

ment of physical ailments—except what has been termed "mental" illness, reinforcing the mind/body split. This fragmented approach to the health of the individual and the community has been questioned in contemporary times by a return to earlier worldview, continued into the modern age through alternative systems and traditional practices (even when these practices are considered "New Age").[1] Moreover, despite changes in the practice of medicine, influenced by these movements, the interrelatedness of our diseased planet to the prospect of dis-ease in our lives still falls outside the ideas held by the medical establishment. In her essay "Healing the Planet/Healing Ourselves," Deena Metzger warns: "We are suffering from global fatigue and despair, from cultural self-loathing, from national suicides, all of which leads to serious increases in attacks against life itself" (199). According to Metzger, there may be a connection between the wars perpetrated against our global neighbors and the "war" on cancer—high technology both—and individual disease may be linked to a world filled with communities suffering from, among other things, cultural self-loathing. Not only are our ills individual, cultural, national, and global; there are interconnections between all of these and the diseases we contract, from disorders of the mental/physical self to the breakdown of the body/mind. Metzger compels us to look at our own personal dis-ease (she deals with women-centered breast cancer) in relation to the global sickness that appears to be over-taking the planet (pollution, environmental poisons, high-tech wars, violence, plaguelike diseases such as AIDS and cancer). One aspect of this personal/global dis-ease, according to the authors examined in this study, is marginalized within the construct of Western individuality—the concept of being culturally ill. This link, to which Metzger, who is Jewish, alludes in her statement on "cultural self-loathing" but does not specifically address, must be part of the global healing of our planet.

But how does one start? Metzger centers her discussion on women's healing powers and the creation of thought-narratives of wellness, specifically in terms of cancer as a symbol of our lifestyle diseases. Taking this notion of visualization and alternative ways of thinking through healing and disease a step further, there are sustained written narratives that address at least one of the problems Metzger poses, that of cultural self-loathing and the disorders symptomatic of it: nervous breakdowns, alienation, depression, and the physical ramifications of these and other emotional illnesses. In reading and teaching women's novels that could easily be described as wellness narratives, I began to perceive a pattern in the work of writers from diverse cultures/ethnic minorities when they wrote about these cultural disorders, prompting a series of questions: Why are women, in particular, writing about healing in this way? Why is the novel their apparently preferred form of expression? What makes women from oppressed social groups existing within the hegemony of a dominant culture write about the traditional cultural base of what is often called "alternative healing"? These writers appear to be exploring a reexamination of women's traditional role of custodian of the culture in order to develop a community-based model for healing the culturally ill through their writings. These writings move beyond relating solely personal health to our global condition. As Metzger intimates, they address head-on the diseases that come from our "cultural self-loathing" and then begin the process of a healing discourse to cure the culturally ill. For people from oppressed cultures, this means reclaiming personal wellness through self-esteem and the "discredited" knowledge (to quote Toni Morrison) of a culture's healing practices.

My purpose in this book is to examine women writers from diverse ethnic backgrounds as cultural workers who aim, through their writings, to heal self and community from these socially constructed diseases. The novels span a geographical space from the United States and the Caribbean to the Pacific Rim. Yet in each novel the protagonist moves from a state of mental/physical disease toward wellness through a reconnection with his/her cultural traditions and the healing practices of that culture. In the African-based cultures of African American Toni Cade Bambara and Jamaican Erna Brodber, in the indigenous worlds of Laguna Pueblo Leslie Marmon Silko and Maori Keri Hulme, and in the Jewish traditions of Jo Sinclair/Ruth Seid, these women writers produce wellness narratives that explore the role of woman as healer to cure cultural dis-ease.

Medical anthropologists have investigated the various healing practices of the cultures they research and have demonstrated how culture affects the way in which individuals perceive illness and good health; women scholars in various disciplines, as well as writers of popular self-help books, have begun to reclaim the historic role of women in the healing arts. The focus of this study, however, is the juxtaposition of these two healing modes in relation to literary praxis as part of a holistic way to cure dis-ease in oneself and one's community. Terry Eagleton has defined the novel as "consolation" (185); however, the works examined here move beyond that notion to the novel as healing discourse. Many ethnic women writers explore the curing of cultural self-loathing and collective self-hate within a storytelling ceremony. The writers in this study (re)envision the novel as a literary formulation of traditional chants and talk stories used in the process of curing the culturally ill. Through this process, the denigrated healing traditions of suppressed worldviews become the basis for repairing fractured communities and dis-eased cultures.

In seeking to bridge the two modes of alternative healing, especially in relation to dominant medical practice, I have found it too easy to slip into the same set of binary oppositions that these healing modes seek to displace. Binary modes of thinking have produced oppositions such as traditional/modern, magic/science, and health/disease, in addition to the most persistent: male/female. These oppositions have structured and informed medical thinking and practice in the twentieth century. Traditional practices by both men and women, within a worldview inclusive of personal, spiritual, and community-based healing resist these oppositions and seek to incorporate knowledge and learning from different sources (although, like any paradigm, culture-based healing can also rigidify as it is reified by participants). Since our own language is defined by difference, and a kind of exclusion structured by technology and its masculinist definitions, it is often hard to avoid the same polarities—an essentialist mode that privileges pre- over postcolonial society, traditional over modern medicine, magic over science. This, of course, merely reverses the original opposition rather than displacing it. One way of breaking down these binary oppositions is through creative fiction, in this case the novel. Precisely because the language of novels is metaphorical and interpretive, it allows a displacement of these oppositions so that a healing discourse can be attempted and even achieved. Reconstructing ways of knowing through a healing discourse may lead to a better understanding of these socially constructed diseases.

In *Women's Ways of Knowing*, Mary Field Belenky et al. speak of a method, "constructed knowledge," which, they say, women have practiced historically but have been educated out of, and are now beginning to return to, despite external societal structures that frame binary thinking: "Constructed knowledge . . . [is] an effort to reclaim the self by attempting to integrate knowledge . . . , weaving the strands of rational and emotive thought and of integrating objective and subjective knowing. . . . During the transition into a new way of knowing, there is an impetus to allow self back into the process of knowing, to confront the pieces of the self that may be experienced as fragmented and contradictory" (134–136).

Allowing the "fragmented and contradictory" into the discourse of knowledge has been at the heart of women's and traditional ways of healing, as reflected in the interplay of literary language. Trained as an academic critic rather than as a creative writer, I am limited by language and method in my attempt to produce the knowing discourse I find imperative for exploring the complexities of understanding cultural illness and healing. However, as creative artists, these five authors resist this linguistic stranglehold through their wellness narratives. They transform binary modes of thinking in both form and content, and create stories to begin this healing discourse—one in which critics and readers alike can participate.

One other concern that needs to be addressed at this point is the question of culture. The overarching vision of all the works analyzed is that to be well at all one needs to be well culturally. In each novel, the protagonist returns to the healing traditions of his/her own culture to cure dis-ease. But is the concept of "one's own culture" overdetermined? Raymond Williams defines "culture" in relation to the "variability of its shaping forces": "The idea of a fundamental social process which shapes specific and distinct 'ways of life' is the effective origin of the *comparative* social sense of 'culture' and its now necessary plural 'cultures'" (*Marxism* 17). In his examination of culture and interactive "plural" cultures, Williams demonstrates how alternative cultures exist both within and in opposition to the dominant culture. He states further that the variety of cultural practices from competing groups remain despite an effective dominant culture's process of identifying among traditions the "selective tradition" always passed off as "the significant past." Williams states: "But always selectivity is the point: . . . certain meanings and practices are chosen for emphasis, certain other meanings and practices are neglected and excluded" (*Problems* 39). Nevertheless, alternative traditions and practices survive whether they are residual (from previous social formations) or emergent (new practices, often related to residual structure—New Age medicine is an example of this). As Williams notes, talking about and identifying culture is a complex issue, not only between the dominant culture and competing alternative/traditional systems, but within the hegemony and those systems as well. Many contemporary scholars of cultural studies have noted the interrelatedness of varying cultures within a society; moreover, often there are disagreements as to what makes up the boundaries of cultures as well.[2] Culture, defined this way, is not static; in a postmodern age, we are painfully aware of the inter/cross/trans aspect of cultural identity. So an individual's subject position in juxtaposition to one's ethnic group is always a tenuous matter, dialectic at best. The notion put forth in Goldberg and Krausz's *Jewish Identity*, that the concept of ethnicity, in this case Jewishness, has changed in the postmodern era, and therefore is a linking of "descent" (who my ancestors are) and "assent" (what I choose to call myself), within the context of my historical circumstances (my physical attributes and familial identification, linked to how I am perceived by the society around me). Therefore, as this book demonstrates through an examination of particular ethnic groups and identity markers, the concept of culture as defined by this study expands out from descent, but is not limited to assent.

So what does this mean in relation to the overarching concerns of these authors and this book? For the five writers—Brodber, Bambara, Silko, Hulme, and Sinclair (Seid)—as well as for many of the other authors mentioned in this study, the healing process at the center of the texts is grounded in the suppressed traditions of their specific culture group. Although one could read this ostensibly linear relationship as an essentialist notion of self and culture, it is clearly a much more interactive process, since these texts resist a linear notion of what culture is. For example, Toni Cade Bambara, in *The Salt Eaters*, centers her text on the African healing traditions embedded in African American communities; however, her overwhelming wellness narrative includes other healing acts as well—from psychiatry to Asian and Native American practices. In another example, one of Keri Hulme's main characters in *the bone people* is a young boy of European heritage who is healed by a blending of Western and Maori medicine, complicating the linear formation identified in the conception of being healed through your own culture. The whole conceptualization of Native American traditions in our postmodern societies is clearly overladen with both Anglo and Hispanic colonial inheritances. I suggest these complications to displace the sense of a unified self in terms of cultural healing. As this book demonstrates, being well personally is associated with being in touch with oneself and one's heritage, however complicated. Whatever has been excluded, effaced, or submerged through hegemonic dominant cultural practices must be revived to heal self and community. This notion of wellness is at the base of these narratives as they lay bare the biases and prejudices that cloud our path toward health, and revive other ways of knowing that have been discredited by the "anonymous authority that confronts us in the pronouncements of science" (Gadamer 3).

This book addresses three areas relating to the wellness narratives: 1) the cultural dimension of the healing process in relation to both Western and alternative modes of medicine and the complexity of that aspect of the human condition; 2) the role of women as healers in various traditional and contemporary cultures, and the ways these women writers have reclaimed that tradition; and 3) literature as it complements the traditional healing arts, particularly the curative power of the word, in relation to the unique way women writers have adapted cultural healing ceremonies in their texts.

The Cultural Dimensions of Healing

At the beginning of *Philosophical Hermeneutics*, Hans-Georg Gadamer posits what he considers the central question of the "modern age": "It is the question of how our natural view of the world—the experience of the world that we have as we simply live out our lives—is related to the unassailable and anonymous authority that confronts us in the pronouncements of science" (3). Gadamer raises this question to challenge the binary opposition between scientific knowledge and the hermeneutic tradition, of which literature is a part; however, this question also exposes polarities in the concept of science itself. We can perceive science, especially medical science developed in the twentieth century, as a hegemonic structure that regulates the processes of medical practice and excludes other systems of knowledge and healing. Although, as Williams notes, in any hegemonic cultural system there are always alternative and oppositional practices, the dominant structure, in this case, the biomedical model, is what Williams identifies as "the selective tradition" (*Problems* 39).

Arthur Kleinman, in his study *The Illness Narratives: Suffering, Healing and the Human Condition*, comments specifically that the biomedical model of healing (the selective tradition), despite advances in the control of physical disease, "has turned its back on the purpose of medicine" (254). For Kleinman, there is a clear dichotomy between this model and the "broader biopsychosocial model" for primary care that he and others propose (6). This difference reflects the opposition exposed in the women's wellness narratives analyzed in this study:

> For members of Western societies the body is a discrete entity, a thing, an "it," machinelike and objective, separate from thought and emotion. For members of many non-Western societies, the body is an open system linking social relations to the self, a vital balance between interrelated elements in a holistic cosmos. . . . The body-self is not a secularized private domain of the individual person but an organic part of a sacred, sociocentric world, a communication system involving exchanges with others (including the divine). (11)

In response to what he sees as a turning away from the purpose of medicine, Kleinman and others have begun to incorporate other approaches to healing, developing a paradigm shift to include all the linking aspects of a person's being in healing, resisting the mind/body split inherent in the philosophies of Western culture since the seventeenth century.

In viewing medical practice in this way, the importance of a cultural dimension in healing is evident. As Peter Lichstein comments in "Rootwork from a Clinician's Perspective," even allopathic medical practice is based on certain cultural perspectives: "Like all belief systems, the biotechnical approach is value-laden and culturally determined" (101). Like Kleinman, Lichstein also argues for a more holistic approach as a way for the patient to connect to the "power of medical therapies to restore homeostatic balance and health" (115). As the field of medical anthropology has developed, this important aspect of physical and societal well-being is being brought to the forefront. According to Cecil G. Helman in *Culture, Health and Illness*, anthropologists have pointed out that "in all human societies beliefs and practices relating to ill-health are a central feature of the culture." Furthermore: "The values and customs associated with ill-health are part of the wider culture, and cannot be studied in isolation from it. One cannot understand how people react to illness, death or other misfortune without an understanding of the type of culture they have grown up in or acquired—that is, of the 'lens' through which they are perceiving and interpreting their world" (7).

To students of cultural studies, these pronouncements may be self-evident; however, within the biotechnical model of medical practice, the relationship of culture to the patient's "physical" disease has not been considered an objective category until very recently. Anthropological studies have tended to address merely how different cultural groups deal with diseases, rather than exploring the cultural component of specific diseases themselves and of overall health and well-being.

In addition to failing to address a cultural aspect of health and identity, doctors and medical practitioners have difficulty accepting certain aspects of the cultural dimension of healing, such as those practices considered outside the realm of science. For lack of a better term, we might call them the spiritual aspects of healing, those areas not easily quantified by scientific method.[3] Both Kleinman and Lichstein acknowledge a patient's belief in these extrascientific occurrences, but neither clearly accepts these practices (like the rootworking Lichstein describes) as an actual part of a holistic medical system. Within a scientific worldview, one can aim to heal the whole person, but what happens when the spiritual aspect of holistic healing is rejected as part of the healing process? In *Planet Medicine: From Stone Age Shamanism to Post-Industrial Healing*, Richard Grossinger identifies this restriction: "Even in its most humanitarian application the medical establishment is limited and conditioned by the cultural beliefs and taboos within which it operates" (15). Because of the taboo against integrating the spiritual (except for allowing a space for Christian "prayer"), doctors part company with much traditional healing. Practitioners commonly use words, chants, and ceremonies as the tools that have the power to heal, linking their treatments to the spirit world. At this point, to use Williams's theoretical foundation, alternative practice becomes oppositional.

In *African Philosophy, Culture, and Traditional Medicine*, African philosopher M. Akin Makinde agrees that the theories and practice of medicine have a cultural dimension, and he grounds his discussion in African traditional healing systems, specifically Yoruba. (The diasporic versions of these practices are examined in the chapters on Bambara and Brodber.) Makinde notes that the dismissive way dominant medical practitioners have of calling the "supernatural" aspects of African healing "magical" has led to a value-laden distinction of scientific versus nonscientific. With wry humor, Makinde uncovers both the tautology and the binary opposition in this presumption when he counters: "Although a scientist may argue that it is pretty obvious that there are good scientific reasons to prefer science over magic, presumably, there would be good magical reasons to prefer magic to science in certain cases and circumstances" (92). A doctor himself, Makinde understands the advances in Western medicine, but he also sees, as do Kleinman and Lichstein, that the biotechnical model of medicine has its own belief system and has left out what it cannot explain. He takes this a step further than the other two by commenting on Western's medicine's failure to account for or investigate traditional medicine, contending that an integration of the two systems would allow a better understanding of the possible ways to heal the whole person as well as a fuller comprehension of the human condition.

Makinde's work points to issues encoded in these women writers' wellness narratives. If there is a major cultural dimension to healing, and there are non-Western cultures that accept the supernatural as part of the healing process, then the binary opposition of science versus magic needs to be displaced so that one can be well in the fullest sense of the word. Makinde's philosophy presents evidence to substantiate the possibilities the writers describe in their wellness narratives. Through their texts, these writers are part of a process aimed to tease Western medical practice into a paradigm shift, uncovering from all sides the limitations of the biotechnical model of medicine.

Makinde, as noted above, bases his argument on African healing strategies. In another example, Kleinman notes that in the Navajo world, for example, "bodily complaints are also moral problems: they are icons of disharmony in social relationships and in the cultural ethos" (12). As is evident in the chapter on Silko's *Ceremony*, Laguna Pueblo and Navajo healing practices are based on restoring balance, not merely between the individual and the community but also in relation to the natural world. Moreover, as illustrated by Hulme's *the bone people*, the four components of Maori health—the spiritual (*te taha wairua*); the psychic (*te taha hinegaro*); the bodily (*te taha tinana*); and the familial (*te taha whanau*)—are integrated to produce a healthy person. In each of these examples, the cultural base of healing strategies is emphasized. The practitioner's healing of the unwell individual cannot be understood in isolation but must be completed in context of culture, even when it may be cross-, trans-, or intercultural.

Still, these wellness narratives are not directed solely at medical practitioners, but also at the patients, the culturally ill, as well as the larger community, the readers. The texts speak to a community of readers often coming from diverse backgrounds—ones they were born into or acquired, raising again the linked notions of descent and assent—who must relate to those cultures in order to be well. These wellness narratives begin to bridge the gap between disease and health, displace the binary oppositions identified in the mind/body split of allopathic medical practice, and begin a process of cultural healing through what Belenky et al. call "constructed knowledge."

Women as Healers

In the beginning of *Medicine Women, Curanderas, and Women Doctors*, Perrone, Stockel, and Krueger call "scientificism" a bias (9) and note that "the inclusion of psychological and spiritual forces in healing is a major shift from the AMA model, which disregards the spiritual-social factor involved in the causes and cures of illnesses" (14). The model of conventional medicine restricts the relationship of healer to healee, and this limitation excludes both the role of the male healers (whose traditions have been lost in their evolution as "doctor") as well as the vibrant position of women in the healing arts. *Medicine Women* examines the position of women healers today, including doctors, although they limits their nonmedical investigations to the Native American medicine women and Hispanic curanderas, who base their healing on spiritual Catholicism syncretized from similar Amerindian traditions throughout the Americas.[4] "A medicine woman's power comes through her spirituality evidenced in the healing ceremonies she performs" (9). These authors make the explicit connection between Amerindian cultural healings and women healers, emphasizing the importance of the healing ritual. Although the wellness narratives in this study are specifically examined as healing ceremonies in the next section, this part of the introduction probes the similarities between women's and cultural healing, the role of woman as healer in pre-Western and residual traditional cultures, and women's position in the emergent/oppositional/alternative healing practices that resists a restrictive biomedical model.

In her introduction to *The Women's Book of Healing*, Diane Stein comments that women's healing, with its emphasis on "the unity of body, emotions, mind and spirit, on the seen and the unseen," is clearly an alternative to what she calls "patriarchal medicine, with its fragmentation of body and spirit" (xviii). It is relevant to note here that this idea of "patriarchal" medicine is Western in concept, since earlier traditions would have clearly defined roles for both men and women healers, as exemplified by the male healers explored in the novels, such as Betonie in *Ceremony* and the kaumatua in *the bone people*.

According to Jeanne Achterberg in *Woman as Healer*, the practice of women healers is "likely to reflect a broad sense of healing that aspires to the wholeness or harmony within the self, the family, and the global community" (4). Achterberg significantly comments that this approach to health is "antithetical to the cosmological structure that binds the Western world" (3), while other cultures "more adequately reflect the positive characteristics of the feminine aspects of healing" (2). The binarisms of Western masculinist thinking have separated male and female healers into male doctors and female caregivers, so that the whole concept of traditional healing has now been conceived as feminized; therefore, contemporary women healers, both Western-trained like Achterberg and alternatively educated like Stein, link this rather essentialized notion of the feminine to specific traditional models from pre- and non-Western cultures, in which women fulfilled their role as healers. However, like Stein and others, including the male doctors cited above, Achterberg demands a paradigm shift, so as to rebalance the notions of health within the human condition: "In order for true progress—true healing in a global sense—Western cosmology must change" to allow a more fully realized concept of wellness (3).

In *Woman as Healer*, Achterberg focuses on the role of women in the healing arts and states definitively: "Women have always been healers. Cultural myths from around the world describe a time when only women knew the secrets of life and death, and therefore they could practice the magical art of healing" (1). Not only does this relegate the male healers' role to silence, but the folkloric tone of this sentence grates against the confines of scientific investigation as well as so-called objective Western history. However, Achterberg is responding to another binary opposition encoded in Western practice: history vs. myth. Much of the "herstory" of women's healing practices comes from this realm of legend and myth. The bias of historical scientism is linked to the patriarchal structures of modern medicine.[5] In other words, in another world, women (and men) were free to practice healing arts, not solely as alternative practice: "Since the vocation of healer, particularly, is associated with the sacred, and the healing beliefs of any culture directly reflects the nature of the gods, only in those times when the reigning deity has had a feminine, bisexual or androgenous nature have women been able to exercise the healing arts with freedom and power" (Achterberg, *Woman* 3).

The relationship of the spiritual essence of a culture to its healing arts is evident today in most women's writings about health. Stein comments that, however it is envisioned, women-based healing is connected to some form of spirituality; often there is a relationship to a goddess (surely we can inscribe in today's medicine a mirroring of a patriarchal god in the role of the physician). Stein also notes that these female deities were frequently associated with earlier "matriarchies" (21–22). Whether we accept this notion of matriarchy or the broader term, "matrifocal," women's healing conjoined both the maternal aspects of the female self and the spirituality of traditional cultures, in which traditional healers included both men and women. My language in exploring the parameters of what is presently called women's healing has been generalized up to this point; however, as I examine the wellness narratives of the writers in this study, the specifically culture-bound aspects of women's healing will be made clear. It is significant that the broad theoretical precepts of women's healing connect well with the tenets of traditional healing arts.[6] The holistic notion in women's healing that one cannot be well without a relationship to the spiritual self, family, and community resonates with the cultural dimension of healing examined in the first section of this introduction.

In *Woman as Healer*, Achterberg focuses explicitly on the changes of women's role in the healing arts in Western culture, especially in relation to the development of "experimental science." She supports her statements by citing Gerda Lerner's extensive study of women's history in regard to the rise of patriarchy/monotheism, exposing the binary oppositions that exist within the context of Western philosophy: "[By the Middle Ages], the view of the world became fixed, distinguished by 'setting apart of all pairs of opposites—male and female, life and death, true and false—as though they were absolutes in themselves and not merely aspects of the larger entity of life,'" (Lerner, quoted in Achterberg 13). These changes in Western societies as they developed, especially the oppositions of male/female and culture/nature, further isolated women from the healing art of medicine as it evolved within an "enlightened" scientific worldview. For in that transitional time in the seventeenth century, when women as a group become associated with the unscientific and so-called demonic aspects of the natural world, their healing powers were also both discredited and feared (this reaction mirrors attitudes toward traditional healing from oppressed/colonized cultures as well). As Achterberg notes, "Men feared—and tried to bar from the new scientific worldview—women's intuitive nature, as well as their strong sense of the inherent link between humanity and the earth" (*Woman* 64). In the case of women's role in contemporary health care, it is evident what happened to women healers after this major paradigm shift: Women were relegated to the most menial tasks in the healing profession, especially in the United States, where, for the most part, hegemonic allopathic medical practice is still sanctioned by the state.

In contemporary discourse on feminism, there is an underlying principle that women's culture is nurturing, communal, and closer to the natural world than the world of men. Juxtaposed to this view (since feminism is hardly a monolithic ideology/methodology) is a strong resistance to biological interpretations of gender categories: women as nature itself, somehow dominated and subdued by the mind of man. This tension in feminist thought has its origins in the rise of the Enlightenment, which identified men's superiority as resulting in part from the fact that women were closer to the earth and needed to be controlled for the advancement of civilization. This masculinist viewpoint is an ironic twist of earlier cultures' understanding of the role of women, as Achterberg notes: "Woman unfortunately was enslaved by the seventeenth century metaphor linking her to nature, instead of enthroned by it, as she had been much earlier" (*Woman* 103). Today we find ourselves replicating this kind of binary opposition, which is problematic either way. To return to Williams's notion of hegemony: As the medical establishment became entrenched and the role of male healers within a traditional context was effaced, the role of women healers was defined only through the limitations of allopathic medical practice, either within the system by their secondary roles as caregivers or in opposition to it in the realm of traditional or alternative medicine.

Women healers are presently a major force in the revitalization of the healing arts and in questioning dominant medical practices, which is even being challenged from within the ranks of the medical establishment. Not only are they looking back into the residual systems of their own cultures, they are crossing cultures to explore healing practices denied by the AMA and similar models in other countries.[7] As Stein, one of the major writers in this popular health movement, notes: "Individually and cross-culturally, women's healthy power-within skills and values, her lost, ignored and repressed knowledges are being re-learned, re-claimed and re-gained. . . . It's a re-turn to ancient (and present and future) women's healing roles . . . [and] a refusal of the medical patriarchal system's split between total power-over of the doctor and the total power-lessness and passivity of the patient" (xix–xx).

In resisting the secondary position to which women as patients and caregivers have been relegated to in the medical establishment, these practitioners often integrate another type of traditional healing, "oral medicine," as M. Akin Makinde calls it (92), linked to the power of the word. The healing discourse that comes out of this process is the focus of this book, and it is through that medium that the writers present these wellness narratives to heal the culturally ill. The next section explores literature's relationship to the healing arts, the importance of language as part of a cultural move toward health, and finally the healing process these writers take us through in their wellness narratives.

Literature as a Healing Art

In *Literary Theory: An Introduction*, Terry Eagleton expounds on what he sees as the psychological root of all narratives. He refers to Freud's *Beyond the Pleasure Principle* by describing "the first glimmering of narrative [as] the shortest story we can imagine: an object is lost, and then recovered. . . . "But even the most complex narratives can be read as variants on this model: the pattern of classical narrative is that an original settlement is disrupted and eventually restored. From this viewpoint, narrative is a source of consolation" (185). The notion that a narrative, in this case a historically specific form like a novel, can be a source of consolation, recovering what has been lost, is directly linked to the wellness narratives I identify in this study. These writers have chosen the novel as the form for these wellness narratives because a novel is a sustained narrative, as opposed to a short story, for example. Furthermore, even nonlinear novels tend to be representational, developing the oral medicines of storytelling rituals to include the power of the word as well as the context of the story itself. Finally, the contemporary novel contain within its genre the freedom to reconstruct reality as a counterhegemonic tool through magical realism and other stylistic innovations and language appropriations, not available within the restrictions of a genre such as autobiography. Therefore, as in most sustained narratives, what is lost in these novels is myriad and complex, but what the author attempts to recover through the novel's healing discourse is the health of the cultural self and community, at least on a metaphorical level.

The use of literary metaphors in medicine is a age-old tradition, but recently, as the medical paradigm shifts, it has received greater attention.[8] According to the authors of *Bridges of the Bodymind*, one of the first treatments for disease was imagery, originating in Egyptian hermetic principles: "Ill health, it was believed, could be overcome by visualizing good health . . . or by envisioning a healing God" (Achterberg and Lawlis 27). Language has always been a part of the healing process, even when it has been used to obscure meaning through euphemism or jargon. Grossinger, in *Planet Medicine*, notes the significance of language in comprehending our good health and disease: "We assume we know disease by the feel of the internal organs of our body. But that is not true. . . . [It] must first be brought to the surface, as concepts, as language with one's self, and, finally, as language with the society and its doctors" (16). One might say that we don't even know how we feel without language, and metaphorical language at that. The body's language needs to be decoded through image and symbol, whether by the person who is ill or by the healer; in traditional systems, both work together. The discourse of healing, including medical language, because it must be structured around symbol and image, metaphor and simile (describing how you feel, what the pain is like), is primarily literary.

In *The Illness Narratives*, Kleinman makes these general statements more explicit concerning medical practice. In the dialogue between doctor and patient, the patient's "tale of complaints becomes the text that is to be decoded by the practitioner cum diagnostician" (9). For Kleinman, "Symptom and context can be interpreted as symbol and text. . . . The text is laden with potential meanings, but in the symptom-symbol only one or a few become effective" (42). In the discourse of patient and practitioner, meaning is exposed. Furthermore, Kleinman suggests, the illness complaint itself is an enigmatic narrative: It is hoped that something lost, in this case one's health, can be regained through the doctor's interpretation: "Thus, patients order their experience of illness—what it means to them and to significant others—as personal narratives. The illness narrative is a story the patient tells. . . . The plot lines, core metaphors, and rhetorical devices that structure the illness narrative are drawn from cultural and personal

models for arranging experiences in meaningful ways and for ef-
fectively communicating those meanings" (49).

Unfortunately, Kleinman notes, doctors with medical school
education "are not trained to be self-reflective interpreters of distinctive systems of meanings. . . . They have been taught to regard
with suspicion patients' illness narratives" (17). This suspicion of
the doctors was forcefully documented in Charlotte Perkins
Gilman's well-known narrative "The Yellow Wallpaper," in which
her narrative was silenced by husband and doctor alike. So, despite the importance of narrative interpretation within medicine
and the healing process, many practitioners throughout the development of the allopathic model had neither the inclination nor
the education to develop the necessary skill. Furthermore, the move
in the mid-twentieth century toward more specialized, techno-
logical skills added to an already serious lack of communication
between patient and doctor. Departments of medical humanities
are now attempting to bridge that gap in communication, lost in
the mechanical treatment of humans and so integral to modes of
traditional healing.

Kleinman, in addressing the paradigm shift away from a merely
quantifiable approach to healing, focuses on the literary tools that
can be used to (re)create a more integrated healing practice. The
study of literature has always included a cathartic aspect that comes
from a complete emotional identification; through what might be
called a "physiological metaphor" (Holman 84), we can learn how
something feels without actually experiencing it, and through those
feelings we deal with the conflicts and problems in our own lives.
If we connect that to Eagleton's supposition that the novel is a
form of consolation, we can begin to comprehend how this kind of
metaphor functions within a conventional literary context. However, the authors in this study take the cathartic aspect of the novel
a step beyond the notion of using literary metaphors for the discourse of illness; one major aim of each of these novels is to develop a discourse of healing, and on some level, each author creates
a healing ceremony as part of the novel's structure and content,
integrating the storytelling tradition of healing rituals into the consolation narrative of the novel itself. In this regard, these writers'
cultural interpretation of health reflects the paradigm shift occur-
ring in medical practice today. Still, there is no easy transition in
this paradigm shift, and the collision that occurs when differing
worldviews clash is revealed through the novel's form and language,
laying bare the site of the displaced oppositions of traditional/

Western medical methodologies. As poet and metaphysician Elizabeth Sewell states in "Preliminary Reflections on Magic and Medicine": "Any attempt to shift method cannot be accomplished
through critical expository prose addressed to the isolated reason"
(80). Sewell comments on the alienation of the healing arts from
the medical profession, noting how in "our particular culture the
physician as healer and the artist as healer have diverged so greatly
over the past centuries" (159). A new paradigm shift, suggests
Sewell, must incorporate both methodologies, including literary
language linked to the spiritual base of traditional medicine. What
Sewell suggests here is that there once was a deep connection between the artist and the healer, and the interchange of medicine
and creative orature/literature ("orature" being the term for oral
creative art as "literature" refers to written creative art), squelched
by the dominant modes of experimental science, may offer a broader
and more integrated view of health. As do the other participants
in Trautmann's *Healing Arts in Dialogue*, Sewell explores the relationship of literature to medicine, but Sewell, like the authors
examined in this study, takes the discussion further. Sewell addresses the power of words in healing, especially the concept of a
healing discourse of magic and the spiritual world. This language
is related to Makinde's concept of oral medicine, and that aspect
of the healing process is encoded in a traditional worldview.

In *African Philosophy*, Makinde states that a major problem
in developing complete systems of healing within an African context is the issue of language: African doctors, scientists, and others are "forced by language to depict their conceptions of reality in
the language of foreign cultures as opposed to the language of their
own cultures" (10). This comment relates to a broad-based problem often cited by those writing in a colonial language. It is particularly potent in relation to both Western scientists' resistance
to a spiritual aspect of medicine and the signification of language
in traditional medicine. Makinde states that while herbal treatments can be tested in laboratories, the basis of Western scientific
practice, oral medicines (called "magic") cannot, and therefore are
unquantifiable from a Western perspective. Nevertheless, Makinde
stresses the necessity of words in traditional healing, and he articulates a healing discourse as he characterizes the use of oral
medicines as a major part of the healing process. "[Unlike the scientific method,] oral medicine implies the existence of latent kinds
of natures which mystical research contemplates as magical or supernatural. Thus, oral medicine . . . has its metaphysical foundations

in the nature of things. In addition, oral medicine demonstrates to the fullest the power of words" (92).

Although disregarded by dominant medical practice, this aspect of the healing process, germane to the writers' aims, is in some way integral to all of the cultures explored in this study. As Makinde so eloquently explains, oral medicines are of paramount importance in many African societies (I include African-based cultures as well). For example, in *Roots of Jamaican Culture*, Mervyn C. Alleyne comments on the Jamaican belief in the "magical power of the word" (105). He states further that particularly in Rastafarian culture (aligned to an African worldview), words have power to "evoke, and in a sense, to be the thing meant" (147). This view is both metaphorical and metaphysical, resisting certain poststructural assumptions that words can never truly *represent* what they mean. In each of the cultures addressed in this work, the word is in some way sacred and has healing capabilities. In both Maori and Native American traditions, there are sacred words and incantations that are part of the healing act; moreover, words can also cause damage, can create an identified evil. In Jewish culture, the culture most closely linked to Western tradition, the power of words beyond their use as signifiers is evident, especially in regard to what Freud called his "talking cure"—psychoanalysis. Most significantly, these views of words and language are integral to the whole concept of healing with images and symbols, relating back to the ancient Egyptian, early Judaic, and other Semitic concepts of imagining health.

In *Bridges of the Bodymind*, Achterberg and Lawlis tell us that "each cell possesses memory" (1). This simple sentence begins to steer our perception away from the notion that only the mind has memory, can think; it begins to repair the body/mind split, so prevalent in Western societies and antithetical to an integrated healing system. Especially relevant for this study, this sentence encodes a method for revisioning the relationship between artist as healer and physician as healer, as identified by Sewell. Through the concept of oral medicine and the language of that process, we begin to reconnect. However, as Sewell and others have pointed out, in order to take the next step we must find a new discourse in which to incorporate both traditional systems of healing, so adept at oral medicine, and established scientific method. As Grossinger notes, neither those of the dominant culture nor those affiliated with residual traditional cultures can go back to a "primary symbolic process" of an earlier time: "If visualizations and symbols are to work, they must contain within them exactly those things indigenous to us" (70). Inscribed in this concept is the linkage between language and healing within our contemporary context. This concept of a new indigenous approach to health care also allows for the incorporation of cultural and gender applications of oral medicines into the relationship of these healing practices to a changing medical establishment.

One major outgrowth of the changing medical practice, which has remained in residual healing traditions, is the notion that a cure is linked to stories of healing. Perrone, Stockel, and Krueger, in *Medicine Women, Curanderas, and Women Doctors*, comment about the significance of storytelling in Amerindian healing systems: "Belief in a cure is enhanced by hearing stories about the usefulness of that cure" (10). In many of the cultures discussed in this book, healing ceremonies are intertwined with storytelling. It is possible to extrapolate, from the actual storytelling aspects of the healing ceremony itself, the way these novels function as wellness narratives, stories of healing. In this study, the texts examined contextualize new kinds of healing ceremonies and rituals through their discourse. Using a language unlike that of expository prose and scientific method, these works expose another, less linear language of symbol and visualization, a way of knowing the healing process through oral medicine.

At the end of "Medicine as Interpretation," Gogel and Terry put forth a caveat concerning the relationship of literature and medicine. The problem they see is not in theory but in praxis: "The physician must take practical action after his [sic] interpretive work, something which the critical reader in the humanities usually does not do" (214). However, these wellness narratives challenge that basic assumption: In the writing itself there is a move toward linguistic praxis, toward "practical action" of another sort, a novelistic discourse to envision cultural healing. Grossinger comments that medicine "embodies the most powerful metaphor for transformation we have, healing becomes a paradigm for both social revolution and self-development" (xxiii). In each novel addressed in this book, the author creates a different story of healing that, on one hand, begins to develop a cure for the protagonists, and on the other, explores the social constructs of cultural disease. All the authors aim to find a new language and context derived from cultures formerly denied, so that readers may begin a similar process. For these writers, the novels work dialectically as a healing discourse that might aid in a further integrated medical practice as it works toward curing the culturally ill.

Curing Dis-Ease

This book places five writers from different parts of the world in an intertextual dialogue on cultural healing. Their wellness narratives incorporate aspects of the self, family, culture, and community into an empirical model of health, resisting the polarities described in the opening of this introduction. In the analysis of these texts, I hope to point to a multivocal healing model, intended to cure the culturally ill, that responds to the questions raised by doctors and patients alike, by Kleinman and Grossinger, Makinde and Sewell. The interdisciplinary and cross-cultural approach to this collection is also reflected in my own methodology, which links feminist and cultural literary theories with developments in medical anthropology, psychoanalysis, and traditional healing strategies. Each chapter explores women's unique contribution to health, while relating the women in each novel to a specific culture and its healing practices, including Freud's talking cure, as part of a holistic system for healing both mind and body. Although the majority of disorders addressed by these authors reflect socially constructed diseases such as nervous conditions, depression, "mental" breakdowns, and the physical symptoms of those body collapses—stomach disorders, excessive scratching, loss of appetite, vomiting, and catatonia—the authors also address major illnesses, such as cancer and diabetes, in relation to their cultural components.

Part 1 of the study, "African-Based Healings," includes two chapters dealing with the culture of the African diaspora in the act of retrieving recursive traditional healing strategies and practices: Jamaican Erna Brodber's *Jane and Louisa Will Soon Come Home* and African American Toni Cade Bambara's *The Salt Eaters*. At the beginning of each of these works, the female protagonist suffers from a mental/physical breakdown, and such traditional healing practices as a laying on of hands and ritual cleansing lead each back to her African-based culture, from which she has been estranged, and toward health. Brodber's text reconnects the Jamaican present with an African past, and the personal healing reflects a healing of the rift of the diaspora. The latter work by Bambara is more expansive, incorporating other healing practices, but the text is still grounded in the reclaimed heritage passed on by African American women since the slave ships crossed the Middle Passage. Part 2, "Indigenous Curative Methods," includes two chapters that discuss indigenous healing by native peoples, dealing with the disjuncture of their colonial past through traditional practices recovered from the hegemony of the dominant culture. Chapter 3 focuses on Native American healing, especially Laguna Pueblo and Navajo, in *Ceremony* by Leslie Marmon Silko. Tayo, Silko's protagonist, overcomes his post-traumatic stress syndrome which he suffers as a result of having fought in World War II, through the women-centered healing practices within his own culture. However, like the novel *House Made of Dawn*, by her predecessor N. Scott Momaday, Silko's wellness narrative is also a microcosm for a healing process for the general dis-ease of the Native Americans, whose history has been one of oppression and enforced cultural denial. Through the talk-stories of the elders and the re-creation of the immemorial tales, and the working together of male healers and female spirit guides, the novel presents a ritual ceremony of healing the self and community (and possibilities for the planet). The fourth chapter examines Maori healing in New Zealand through Keri Hulme's *the bone people* and makes the most explicit connection between both physical and mental health and cultural identity. The three main characters, a Maori man who is emotionally disturbed and a child abuser, a mixed Maori-English woman with cancer, and a battered European orphan boy, move toward health through accepting Maori cultural traditions and cures. Part 3, "Cultural Linkages," begins to bridge the gap between models of conventional medicine and the traditional practices of the earlier chapters. Chapter 5 explores a cultural healing in an ethnically "in-between" group, the Jews, in Jo Sinclair/Ruth Seid's *Wasteland*, which details a "passing," broken man in narrative discourse with his psychiatrist. Although included as part of biomedical model limited to personal mental disorders, this healing through psychiatric methods identified in the text illustrates a holistic, familial, and cultural process with its origins in Jewish history. The Jewish protagonist begins a healing process for mind and body as he answers the questions of the psychiatrist; the oral medicine is enhanced through the aid of his lesbian sister, who acts as the psychiatrist's liaison to help her shattered brother become whole.

The conclusion to this study addresses the relationship of these wellness narratives to the changes in our approach to health, and interrogates the implications of these novels in terms of what it means to be well. The models presented go beyond a kind of cultural self-help book to open avenues of discourse on how culture affects our health and the health of our communities, raising the question of how these models may hold promise for both cross- and transcultural healing. Furthermore, the study aims to focus on a rebalancing of what are usually called masculine and feminine aspects of the healing process through a (re)examination of the roles of the male and female healers in the works. Finally, the healing discourse of these novels is linked to the possibilities of breaking through the boundaries that limit discussions of culture and health.

Taken together, these five wellness narratives constitute a sustained response to our dis-eased condition, particularly the "cultural self-loathing" noted by Metzger. Despite the differences of culture, "race," geography, and historical circumstances, the women writers examined here present models for wellness that are surprisingly similar in their examination of the basis of cultural illness and its effects on the individual and the community. Through what might be considered an unlikely source, these writers provide a unique approach to considering problems of world health, cultural dis-ease, and personal dysfunction. This book aims to add to the general discourse on the cultural basis of illness, the holistic nature of healing, and the writer's role in reviving more inclusive strategies for healing ourselves, our communities, and the planet.

Part One

African-Based

Healings

1

Reclaiming

Residual

Culture

African Heritage as
Caribbean Cures
in Erna Brodber's
*Jane and Louisa Will
Soon Come Home*

Contemporary women writers in Africa and
the Diaspora have begun to explore the roots of their heritage to
find a cure for cultural malaise they have found in their communities. Tsitsi Dangaremgba, taking her title from Fanon's famous
statement "The condition of the native is a nervous condition,"
addresses the emotional diseases brought on by colonialism in
her novel of Rhodesia/Zimbabwe, *Nervous Conditions*. Although
she does not present a way to heal these disorders in her work,
West African writers, both male and female, have often returned
to their still intact traditional cultures to heal the wounds caused
by five hundred years of penetration by traders and, later, colonists.[1] Although separated by time and space, Black women writers in the United States and the Caribbean are investigating aspects
of their African past that remains within the culture to understand both the postslavery and postcolonial disorders that plague
their communities. Toni Morrison, Alice Walker, Gloria Naylor,
and Sandra Jackson-Opoku in the United States, Jamaicans Olive

Senior and Michelle Cliff, Trinidadian Merle Hodge, Guadeloupian Simone Schwarz-Bart, Haitian Edwidge Dandicat, and Guyanese Denise Harris (Wilson Harris's daughter) in the Caribbean are trying to find a usable past in order to create a healthier future. Although Cuban American author Cristina Garcia does not develop her use of African-based Santeria as a model for healing her characters in her novel *Dreaming in Cuban*, Barbadian American writer Paule Marshall, in her trilogy that culminates with *Praisesong for the Widow*, directly relates being a healthy individual to understanding one's collective history and taking a spiritual "middle passage" back to Africa. Two African-based cultures— Afro-Caribbean in Jamaica and African American in the United States—are evoked through two fully sustained wellness narratives, Erna Brodber's *Jane and Louisa Will Soon Come Home* and Toni Cade Bambara's *The Salt Eaters*. For African-based cultures in the Americas, both the concept of cultures ill from oppression and the importance of residual healing traditions are explicitly exposed in these novels; furthermore, in these cultures, the role of woman as writer and protagonist replicates the role of woman as culture-bearer and healer in the African societies from which these new cultures are partially derived. An examination of African-based cultures in the Americas reveals the recursive healing practices still vibrant in many African societies, while at the same time it makes manifest those aspects complicated by migration, transplantation, and cross-cultural interactions. Finally, these works exemplify a hidden legacy for the most part effaced from dominant history, including medical history; and the healing process (outside the scope of biotechnical medicine) articulated in the novels moves toward a restoration of both the individual and the community made ill by the historicity of the trauma of the slave trade.

This chapter examines the first of these two cultures, Afro-Caribbean, and the novel *Jane and Louisa Will Soon Come Home* (1980) with selected references to Brodber's other healing narratives, *Myal* (1988) and *Louisiana* (1994). Brodber's focus on the linguistic thrust of the cure of cultural dis-ease is a fitting place to begin the exploration of women writers' contribution to healing the planet. In the first two novels, Brodber works as a myalist (Jamaican traditional healer) to cure personal and cultural disease through a (re)writing of language and a revisioning of the cultural imperatives that have guided both therapists and social workers, the area in which she was trained. In "Fiction in the Scientific

Procedure," Brodber identifies not only her own dis-ease in relationship to her boredom with the apparently useless research on
poverty in the slums of Kingston, but also the process through
which she came to understand writing fiction as a healing tool:
"Boredom with a social scientific methodology devoted to 'objectiv-
ity' and therefore distancing the researcher from the people . . . led
me to fiction. To defeat my boredom, I developed the habit of writing down my feelings before entering the field. . . . This activity was
to me like vomiting and defecating, and I flushed away the effort.
[However,] fiction was to become not just the outcome of the act
of cleansing, but something of intrinsic worth" (165).

Brodber describes her bulimialike activity, replicating a predominantly female socially constructed disorder. She then develops a healthier response, using the writing as not only a personal
but also a communicative cure. Brodber began to retain the bits
and pieces of these curative writings and wrote her first novel as a
kind of case history. The novel presents a layered bildungsroman
that centers on the transformation of the confused sexual and cultural identity of the protagonist, Nellie; it develops from Nellie's
disjointed narrative of her breakdown to a curative process that
uncovers her own, her family's, and her nation's trauma of separation from their African heritage and its healing traditions. As other
critics have pointed out, the novel is semiautobiographical in its
approach and focus.[2] Brodber, however, translates these events into
a "culture-in-personality study" that focuses on the power of the
word/narrative to become a "transforming work for the therapists
and through them the clients with whom they would work" ("Fiction" 166).

To ground this discussion within its literary and cultural context, I define some aspects of health within an African worldview
and its Caribbean appropriations. Evelyn O'Callaghan, in her article "Interior Schisms Dramatized: The Treatment of the 'Mad'
Woman in the Works of Some Female Caribbean Novelists," identifies a pattern in certain West Indian women writers, including
Brodber, of female protagonists who are in the throes of mental
collapse. O'Callaghan starts with Jean Rhys's *Wide Sargasso Sea*,
a well-known portrait of the destruction of social and personal
identity through the most intimate of colonizations in the rewriting
of Bertha's story in Charlotte Brontë's *Jane Eyre*. She further focuses on female protagonists of African descent who descend into
psychic and physical collapse, such as Telumé in Schwarz-Bart's
The Bridge of Beyond, who is healed, and Toycie in Belizean Zee

Edgell's *Beka Lamb*, who is not, in terms of perceiving their disorders within a social context, linking sexuality with group identity. Then she asks a question germane to the concerns of this book: "What is the significance of this recurring presentation of the female in a state of psychic collapse? [and] are these representations of mental illness medically credible?" (90). O'Callaghan rightly sees this disorder in the female character as a "social metaphor" for recurrent breakdowns in postcolonial Caribbean society; however, it is the second part of the question that is addressed here: Does only one system of medicine hold the answer to that question? For these next two chapters on writers from the African Diaspora, I turn to the formulations of traditional medical practice within an African context to foreground discussion, and specifically in this first chapter, to elucidate the "mental" disease to which Nellie succumbs.[3]

In *Anthropological Structures of Madness in Black Africa*, I. Sow defines a basic tenet in African concept(s) of identity. Within the structure of traditional life, one must not only be born "biologically," but "one must be born socially as well" (147). This concept is linked to the relationship between past and future generations through the role of the ancestor, whose importance is evident in much of the Caribbean as well as U.S. African American society explored in chapter 2. Sow emphatically states that "it is impossible to think of African psychology and, *a fortiori*, African psychopathology without references to the anthropological structures of the self in the various stages of traditional life" (125), including the antecedents and the unborn. Black African thought (despite the obvious variations in societies within sub-Saharan Africa) derives its principles from "symbols and myths (merging into one the universe and the society in which the African person/personality is formed) as well as from a collective ritual" (125). Therefore, the health of an individual person is directly linked to the health of the community and the culture. Furthermore, in "such an all-encompassing anthropological perspective, sickness is, even more patently than elsewhere, inextricably bound up with the cultural context" (170).

The role of traditional healing in the African Diaspora, examined in both novels and in these first two chapters, is based on concepts governing the healer and the diseased person within an African worldview. According to Sow, within the concept of disease, there is always something beyond the immediate symptoms. In the patient's dysfunction, "a latent dimension always lies hid-

den" (62), and "the role of the practitioner is always that of someone whose task it is to bring to light (and lay bare) the fundamental conflict that has caused the patient to be personally afflicted"
(63). For this to occur, the traditional healer must also be operat-
ing within the constructs of the culture, and it is his/her job to
help the patient return to health. Rather than isolating the specific behavior and disease of the patient, the traditional healer acts
to restore balance in the patient in terms of realigning self and
community. S/he "takes the patient out of dysfunction back into
society, and both are changed from the experience" (Grossinger
34). What is revealing in this concept is that both the patient and
the healer are transformed by this process, and through it, the community as a whole becomes healthier as well. As identified in the
introduction to this book, this traditional concept of healing dif-
fers greatly from Western practice in which, according to Richard
Grossinger, patients are prescribed a quick cure that does not re-
quire them (or the doctors) to change, thus ignoring "the message
of alienation of which the illness is an embodiment" (34).

As with other survivalisms, aspects of an African worldview
are retained in the concepts of health and disease in the Diaspora.
In *The Roots of Jamaican Culture*, Mervyn Alleyne devotes his
study to the "transmission of what I shall call an African culture
to Jamaica and the evolution of that culture in Jamaica" (vii). Since
the site of *Jane and Louisa* is Jamaica, Alleyne's study presents
both a broad-based diasporic perspective and cultural specificity.
He comments that the relationship to both an African present and
past is complicated, but he centers on an African worldview, which,
in Jamaica, is linked to informed populations, specifically certain
Afro-Jamaicans and the "folk" (157). Alleyne describes the
individual's relationship to health, in much the same terms as does
I. Sow, identifying community and ancestral bases of wellness.
Since the structure of traditional life in Jamaica is "essentially
communal," when someone has a health problem, "the first person to be contacted, outside the immediate family, is the spirit
leader. . . . The next step would be to arrange a ritual or ceremony,
and this would involve the whole group" (Lewin, quoted in Alleyne
156). Alleyne also notes that, as in many traditional African cultures, it is difficult to separate the religious/spiritual aspects from
the medicinal and biologically based aspects of healing. Although
it is not always the case, more often than not the role of the spirit
leader in the community is filled by an older woman, even though
traditional healers, obeahmen, and myalists can be male.[4]

One major aspect of this healing process is the importance of "oral medicine" as identified by Makinde: "In the context of African traditional medicine, the power of words and meanings, bearing on human happiness, misery, sanity, and insanity, is enormous" (97). This attention to the language of healing in its most explicit terms was rejected by the strictures of scientific rationalism imposed upon the healers by the colonial regimes. As Sow notes, in trying to recover those aspects of healing lost in the move toward allopathic medicine, that for the traditional healer, words through the "chants and invocations, make up a language of secret symbolisms" that "activate and strengthen the therapeutic action of the medicines" (98). The importance of words for evoking health within an African worldview was part of the cultural transmission that the enslaved Africans brought with them to the Americas. Helen Tiffin, in her study of Caribbean literature, notes that "within the folk tradition, language was (and is) a creative act in itself; the word was held to contain a secret power" (35). More specifically, in his section on the rise of the Rastafarian movement in Jamaica, Alleyne states that in Jamaica the Rastafarians are those who most closely identify themselves with an African past, and the Rastafarian belief in the magical power of the word is an "African continuity upon which Rastas successfully built" (147). According to Alleyne, they believe in the "'evocative power of the word,' i.e. the power of the word to evoke and, in a sense, to *be* the thing meant" (147). The efficacy of words to evoke health indicates a direct link between the healer's words and the diseased person's feeling; what the Rastas would call an "overstanding" of language (overstanding because it encompasses all rather than being under) in relation to the forces of the natural/supernatural world is broader than conventional concepts while resisting certain poststructural notions of representation:[5] "Words, in this regard, *are* these forces rather than merely symbolizing them" (Alleyne 148). As Paule Marshall states in "From the Poets in the Kitchen" and in interviews with Bambara in the next chapter, words were the only weapons the women had to use in trying to resist the cultural disease of their communities and to create a healthy environment. However, this also means that words have the power to affect health, both positively and negatively.

Elsewhere I have explored in detail the conflict of Caribbean writers in regards to the use of English as a medium for their writings.[6] Here it is addressed cursorily in relationship to the other role of language—as part of the cure. Caribbean authors who write in English must confront the basic contradiction in the language in which they write: a language, as poet Marlene Nourbese Philip asserts, "which has sought to deny us" and is an "foreign anguish" ("Earth and Sound"). The correlation between the language developed out of a culture and that society's accepted sense of reality is clearly marked. For the people of the Caribbean, and especially for writers, there is a definite distortion in this correlation. The literary language available to them reflects the internal domination inscribed in it. The break in the correlation of language and accepted reality at once subjugates and debilitates. Caribbean writers face their most challenging goal in dismantling the colonial legacy of their language. The oppositional difficulty of language interpretation in some of the writers, such as Brodber, George Lamming, Jamaica Kincaid, Edward Brathwaite, Derek Walcott, and Wilson Harris, extends beyond access to this milieu to the basic contradiction in their use of English. Writers like Brodber and Wilson Harris especially are well known for their extensive use of metaphor; both writers strive to break through the conventions of Western thought to unmask what has heretofore been suppressed, necessitating revisionist metaphoric activity. Harris explains that he needed a way to disrupt and transform the imperial language of the colonizers: "I had to unlearn what I had learned. I could not just write 'The river is dark; the trees are green.' One of the tasks that began to haunt me personally is how to write that."[7] Helen Tiffin, in "The Metaphor of Anancy in Caribbean Literature," notes: "Metaphoric activity in post-colonial writing is thus likely to be more culturally functional than poetically decorative, more self-consciously concerned with the problem of expressing the new in the language of the old, and more concerned with the importance of language, art, literature not just as expressions of new perception or paradox, but as active agents in the reconstitution of the colonial psyche, fragmented, debilitated, or apparently destroyed by the imperial process" (Tiffin 16).

As Tiffin notes, the colonized psyche is debilitated and diseased by the violent imposition of the dominant culture. However, through the use of metaphor as an imaging process by which to heal the wounded tongue, the language itself can be transformed into a healing narrative in which to reconstruct the fragmented self.

Contemporary women writers in the Caribbean have begun to reconstruct this worldview and perceive their own literature as a way to heal their communities, to create metaphors of healing, to make the word evoke the thing meant—in this case, to cure the (neo)colonial fractured psyche. According to Trinidadian writer Merle Hodge, there is no contradiction between writing and attempting to improve the quality of life for the people of the Caribbean. She notes a relationship between social problems in the Caribbean, including dysfunctions in "mental health" ("Challenges," 204), with the "suppression of Caribbean culture" (203).[8] Hodge states most forcefully: "[T]he power of the creative word to change the world is not to be underestimated" (202). Her own two novels, *Crick Crack Monkey* (1970) and *For the Love of Laetitia* (1993), explore the alienation of the young protagonists, Tee and Laetitia, from their cultural roots through Western education, although the later novel presents a more positive return and potential healing of the main character, Laetitia. For Hodge and others, fiction becomes a tool for political protest (for which it has a long history) and a way to help heal the fractured psyche of the individual and the nation as well. Carolyn Cooper, in "Afro-Jamaican Folk Elements in Brodber's *Jane and Louisa Will Soon Come Home*," comments on Brodber's use of language as a healing process: "The therapeutic power of the word is the subject and the medium of Brodber's fictive art" (280). Like the other writers in this study, Brodber writes not only to keep her own "sanity" ("Fiction" 165), but to create a story of healing and apply her words as the medium to heal her community.

Jane and Louisa, Brodber's first novel, has similarities with other first works by Afro-Caribbean women, such as Hodge's *Crick Crack Monkey*, as well as Michelle Cliff's *Abeng* and Jamaica Kincaid's *Annie John*; it is semiautobiographical and features a young woman narrator who is forced to deal with the clash of cultures, often losing the nurturing aspects of her childhood as she moves up in education and class. In *Jane and Louisa*, the growth of Nellie, the narrator, as a woman and a sexual being, mirrors the development of her identity, as Jimmy Cliff sings it, as "a true born Jamaican." Furthermore, this growth is connected to her throwing off the disfiguring mask of the dominant culture and the re-creation of her uncovered past through an under/overstanding of personal and community history—in this case, through violently fragmented childhood memories. The healing powers of the novel come from linking Nellie's own breakdown and recovery with the disease of her nation, whose populace is suffering from the same dysfunctions. The novel, particularly at the beginning, is extremely dense and difficult to understand, since it is narrated by Nellie during her psychological breakdown and extremely metaphorical. To disrupt the colonial, linear conception of time, Brodber constructs her narrative so that it lacks a coherent notion of chronological time. It is often unclear whose voice from the past Nellie is remembering, and the narrative includes an extensive use of the metaphor of the kumbla, which is usually defined as a rounded container like a calabash but also the rounded body of the white-spun cocoon of the August worm. The novel appears more coherent to the reader toward the end, as Nellie teaches us a new language. Through an African-based healing ritual, she begins to tie in all the strands of her past life with the help of a Rastafarian folk healer, her friend Baba, and her spirit guide, ancestor Aunt Alice.

The movement toward wholeness at the end of the novel, mirroring the changes in Nellie's personal development, also functions linguistically in terms of Brodber's disruption of the alien use of English as her medium for writing and her use of the magical power of the word to help us envision a healing act. As the novel unfolds, Nellie takes us through a spiral backward into her life, from her detached memories of her life in Jamaica and overseas, to her breakdown while she works with an activist Marxist group in the slums of Kingston, and finally to her spiritual healing. As readers, we have to reconstruct this at first incoherent narrative as she liberates the language from debilitating colonial constructs. The opening paragraph of the first section of the novel, "Voices," presents no specific characters and little of the narrator Nellie, just an undetermined "we" whose colors are metaphors for the class and race conflicts in Jamaica: "So we were brown, intellectual, better and apart, two generations of lightening blue-blacks and gracing elementary schools with brightness. The cream of the earth, isolated, quadroon, mulatto, Anglican. But we had two wiry black hands up to the elbows in khaki suds" (7).

For readers, it is unclear exactly who the "we" are, and what is the relationship to the "two wiry black hands" of a darker-skinned maid/mother/grandmother, whose hands wash clothes in dirty water the color of these children's skin (this British military cloth ironically named for the light-skinned). But it is evident, without our knowledge of who is speaking or where the scene takes place, that light-skinned children are privileged on one hand, yet their coloring is metaphorically that of dirty water on the other.

O'Callaghan notes that Brodber is one of the women writers who uses the "psychic damage and distorted self-image of the individual as metaphors for a kind of pervasive 'illness' to which our societies are prone as a result of the colonial encounter" (104). Nowhere is this more evident in the novel than in the linguistic disruption of the narrative. Sentence structure is linked by loosely connected metaphors, and the imposition of the dominant colonial culture pervades the characters' discourse. Nellie speaks in Jamaican Standard English, derived from that discourse, but included in the novel is Jamaican Creole, or what Edward Kamau Brathwaite calls "nation language," a language for the nation. It is one way the reader divines who is speaking, but it is also representative of the class-and race-bound society of Jamaica. This linguistic spectrum, related to the class and color structures imposed by the former colonialists and neocolonialists, illustrates both the dysfunction and, later, the potential for healing the community. In the novel, the tension between the upwardly mobile khakis whose English is a source of pride and the darker-skinned folk, who detest the pretension of these speakers yet are painfully aware of their privilege, is played out in Nellie's colonized-schizoid consciousness as we follow her descent into a catatonic state. Here the incoherence of the language and the disembodied voices present English as a source of anguish to the narrator. All around her, Nellie witnesses the silences imposed by the conflict of gender, color, and class-bound language, determined by the "standard" dialect of schooled Jamaican English, and as she returns from abroad she sees people "waiting. Perhaps for language" (41). She is disturbed by these silences and by the lack of a language to represent her nation, a language that is not class, color, and gender bound. The resistance to the community-born Creole, informed by residual African languages, and the dominance of the colonial so-called standard English leaves no voice for Nellie. Merle Hodge, whose character Tee in *Crick Crack Monkey* is also torn from her (grandmother) Ma's Creole words and stories by the linguistic separation of schooled English, comments on the antagonism toward the use of the national language, Creole, which expresses *"our personality, our worldview in a way no other language can"*: "Think of the implications for our mental health—we speak Creole, we need Creole, we cannot function without Creole . . . but we hold Creole in utter contempt" ("Challenges" 204). Furthermore, the African-based syntax and other holdovers in Creole, according to Maureen Warner Lewis, are the basis for "the African language" in which one communicates with the ancestors ["If you cyan talk de African language to dem/wha' you gwine tell dem?"] (70). Evidently, as both Hodge and Lewis infer, this language conflict has grave consequences for Nellie's mental/physical health. However, the existence of this language allows a space in which to reconnect to the healing attributes of the ancestors within the Caribbean, a relationship more problematic for African Americans in the United States, as chapter 2 will demonstrate.

Through this linguistically charged narrative, Nellie presents a family and culture in conflict. Her childhood memories are metaphors that sift through the disjointed images of her fractured psyche. The safety of the mother's love becomes evident, although there is no mention of a mother: "Ever see a fowl sitting on eggs in cold December rain. We knew the warmth and security of those eggs in the dark of her bottom" (9). This metaphor creates a safe space for Nellie in her memories of the "beautiful garden" of childhood; however, inscribed in the image is the precariousness of these khaki children's protected position, perched between two hostile cultures. These memories form a discourse both conflicted and potentially empowering. The values learned from "the pale faces" (30) set up the rigid standards of assimilation into an aspiring Eurocentric culture, in contradistinction to all the customs and prescriptions of the Afro-folk in her family and community, who give advice concerning both the living and the dead: "Our dead and living have no stone encasements. . . . Step warily" (12). The two sets of advice appear contradictory, oppositional, and Nellie is unable to find a space in which to grow as a healthy adult. Moreover, Nellie receives no valid explanation from her family about her noticeable growth into womanhood, protected by the kumbla of cryptic words. The contradictions of familial advice in terms of her own development and the imposed silences of her family's past, particularly the loss of African heritage, impair her ability to communicate.

The central metaphor of the novel is that of the kumbla, presented in the traditional Anancy story "Go Eena Kumbla." This tale of Anancy, the West African Akan trickster figure transported to the Caribbean, is a break in the plot line, but is intricately connected to Nellie's protective family structure as well as her stunted sexuality and cultural denial. In "The Metaphor of Anancy in Caribbean Literature," Helen Tiffin comments that for Caribbean writers, Anancy the spider "becomes a very complex metaphor and archetype for the Caribbean experience"; on one hand, Anancy represents "the fossilized past of the colonized" and on the other, "a possible source of fresh creative energy" (17; 35). Unlike the role of Grandmother Spider within Native American tradition whose humor and power is generally perceived as positive, Anancy's role as trickster in the Caribbean also contains in it a static notion of the African past. The Anancy story of the Kumbla creates a similar dialectic in *Jane and Louisa*. In the story, Anancy and his children are caught stealing fish from the powerful Dryhead. To save his children from being eaten, he hides the others and takes only his eldest son with him before the captors. To fool Dryhead, he brings out his son, pretending he is one of the other children. Each time the son comes forth disguised, Anancy shouts a supposed curse, "You face favor... go eena kumbla," which means, in code, that the son should "change colour" and disguise himself as another of the children. Dryhead then allows Anancy to leave only with his eldest son, but in fact all the children are saved (123–130). In the Anancy story, the kumbla works as a protective covering, which fools the enemy. However, as Tiffin notes about the Anancy figure in the Caribbean and Michelle Cliff has identified about the abeng, the kumbla also has a dual meaning in the novel: It is both a protective device and a metaphor for suffocating cultural dis-ease.[9] Nellie's own kumbla, described as a "round seamless calabash that protects you without caring," becomes a symbolic rendering of the August worm's spun cocoon, and as Nellie further notes: "they usually come in white" (123). The kumbla is a disguise that works as a metaphor for the way that Caribbean women protect their children in a manner similar to Anancy's protection of his son. Specifically, for young girls, the kumbla is also used as a way to protect them against the onslaught of male aggression (or even their own sexual yearnings). But while the kumbla protects, it can also "disfigure" (Cobham 34), linking sexual repression with a rejection of cultural identity, a changing of color.

Nellie's kumbla is constructed as she is given over to her khaki, assimilated, and psychically disturbed Aunt Becca—who speaks of others in her community as "those people" (17). Nellie's confusion when Aunt Becca refuses to allow her any association with her childhood companion Baba is linked to his place as child of "those people" and Becca's own admonition that everything is "trying to spoil your life" (18). And Nellie's response is to accept the prescription, but also to feel caged in, claustrophobic, physically sick, without a voice: "Is there no way out Saviour Divine? Let me try and hold it in. But I'm going to vomit. . . . Vomit up a scream" (19). Furthermore, Nellie's awakened sexuality is twisted into horror by Becca's repressive Anglican values and her own confused sense of sexual identity. Her natural feelings become something to be ashamed of, as she learns that to "touch is to contaminate" (23). Nellie's mother's is also complicit in this process of kumblalization, as identified here: "You feel shame and you see your mother's face and you hear her scream and you feel the snail what she sees making for your mouth. One long nasty snail, curling up, straightening out to show its white underside that the sun never touches. . . . Vomit and bear it" (28). The image of the snail calls forth violent sexual objects—tongues and penises used only for abuse; Nellie's response to sexual awareness is to vomit and bear it. The use of vomiting to regain control of one's life is the basis of the disease bulimia, often associated with young women on the verge of adulthood and linked to sexuality. In this passage, the sexual metaphor of the snail is clear enough, but what adds to the linguistic complexity of the passage, whether it is real or imagined, is that the "underside" of the snail also exposes another penetration—that of "white" domination. Vomiting, which Brodber identifies as a metaphor for her writing, can be a way of cleansing oneself of dominant cultural oppression, as it does for Avey in her passage to Carricou and her ancestors in Marshall's *Praisesong for the Widow.* However, a bulimic response can also be devastating, especially for a young woman. In Dangaremgba's first novel, *Nervous Conditions,* one of the characters, Nyasha, almost dies from trying to vomit out the offals of the colonial system in Rhodesia, imposed on her by her Eurocentric, patriarchal father, Babamukuru.

Like these authors in the United States and on the African continent, Brodber defines Nellie's disease by linking bodily (dys)function with emotional/mental stress and sociocultural dislocation, arising from that colonial/Eurocentric heritage. This linkage is further explored in Leslie Marmon Silko's *Ceremony,* in which the male protagonist, Tayo, also vomits up his severe dislocation in his home after fighting in World War II. One of the ironies of Nellie's disease is that even her role as doctor cannot help her, but her place of learning makes her more ill. When Nellie goes to study medicine in the United States, we learn little of her educational experiences and practice; however, we do witness her reactions to race relations in the hospital where she works. As Marshall and others have noted, the move from the Caribbean to the United States is a further dislocation because of the rigidity of racial lines drawn.[10] However, although Nellie is separated from the Black American workers in the hospital by class, they are the only one who acknowledge her: "They are proud of me for I am a doctor and their own" (33). As a child growing up in Jamaica, Nellie is privileged, "khaki"; however, when she goes to the United States, she recognizes her connection with other people of the African Diaspora, and this drastically changes her self-image. Her confrontation with explicit racism causes her to be ill, with a lump in her throat: "But that lump is anger. Research labs now link repressed anger with cancer and the cancer must out with a surgeon's knife" (32). The linkages of tumors with cultural disease is most explicitly evoked in chapter 4, on Keri Hulme's *the bone people*, but here the tumor is a metonym of racial antagonism with which Nellie finds herself surrounded and her own confusion of class issues from her childhood in Jamaica. Nellie's identification with "her people," the black ones Aunt Becca called "those people" and tried to keep her away from, helps her to extricate the lump in her throat: "I emerge from this surgery, black, taken now for an African" (33). Her renewed bonds with her African heritage, via Blacks in the United States, cures her for the moment of that carcinogenic lump of anger within her. Still, these links with African Americans during her stay in the United States are not enough to heal the wounds both she and her nation suffer, for as she notes, "I am not at home" (33). This experience politicizes her, nevertheless, and she returns to Jamaica not as a doctor but as a Marxist community activist, who ironically is unable to connect to that heritage passed on by the folk she is trying to help.

When Nellie returns to Jamaica, she joins a radical political group, and goes to the Kingston slums to lives in one of "yards" that Brodber, as a sociologist, had studied. As is true for Clare in Cliff's *No Telephone to Heaven*, the return of the intellectual poses stark choices, and despite good intentions, s/he is often separated from those with whom s/he wants most to connect. Although in her last novel, *Louisiana*, Brodber's characters come to link spirituality to their activism, in this case, neither Nellie nor the other members of the Marxist group are comfortable with the "people": they objectify and look down on them (50–51). Moreover, these alienated intellectuals, exemplified by her boyfriend, Robin, have lost the language to communicate: "My young man talks in an unknown tongue . . . words like 'underdevelopment', 'Marx ,' 'cultural pluralism'" (46). Ironically, the members of this group do not understand what they can learn from the people in the yard; ironically, it is they, rather than the folk they reject, who "have no culture at all" (51). In one of her sociological studies, "Oral Sources and the Creation of a Social History of the Caribbean," Brodber identifies those assimilated Jamaicans, like the character Nellie, as dispossessed and isolated from the sustaining roots of their culture; furthermore, she warns, the intellectual history that helps maintain their "social position does not mirror [their] past" (2).

Carolyn Cooper interprets Brodber's analytical comments in regard to Brodber's own creative fiction and further links the understanding of cultural history to personal health: "Eurocentrically disposed Caribbean intellectuals, like Nellie, must revitalize the severed linkages with the nurturing folk culture, for sanity's sake" (281). As she slowly succumbs to the physical symptoms of her cultural disease, Nellie perceives the actual death by fire of her lover as a symbol of the inevitable path for her and the other dried-up intellectuals; her own comprehension of this profound linguistic and cultural chasm is, in actuality, making her ill. Furthermore, the way in which the intraracist precepts that she carries from her upbringing and education intertwine with her stunted sexuality gives her no room to be a well person within a community, as defined within an African context.

As Nellie breaks down, she becomes almost zombified as she tries to work with the people in the yard from whom she is alienated. In her psychotic state, Nellie becomes frightened of the people whom she lives with in the "hall," those whom she loves and wants to save. The hall itself becomes a symbol of her fear and she sees it as "a living animal" from which she shrinks. In Sow's terms, it is possible to identify her perceptions of the hall as well as her reaction to the people who live there as part of a certain kind of schizophrenic isolation: "In Africa, someone who places himself [sic] outside the community, in one way or another, loses his quality of human being and becomes a kind of reincarnation of evil spirits, shunned and feared by all" (155). For Nellie, the hall has lost its humanness and is to be shunned; however, it is really Nellie who can no longer make human contact. In Brodber's second novel, *Myal*, this condition takes its most extreme form in the zombification and possession of the character of Ella; in this novel, Nellie descends into a catatonic state.[11] Each of her three novels presents a physical/emotional descent and a curative assent that leads into cultural awareness and renewed health. In this novel, despite/because of her breakdown, Nellie begins to have a budding awareness of the relation of the people in the hall to her disease, linked to hidden legacy of her past: "These people were to me neutral patterns of sounds and smells, visual memories from my long past" (73). At this point, however, she does not understand the significance of this statement for her potential healing; it will take a further process, guided by Baba and ancestor Aunt Alice, to lead her toward wholeness.

As Nellie defines for herself the symptoms of her collapse, she returns to a recurring signifier—the cancerlike lump of anger in her throat—along with manifestations of psychosis, like her compulsive scratching. As she details the failure of her attempts to control these symptoms, she tries to justify her increasingly bizarre behavior: "My little scheme for personal discipline was pointless; might as well scratch too. Moreover, if my fingernails tore my skin as sometimes happens on those occasions, that would no doubt help to dissolve the lump now beginning to gather in my throat" (65-66). Nellie self-diagnoses her breakdown only in terms of the death of her lover, Robin; revealingly, her role as doctor never enters into her own understanding of her illness. Further, the doctors who attend to the final stages of her collapse also misdiagnose her, treating only the somatic aspects of her illness. They identify her as "diabetic," even though she has not had diabetes before; this incomplete diagnosis, according to Katon, Kleinman, and Rosen, is common in cases of depression (129).[12] Within the context of this novel, Nellie's depression reflects the larger dysfunction of her community, and she needs more than allopathic medicine to be healed. For "sanity's sake," her healing involves a reconnection with the community from whom she has been estranged.

In "Autobiography, History, and the Novel: Erna Brodber's *Jane and Louisa Will Soon Come Home*," Joyce Walker-Johnson expands the genre of autobiography within a West Indian context as communal as well as personal (an African-based concept), and she comments, using the metaphor of cell reorganization: "[In regard to] Brodber's concern with communal ancestry. . . , it has been generally recognized by her critics that Nellie's search for autonomy represents more than a search for a personal direction. . . . Furthermore, Nellie's attempt to free herself from the safe "womb" of inherited ideas evokes extreme schizophrenia comparable to the confusion and disaffection within the social organism attempting to re-orient itself" (48).

The cultural illness to which Nellie succumbs reflects the disorder in her society, that disease developed from the dislocation of the slave trade and the colonial encounter. Therefore, as is evidenced in all the novels examined in this book, Nellie cannot be cured outside a community. Furthermore, her movement toward health affects her community and nation, as she is transformed by the (re)wording and (re)writing the stories of the past.

The second half of the novel is concerned with the healing of Nellie and its significance for Jamaicans and all those who suffer from these postcolonial disorders, arising from what Frantz Fanon calls the "nervous condition" of the oppressed. In her narration, Nellie reiterates a thought that is developed in each of the novels discussed in this book: "The practice of medicine is a strange thing and we can't always accept the diagnosis" (67). Relevantly, though, it is not through her own medical education or from the doctors that she gets the correct diagnosis, rather from her childhood companion Baba, one of "those people" from whom Aunt Becca tried to keep her. Baba is identified within what Carolyn Cooper calls a "Neo-African folk aesthetic" (279), and he is also associated with the Rastafarian movement. Like Anancy, Baba is connected to the folk but also is changeable; he can mediate between the past and contemporary Jamaica. When Nellie first sees him again, she perceives him simultaneously as a doctor (surgeon's hands), as a savior (Jesus), as a Yoruba diviner (dressed in a white gown, hair plaited), and as one born of the soil of Jamaica ("soaked in lime"; 63). Baba personifies the linking of the Yoruba tradition of divination with both Anancy and the African-based Rastafarians, and in this novel, his healing capabilities are stronger than Nellie's, despite her medical background. Moreover, Baba is in the tradition of literary Rastafarian healers, like Roger Mais's *Brother Man*.

In the novel, Baba is signified as an integrated person, apart from the alienated intellectuals of Nellie's Marxist group. When Baba first infiltrates the Marxist group, he symbolizes her illness through a carving of a doll (echoes of the vodun dolls that can powerfully affect one's health), and he compels Nellie to see herself as a "cracked-up doll" (69). At first, she is resistant to his healing methods, but after her breakdown, she puts herself in his charge and lets him lead her to health. Baba feeds her, puts her in a safe space for her convalescence, and performs a laying on of hands, similar to the female Balm healers in Jamaica and the famed healer Minnie Ransom in Bambara's *The Salt Eaters*. Nellie reflects: "I had experienced the firm gentleness of his probing fingers. With just his index finger he had probed the base of my skull that day, had made me sweat and broken my fever" (68). She lets Baba guide her healing process because "I knew Baba's past. He knew mine.

On this we shared a common language" (67). Her aim to have her
language correspond to her cultural identity and break away from
the imposition of the dominant culture's loaded words echoes that
of *The Tempest*'s Caliban.[13] In response to Baba's prodding Nellie
out of her kumbla, she curses at him. She stops and says, "I have
been talking aloud. Is that me? with such expressions. Am I a
fishwife?" Baba answers, "Yes it is you. You have found your language" (71). As Leslie Humphrey points out, Baba's Anancy qualities are just what are needed to move Nellie (and consequently
her society) from a "neglected past [and] a dry, static present [to] a
potentially fruitful future" (35). Through the oral medicines administered by Baba, Nellie begins to develop a healing language to
offset the restrictions of the kumbla.

It is at this point that the story of Anancy, "Go Eena Kumbla,"
is narrated, as Nellie examines the properties of the kumbla and
exposes the kumbla's limitations: "But the trouble with the kumbla
is the getting out of the kumbla. It is a protective device. If you
dwell too long in it, it makes you delicate. Makes you an albino:
skin white but not by genes. Vision extra-sensitive to the sun and
blurred without spectacles. Baba and Alice urged me out of mine.
Weak thin, tired like a breach baby" (130).

As she reconstructs her history, Nellie begins to understand
the metaphor of her kumbla as a type of medicine whose cure is as
bad as the disease. Nellie begins to emerge from her personal
kumbla through Baba's "higher science" (67). Relevantly, Baba's
approach to healing has similarities to the balm healers, who developed their Afro-Christian art through the "myalists healing cults
[sic], which emerged in the late eighteenth century," according to
William Wedenoja in the essay "Mothering and the Practice of
Balm in Jamaica" (78). Myalists, as Brodber demonstrates in her
second novel, *Myal*, were men as well as women, but the majority
of those practicing balm have been women. Wedenoja further notes
that "Spirituality and healing are largely associated with women
in Jamaica" (6). Baba has an important role to play in Nellie's healing process, but in this case, as in Wedenoja's observations, the
spiritual aspects of curing come through a woman.[14] As in many
African societies, Baba is the diagnostician, a practitioner, but
Nellie needs the help of the ancestors to secure her healing, and her
dead aunt Alice acts as her spirit guide to unravel and reword family and community history, to lead her out of the kumbla, and
potentially to heal the rift of the Diaspora.

Nellie's kumbla is directly tied to four female relatives and ancestors: her Aunts Becca and Alice, Granny Tucker, and her great-grandmother Tia Maria. Tia and Becca symbolize the damage that the kumbla can do and has done; Aunt Alice and Granny Tucker work as antidotes to Nellie's disease. Nellie describes the kumbla as an addictive drug, used to stop pain but causing the patient another ailment, without affecting the original disorder. She comes to realize that the kumbla has become the personal talisman for her group, and realizes that in her family, "Some people need the protection more than others and use the thing more often and in larger doses than others. But everyone shares the value of its usefulness and the necessity to use it" (142). Clearly, the most addicted in the family is possibly the "inventor" of the kumbla, Nellie's great-grandmother Tia, who marries the white William, "spouting khaki children" (136). Through Tia's story, Nellie's personal and familial trauma is forcibly bound to the colonial encounter and the disaster of the slave trade. Tia's name is symbolic here: The white coffee flower the name comes from is beautiful, but it encodes a visual contradiction, echoing the memory of the slave labor on the coffee plantations. Tia represents the most damaging aspects of this disease caused by European colonialism and its hegemony in that she "had built a fine and effective kumbla out of William's skin" (142). The kumbla, initially used to protect, becomes a symbol of deformed cultural identity. Tia helps develop a new hegemony—that of upper-class, light-skinned Jamaicans—from which she is excluded. She makes herself disappear so that her children (the khaki ones) can make their way into this dominant culture. Her success in spinning kumblas around her children is evident in the use of language: "Tia wanted it so that with a snap of her fingers she could disappear and her children would loom large in their place in the sun. The stranger the words her children spoke, the happier she felt" (139). Their place in the sun, obviously the world of the aspiring bourgeois Jamaicans, has no room for the Black Tia, thus severing the most primal bonding of mother to child, while denying both African heritage and community.

In the novel, Tia symbolizes what Clarissa Zimra calls the "original fable of loss: *le désastre*, the wrenching from Africa, the primal mother" (230). She cannot fulfill her role as nurturer, as mother, since she has severed herself from her children's lives. The white, finely spun kumblas she builds for them harden into "white steel helmets" and isolate them from her. Ironically, the only thing Tia can nurture is the kumbla. However, "nurturing the kumbla is nurturing any vaccine, any culture. Some skins react positively, some don't" (139). The vaccine doesn't take with Tia's own daughter, Nellie's grandmother Kitty, who "liked the music, not of the piano, but of the drums" (139). Tia rejects this daughter who refuses the false protection of the kumbla; nor does it work well with her other daughter, Alice, perceived as "not quite right in the head" because of her links to the spirit world (140). Ironically, the light-skinned Kitty, despite her rejection of the kumbla, is unable to pass on her resistance to her own child Becca: The only one who took her great-grandfather's color (91) also takes the kumbla of his skin.

Aunt Becca, a living representation of the kumbla spun by Tia, is a major influence on Nellie's life, like the assimilated Aunt Beatrice in *Crick Crack Monkey*. Becca's educational process teaches Nellie about the contradictions in her family, but Nellie can comprehend it only in retrospect, through the help of Aunt Alice's spirit vision. Becca is the one who determines how everyone in the extended family should act; her designation as "Aunt Khaki" conjures up all the power of that word. Like the young female protagonists in *Abeng* and *Crick Crack Monkey*, as Nellie develops into womanhood, her own mother gives Nellie to Becca for her indoctrination into the world of the Jamaican bourgeoisie: "Go Eena kumbla for you need to be cleaned. . . . I went with Aunt Becca and the sun" (122). Revealingly, it is Becca who keeps young Nellie from Baba, telling her that "those people" are different. But even for Becca, the kumbla doesn't protect totally, and through Nellie's unraveling of the family history, we come to learn why the uptight, Anglophile Becca is praying in a thatch church, "surrounded by perspiration, drum beat and moaning" (93). Becca suffers from the loss of a future generation, since she chose her kumbla of protected skin over the life of her unborn child, which she aborted because it might have come out too dark. In reconstructing the past, Nellie gains insight into Becca's tragedy and, through the guidance of Alice, begins to recognize the poisonous quality of the kumbla, the antidote to blackness that kills the patient: "With every orgasm, a white lie must be born, an image, a cowl, a kumbla, to cover its fruits. And even with the cunning of the kumbla, the game was lost: it was the womb or its fruits. So Tia had to die so that her children could live. Aunt Becca had to kill hers so that she could live" (143).

These sterile kumblas, originally meant to be a prophylactic, become a poisonous culture, a vaccine worse than the disease (139).

Becca, whose vaccine took too well, tries to find her lost child in the Africanized drum meetings of the thatch church, but it is too late for her. However, because of the positive influences of spirit guide Aunt Alice, Baba, and the memories of Granny Tucker and her culturally healthier cousins, Jane and Louisa, Nellie can begin the process of healing.

Nellie's healing must come through recovering the African aspects of her culture.[15] Baba takes Nellie through part of her healing process, but it is ancestor Aunt Alice who leads Nellie to articulate a new construction of self and society, like Avey's own ancestor, Great-Aunt Cuney, in Marshall's *Praisesong for the Widow*. One of the disembodied voices that Nellie hears when she returns back to Jamaica after her sojourn in the States is that of her now dead Aunt Alice. Nellie says: "I read you Aunt Alice" (40), but neither she nor the reader understands the import of Aunt Alice's intervention at the time. Nellie must take a spiritual journey to make out the meaning of the stories that she is told, the stories to make her well, much like Tayo's interpretive story journey in Leslie Marmon Silko's *Ceremony*, discussed in chapter 3. As Nellie rewords and retells history through her wellness narrative, the novel itself becomes more intelligible to the readers as we learn along with her. The fragmented, chaotic memories of a denied and partially effaced past become comprehensible through Aunt Alice's ancestral guidance. Coming to Nellie in dreams and visions, Alice continues the cure that Baba, through his use of herbal medicines, laying on of hands, and healing words, has begun. Alice, the child "who would never be able to keep house" (140), becomes, both in her life and especially afterward, a guide to Nellie's health. As Nellie works back through her past, "into the beautiful garden," she hears the voice of Aunt Alice leading her to reconstruct childhood and familial trauma.

While Nellie is recuperating at Baba's, she is visited by Aunt Alice under the "transfiguring light" of Brer (A)Nancy. Nellie's vision is telling because it identifies Aunt Alice as Nellie's spirit guide and also reflects examples of the spirit possession that exists throughout Africa and the Caribbean.[16] In Nellie's state, neither asleep nor awake, she enters into a new world. Her description of the world she enters replicates that state of possession needed for induction into the spirit world. As she walks in, suddenly self-assured, she notes in this dreamlike state that she is beginning to find her place: "The light was no brighter but this piece of ground was clearly mine no more or less than anybody else's; I had a right to sense my way in and around bodies and spirits" (75). As Nellie describes the dancing and conjoining of both bodies and spirits, she connects with her ancestral spirit guide, Aunt Alice: "Some people analyze that spirit and perceive each individual atom. Alice could: for how else would she had been able to recognize me and call me by my name" (75) The power of naming and "calling out" someone's name, for both positive and negative uses, is integral in many African cultures and the Diaspora, as well as in other cultures, such as Amerindian societies throughout the Americas.[17] In this case, Alice's recognizing and calling out to Nellie begins a spiritual return toward health. As in Minnie Ransom's relationship with her ancestor Old Wife in *The Salt Eaters*, Nellie learns from her spirit guide, Aunt Alice. Her spiritual travels with Aunt Alice educate her on healing herbs, like the guinea hen weed and the leaf of life, giving her greater vision. On this first trip, however, Nellie perceives only a partial vision of her people; Aunt Alice promises to show her more later (76).

In subsequent visions, Alice tells Nellie to accept the spirits within her and introduces Nellie to her kinsmen coming out of the rocks, "tall, proud, and happy to meet me" (78). This vision of the ancestral family coming to meet Nellie is similar to Kerewin's dream of her Maori ancestors rising from the rocks to greet her in Keri Hulme's *the bone people*. Nellie accepts the spirits, allowing what she has been insulated from by the kumbla to enter into her system, to cool and cure her. Moreover, she recognizes her own and her family's betrayal of those ancestors and the damage it has done to the whole family, who gave up the drums for the piano. But most significantly for her health, and for the understanding of Brodber's readers, Nellie gains an awareness that leads to a healing of her fractured psyche: "I saw that if I knew all my kin . . . I could no longer roam as a stranger; that I had to know them to know what I was about; [that I could nohow] eat my cane nor walk in my beautiful garden unless I walked with them, the black and the squat, the thin and the wizened, all of them" (80). The conclusion of this vision prepares the way to the next section of the novel, "Into the Beautiful Garden," in which Nellie returns to the garden of her childhood, a retelling of family history with "all of them" included.

From this point on in the novel, Nellie is retelling her family history/herstory in her own personal/nation language as part of a wellness narrative. Brodber's wellness narrative moves toward (re)conciliation. The negotiations of the various aspects of her culture are inscribed in a holistic language that has been feminized and Africanized, a language of healing. The orature of her African ancestors, blended with the English (subdued, nonhierarchized) of her European ancestors, produces a new language that incorporates both the khaki and black, moving deftly from Jamaican Standard English to the nation language of Creole. This section refers back to the title of the novel, a British song-game popular in the Caribbean. As Humphrey points out, the use of this ring-game song is extremely symbolical in the novel "due to the combination of its racial origins" (30). Reflecting the changes in the narrative's discourse, Brodber employs this alternative metaphor to that of the kumbla as an example of the potential for integrating the disparate elements of heritage, as the children have always done with the ring-game tradition in the Caribbean, appropriating its Englishness into the Afro-Caribbean oral tradition. Once again, Brodber refuses to reify the African traditions in opposition to the European ones, defining a healing process that is also a healthy creolizing of the Caribbean personality.

The "Jane and Louisa" of the title and the song are transformed in the novel into Nellie's two cousins; they are "in the know" because of living with Granny Tucker, in tune with the African elements of their family. Because of the denial of the African aspects of her past, Nellie does not occupy the important position of title name; that goes to her cousins in the know. Nellie must grow and heal before she can join her cousins in healing her nation. Despite the security of the fabricated "beautiful garden" of her own childhood, Nellie was faintly aware that Jane and Louisa, although orphans, were self-assured and, under the tutelage of Granny Tucker, could see more clearly what was being buried in their history. Nellie thinks back on their visits: "Janey and Louise's visits freed up everybody. Aunt Alice especially. They were tongue to her thoughts" (94). It is revealing here that this matrilineal heritage is passed on from Granny Tucker (of her mother's side) through Alice (of the father's family) and back again to Jane and Louisa, incorporating all of Nellie's extended family; therefore, the healing process that Nellie goes through is inclusive.

The final section, "Jane and Louisa Will Soon Come Home," concerns Nellie's acknowledgment and reconstruction of her cultural his/herstory through the exemplar of Granny Tucker and her charges, Jane and Louisa, who metaphorically have come home. Nellie also is making that metaphorical journey home under guidance of her ancestor Alice. Still, following an African model of generational continuity, Nellie's mother's mother is the only living entry into the more African-based side of her family. As an Afro-Christian, Granny Tucker is linked with the Revivalist movement in Jamaica (Wedenoja 78); this form of Christianity within the African Diaspora, has been syncretized to incorporate much of African traditional religion. (Syncretism and spirit guides within U.S. African American context is further developed in chapter 2.) Furthermore, Granny Tucker is identified throughout the novel with the African aspects of her heritage, and as Walker-Johnson notes, she is only "partially assimilated by European values, despite her strong adherence to the Christian faith" (50). Granny's prayers are direct lines to the ancestors, and her support of Jane and Louisa helps them to be models for Nellie. At the end of the novel, Brodber creates a healing circle and returns to the book's opening; circular narratives are often in the domain of women writers as well as in healing stories. In a return for both the readers and herself, Nellie's story and self are strengthened by the now known "wiry black hands" of Granny Tucker: "Vulnerable as a premature worm, we returned. . . . No paths lay before us. We would have to make them. But we still had Granny Tucker's wiry black hands, strong enough to scrub away khaki suds" (146). Granny Tucker gives the three young women strength to continue, but as Nellie states, there are no paths to follow. To begin a journey toward a noncolonized, healthy society is to forge a new path, and the conclusion of the novel reflects this.

The end of the novel is chantlike, partial, and the last line, "We are getting ready" (147), implies an open resolution, a stepping out of the kumbla, which is a healing process not just for Nellie, her cousins, and the rest of her family, but also for her nation. Nellie has to say good-bye to the restrictive world of Aunt Becca, and she tells her ancestor Aunt Alice and the others that she and her two cousins are just "getting ready," since there are no exact models for this emergent culture, ready to be born. In the final pages of the novel, Nellie has returned to health and takes her place with her two cousins, who were formerly more in touch with their heritage than she. But for all of them (and symbolically, the next generation of Jamaicans), the process of healing themselves and their nation is a course that is just at its beginning, is, in fact, a becoming; the open-ended nonresolution of the novel reproduces that process.

In *Jane and Louisa*, Brodber presents a healing culture-in-personality; in her "twinning of fiction and science" ("Fiction"

167), Brodber creates a novel, which is a becoming, for the characters, the readers, and the work itself. This act of becoming reflects
an African worldview in both art and life, as identified by Sow, in
that the African person is not "a 'completed' system"; rather, "the
human being, as such, is perpetually in the making" (126). And
this perception of the healthy development of an individual, a family, and a nation hinges on the understanding that neither people
nor cultures are static, but are constantly in the process of being
made. For Nellie and her cousins, as for the readers, the movement toward health is linked to a process and a methodology, with
the potential to become. In *Myal*, Ella, who is diseased by the colonial spirit thieves, comes to health through myalism; and through
her healing, she takes on the potential to be a healer herself. In
Louisiana, Brodber's companion text to *Myal*, the protagonist, Ella,
combines spiritual healing with social activism through a relationship with the ancestors. In this earliest work, *Jane and Louisa*,
neither Nellie nor her cousins are identified specifically as healers
or activists, but it is evident that they are the precursors of new
generations, those who will begin to heal the rift of the Diaspora;
they are getting ready to become true-born Jamaicans. The last
image is Nellie's dream about giving birth to a fish (from the Sargasso Sea?) that will not leave the womb; but she is not worried,
because "it will come" (147); this birth is in the process of becoming, reflecting the unresolved ending of the novel. The comparison of writing to having a child is evident in much of women's
literature. One such example is Nigerian writer Buchi Emecheta's
comparison of the birth of a new book with the traditional action
of examining the newborn to make sure s/he has all his/her fingers and toes (*Our Own Freedom* 47). The novel presents the possibility of a healthy becoming of the Jamaican personality.

   In all her novels, Brodber writes about women who, within a
the context of the Diaspora, are in the process of becoming. Linking Sow's term for the African personality with Alleyne's comment that the "language of Jamaica is best understood dynamically
as a 'becoming'" (121), Brodber develops this concept into a
wellness narrative to prepare a "getting ready" for all Jamaicans
(and her readers in general) to begin a process of healing, which is
also a becoming. This notion of becoming disrupts the binary opposition of colonizer/colonized, khaki/black, and disease/health.
Wilson Harris, in "The Complexity of Freedom," emphasizes the
partiality of being and language in a dialogue that heals communities, and therefore, larger societies: "What is required at a certain

level—if a new dialogue is to begin to emerge—is a penetration of partial images, not a submission to the traditional reinforcement of partiality into total or absolute institution; partiality may begin to declare itself for what it is and to acquire a re-creative suscepti- bility to otherness in a new and varied evolution of community" (116).

Harris does not explicitly connect this type of dialogue with a healing of communities, but Brodber does. In keeping with Brodber's aims, *Jane and Louisa* is transforming, not only for the therapists and clients she began to write for, but for everyone, within the context of this postcolonial dialogue. Moreover, the open-ended quality of the work also prepares us, as do the other works examined in this book, to engage with the multifaceted nature of our health. In this area as well, we are just "becoming," getting ready to see health as a process, connected to self, culture, and society: to begin to envision a new model for a healthy cul- ture, through the power of writers and their words.

2

A Laying

on of

Hands

African American Healing Strategies in Toni Cade Bambara's *The Salt Eaters*

In the creation of the African Diaspora, the cultural survivalisms and imperatives carried from the African coast were tempered by the specific cultures from which the enslaved Africans came, as recent studies have shown.[1] Equally important, they were mitigated (and often violently) by the societies in which they entered. In the first part on African-based texts, I focus on healing in the Caribbean, specifically Jamaica; here, my discussion centers on African-based healing strategies of an African American community in the United States, a major site of the development of "Western" medicine, along with more hidden sites of healing, often ignored by the American medical establishment. Chapter 1 examined a discourse of healing through Afro-Caribbean oral medicines presented to the protagonist, Nellie; Toni Cade Bambara's *The Salt Eaters* explores a broader base of healing strategies in relationship to other systems, both conventional and alternative, including Native American. However, as is the case with the other works examined in this book, this novel is solidly grounded in the reclaiming of the healing practices and worldview of a violently transplanted and formerly despised culture group. In *The Salt Eaters*, Bambara presents her own take on Mervyn Alleyne's notion of the magical power of the word in Afro-Jamaican culture to identify an African American wellness narrative. Bambara, a politicospiritual healer, tells us of her impetus for writing: "That's what I work to do: to produce stories to save our lives" ("Salvation" 41). Through her evocation of the language and stories of healing, Bambara, in a literary laying on of hands, begins to develop a discourse to help cure the culturally ill. Significantly, the novel also moves us toward a comprehension of medical performance as envisioned by Makinde, in which biomedical practice joins hands with the traditional healers.

In her use of the magical power of the word, Bambara's aim to heal her community reflects a "prevalent strategy in contemporary Black women's writing," according to Athena Vrettos. Although Vrettos unfortunately does not mention Bambara in her article "Curative Domains: Women, Healing and History in Black Women's Narratives," her focus on Alice Walker, Gloria Naylor, and Paule Marshall, who envision "the fragmentation and alienation of Afro-American culture from traditions of its past as a disease that can be healed, and healed specifically by Black women" (471), can easily be expanded to include Bambara. Vrettos further states: "Through representations of healing, Black women writers seek the inspiration and authority to heal, locating in language a new curative domain" (456). Furthermore, Joanne Gabbin, in "A Laying On of Hands," comments: "[Black women writers] have begun to explore the roots of their cultural traditions and, as symbolic agents in a kind of ritualistic, laying-on of hands experience, are cleansing, healing, and empowering their communities" (246). Along with Marshall's *Praisesong*, Gabbin discusses female empowering texts like Zora Neale Hurston's *Their Eyes Were Watching God*, Margaret Walker's *Jubilee*, and Toni Morrison's *Sula*; however, in her article she does not mention *The Salt Eaters*, a novel that, with the exception of *Praisesong*, deals with healing more explicitly than do the other texts mentioned.[2] Despite the fact that this profound healing text is not discussed in either of these articles, Bambara actualizes these two women's theoretical positions. *The Salt Eaters*, as a healing text, most explicitly relates personal dysfunction to both cultural and global dis-ease. And Bambara, as authorial healer, takes on conventional medicine while creating a strategy for healing in her language and narrative structure. In her woman-centered and African-based discourse, Bambara performs a linguistic "laying on of hands" on her readers and community.

The Salt Eaters, in which two hours of a traditional healing at a community hospital extend out into concentric circles of the lifeblood of an African American community, is a complex novel, considered difficult by many critics and readers. Much of its complexity comes from Bambara's design: "To work at the point of interface between the political/artistic/metaphysical, that meeting place where all contradictions and polarities melt" ("Salvation" 43). But the complexity also derives from Bambara's extensive use of allusions: New Age terminology, such as tarot, chakras, past lives, astrology, from the cultures that New Agers appropriate. Marxist political discourse and underground American resistance; and most important, African-based mythology, cultural traditions, and healing practices. For Bambara, as for her character Velma Henry and the healers themselves, being well is integrally connected to the acknowledgment of one's African heritage. To glean from the Rastafarian vocabulary, Bambara's "overstanding" is that one can "want to be well," cure the "affliction of disconnectedness," and save lives through residual African cultural practices, which often lie dormant in African American communities. The governing force of the novel is a challenge: How, as a culture, in this case, African American culture, do we begin to get well despite "the psychic and spiritual damage that is being done to us?" (Chandler 348).

For Bambara, whose aim is to produce "stories to save our lives," the link between language and healing is paramount. In her creation of this wellness narrative, she begins to work with Makinde's oral medicine in trying to find a language in which to perform the healing. In an interview with Kalamu ya Salaam, right after the publication of *The Salt Eaters*, Bambara details her design for healing her community, as well as the limitations of English as a language in which to conduct the healing. She comments that English (as well as other corresponding colonial languages) "has been stripped of the kinds of structures and the kinds of vocabularies that allow people to plug into other kinds of intelligences, [at a time when] certain types of language 'mysteries'—for lack of a better word—were suppressed" (48). Like her Caribbean sisters, Brodber and poet Marlene Nourbese Philip, Bambara is trying to disrupt the language to overthrow the dominant linguistic stranglehold that makes English a "foreign anguish" through her own metaphoric activity. Bambara tells us how she tries to invent a new kind of discourse that relates back to that other language in metaphors that include both the idiom of science and the ancestors: "I'm trying to break words open and get at the bones, deal with symbols as though they were atoms. I'm trying to find out not only how a word gains its meaning, but how a word gains its power" (48). In searching to find how words gain the power to heal, Bambara, who prematurely died of cancer as I was writing this book, takes on the role of ancestral spirit guide, and leads us linguistically through a healing, decentering both our language and the sense of linear narrative, making the connections to heal the whole person. In her holistic vision, "everything becomes a kind of metaphor for the whole" (Salaam 50). In what Bambara herself calls a "thrown-open" book, she traces the whole through a personal healing, the reconstruction of the community through the medicine people, the warriors, and the artists. Furthermore, she links this growth to combating the "national suicide" that Metzger identifies through our society's environmental disasters and nuclear wastes, especially the environmental racism committed on so-called minority communities.

To uncover some of the layers of this wellness narrative, it may be useful to explore further notions of wellness within an African worldview, in the case, African-based healing practices specific to the United States, especially the Black communities of South Carolina and Georgia's Sea Islands. It is no coincidence that Bambara places her wellness narrative in the Sea Islands, since this has been a site of African-based culture from the moment resisting slaves set up their maroon colonies. Because of this history and the isolation from the mainland, African cultural traditions on these islands have endured in ways distinct from African American experiences in other areas of the United States. According to John Hendrik Clarke's foreword to *Sea Island Roots*, the Sea Islands are a "special case" because the "lack of contact with the mainland helped to preserve some of the important features of their African culture" (vi). A cursory discussion of the history of the Gullah (or Geechie, as members of this diverse group are called in certain parts of this area) gives us insight as to why they are considered the African American culture group most closely related to its African forebears and have "ranked highest on a scale of African linguistic retentions in North America" (Baird, "Guy B. Johnson" 426). According to Lorenzo Turner in his impressive study, *Africanisms in the Gullah Dialect*, Africans "constituted a considerable part of the slave population of Coastal South Carolina and Georgia" (1). Turner and other scholars of the Gullah all point to the certain historical events that made these islands fertile ground for maintaining African traditions. From these historical roots, the Sea Islands developed an emergent culture, based on the West African societies from which many of the enslaved Africans came and explicitly linked to the diasporic culture identified in the Caribbean.

Unlike the case of other areas in the southeastern United States, the number of slaves imported directly into South Carolina in the 1700s numbered around 100,000; moreover, even after the slave trade was officially abolished in 1833, rogue ships still were bringing Africans into the Sea Islands until 1858. These islands, explored and exploited since the 1520s, were originally settled by Barbadian and other Caribbean planters. Furthermore, because of the geographical conditions and the difficulty of the Europeans who were not used to living in subtropical, malaria-infested islands, the white population was far outnumbered by those of African descent, and at times slaves ran plantations for absentee owners, as in the Caribbean. Therefore, the slave system and lifestyles of the descendants of the Africans often had more in common with West African and Afro-Caribbean societies than with those of other slave populations in the United States. Finally, because of the similarities in the coregional forest societies forcibly brought directly to the Sea Islands, the African American culture emerging from different ethnic groups such as the Vai, Mende, Akan, Igbo, and Yoruba, reflected a more homogenous group than did other slave populations in the United States.

Along with Bambara, other contemporary Black women writers such as Toni Morrison, Paule Marshall, and Gloria Naylor, as well as film director and writer Julie Dash, have written of the South generally, and of this area specifically, as a repository of African-based traditions. Furthermore, they have recognized a knowledge of this cultural history as a way to heal fractured African American communities. In *Song of Solomon*, Morrison identifies a Southern base for African culture in her invented Southern town on the Virginia coast, Shalimar, where the Flying Africans returned to Africa leaving a legacy to be uncovered. More specifically, in Marshall's *Praisesong* , the Igbos, after realizing what life in this new land would be, walk back to Africa over water, from Ibo Landing in Tatem, South Carolina (this historical site still exists today, and will remain if people of that community are successful in resisting plans for a waste water treatment plant on the site). Julie Dash's film *Daughters of the Dust* returns us to these same islands and Ibo Landing at an earlier time, when the Peazant family has a reunion both to honor the ancestors and to deal with the children who are about the become part of the famous migration north. Naylor's *Mama Day* is situated on a mythical Sea Island community somewhere between Georgia and South Carolina, and it presents an Africanized community, proud and independent, through the point of view of the Matriarch, Mama Day. In this novel, Naylor pays tribute to this healing place through Mama Day's supernatural powers, and even places her Sea Island outside the realm of US government control, since the Island is in neither South Carolina nor Georgia.

Germane to the aims of this chapter is the retention of African traditional healing systems on these islands, continuing in the area since the 1600s, when enslaved Africans first landed there. In the introduction to *Hoodoo Medicine: Sea Island Herbal Remedies*, Faith Mitchell comments: "That a separate Black folk medicine was recognized even then is reflected in the repeated references made in literature written during the plantation period to herbal medicines used only by blacks" (16). The development of these healing traditions in the Sea Islands is one aspect of a cultural matrix of African American beliefs, identified by folklorist Beverly J. Robinson. Robinson notes that "metaphysical traditions belonging to an African worldview . . . [encompass] the balance of nature and [do] not separate mind and body" (218). African American healing, inscribed by this African worldview, is therefore a sacred act, which "places folk practitioners and their art in the world of the spiritual" (Robinson 219). Twining and Baird, in *Sea Island Roots* further state: "For although they exist in syncretic form, these survivalisms are still eminently functional in the society" (10). The implication here is that sites of healing develop away from sites of advanced technologies, such as cities; however the writers address that in different ways. In *Mama Day*, Naylor's urban dweller, George, has to give up his life to keep the traditions going, whereas Marshall's healed Avey of *Praisesong* returns shamanistically to her urban center of New York City to teach the upwardly mobile African Americans this curative history. Bambara, who like Naylor and Marshall grew up in New York, also saw the site of healing within this rural isolated world in which African traditions remained. As Bambara notes in her essay "Reading the Signs, Empowering the Eye: *Daughters of the Dust* and the Black Independent Cinema Movement," it is this geographical terrain where the descendents of those enslaved can "enact daily rituals of group validation in a liberated zone" (*Deep Sightings* 95). There are these special places, sites of healing that allow for this kind of ritual of community and work as a restorative for past wounds. However, Bambara resists a binary opposition here, avoiding the essentialism that often comes with glorifying the pastoral. The characters in *The Salt Eaters* have clear links to the urban centers, known to many of them, since they not only travel to urban sites of political activism but also have relatives living in the urban North, linking back to the great migration alluded to in Dash's film. Most pertinently, the town of Clayborne is a representation of Frogmore, South Carolina, where the famous Penn Center has existed as a site of both healing and resistance.[3] Furthermore, even in the urban centers, one can worship the ancestors (as many have done, for example, in the Yoruba temples and apartment shrines in New York), expanding the healing traditions outward from the original sites.

The ancestral presence, a major retention of this African worldview is a concept connected to the health and disease of an individual and community. Both African American and Caribbean women writers have looked to that ancestral presence, as Toni Morrison identifies in her essay, "Rootedness: The Ancestor as Foundation." Chapter 1 of this book examines Brodber's development of Aunt Alice as spirit guide and ancestor for Nellie; this chapter specifically explores Bambara's sustained discussion of the Law of the Ancestor, as identified by I. Sow in *Anthropological Structures of Madness in Black Africa*, particularly how the loss of the ancestors brings on illness to a community. In the "reality of the panstructured African universe," according to Sow, the "principles of society, which dictates all sociocultural praxis, have their source in the fundamental law of the Ancestor" (7). Although evoked differently throughout sub-Saharan Africa, the role of the ancestor in most traditional religions is to preside over the welfare of family and community (Adedeji 117). These ancestors in conjunction with the deities of the society affect the collective health of the community and its individual members. In "Ancestors—The Living Dead," Daniel Wambutda details this profound influence on a day-to-day basis: [The ancestors] are expected to guard the interest of the community and to bless the people and their endeavors generally. . . . If offended, however, they can also inflict one form of misfortune or another" (132). Therefore, what we term as psychological/physical disease often comes from an unfixing of the relationship of the person to the society's "collective value system" based on the "order of the founding Ancestor" (7).

Throughout the African Diaspora, ancestor worship has been identified as an integral part of African American experience. In their "New World" incantations, the ancestors are part of a pantheon of beliefs, derived from the West African societies from which they came. One example, identified by Donald Cosentino, is the ancestor belief system of the Fon of West Africa, including the spirits called *loa* (261). Like Ishmael Reed in his comic version of ancestor worship, *Mumbo Jumbo*, Bambara takes this term for the ancestors from its transportation in the Caribbean, most clearly identified in Haitian Vodun. Furthermore, *The Salt Eaters* is inhabited by deities of other West African cultures: Oshun, Ogun, Shango, Oye, Damballah, and Eshu-Elegba (Legba).[4] Bambara, who identifies herself as a Pan-Africanist (Hull 229), states her belief that wellness can only come when a balance with these deities and the ancestors is restored: "We don't call upon those spirits. We don't celebrate those ancestors. . . . More horrendous is the fact that we don't tap into the ancestral presence" (Chandler 348). Bambara's conclusion is that the ancestors in *The Salt Eaters* are offended by the community's lack of reverence and, moreover, that often her community doesn't want to be well.

The relationship of personal and community health to the presence of the ancestors resists a binary opposition in contemporary culture, the separation of medicine and healing from worship and the spirit world. Although certain Christian sects do "faith healing," which encodes an earlier traditional approach linking the healing arts with religion, all aspects of the healing process from bodily remedies to spiritual afflictions are treated holistically within an African worldview. Still, in the Americas, it is relevant to note that the syncretism, which links African and Christian cosmologies, also integrates worship and science in opposition to a Western, modern approach. Peter Goldsmith notes that what has been called "Afro-American religion was not separate but part of a larger complex of thought and behavior broader than what we [read dominant culture] have generally regarded as 'spiritual'" (85). Goldsmith further comments that within this cultural domain, religion and science do not represent separate spheres of influence, tracing this viewpoint back to Africanized lifestyle reconstructed by the slaves:

While their masters carefully distinguished between cures for the afflicted soul and cures for the afflicted body, the African tradition led slaves to recognize multiple and non-contradictory levels of causality. Spiritual and temporal worlds interpenetrated one another, as did present, past, and future. By manipulating these realms simultaneously as they saw fit, slaves recognized the fundamental connectedness of physical, social, and emotional aspects of affliction, while the dominant culture then, as now, failed to see the connections. (88)

Goldsmith's comments are relevant both to Bambara's novel and my own aims in this study. For within the syncretic function, the place of the female spirit guide and diviner is of paramount importance. Within the African American church, women have maintained a role denied to them in medicine. As Achterberg explains in *Woman as Healer*, traditional healers, especially women, went underground with the scientific "revolution" and advent of biomedical production, but still maintained authority within specific communities, even when effaced by the dominant culture. I. Sow identifies the role of healer as part of women's position in traditional Black Africa: The woman is a "prime mover and vital element essential to the good functioning and continuation of social institutions. The source and seat of fertility and prosperity, she is also the guarantor of custom. She preserves the traditional methods of healing" (63; note 2). As in the case of the balm healers in Jamaica, women maintained their position as healers and custodians of the culture throughout the Americas, even though this position was mitigated by various societal constraints.[5] Often the act of syncretizing African traditional practices into the Christian church allowed women to retain some of their authority as healers. Historian Margaret Washington confirms this view in her study "Cultural Transmission and Female Diviners in Gullah Slave Society." In exploring the healing ritual of the "ring shout," Washington notes: "For Africans, the spiritual agency was an ancestor. For the Gullahs, on a conscious level, the agency was the Holy Ghost. In both cases the transmitter between the two worlds was usually a woman" (12). Washington states further: "The female diviner-healers believed in the power of the word and the necessity of harmony between mind and body" (14). Like Baby Suggs in Tony Morrison's *Beloved*, Minnie Ransom is representative of these "diviner-healers," and in her case, Minnie leads the patient protagonist, Velma Henry, toward health with the help of her own spirit guide, the ancestor Old Wife. In *The Salt Eaters*, language, in addition to touch, is the medium in which healing occurs (for the characters as well as the readers).

In the opening of *The Salt Eaters*, traditional healer Minnie Ransom says to her patient Velma, who has tried, unsuccessfully, to kill herself: "Are you sure, sweetheart, that you want to be well?" (1). The disease of the protagonist, Velma, mirrors all the disconnectedness of her community. The term "Salt Eater" has multiple meanings, one of which has to do with the fact that the slaves who ate salt were unable to fly back to Africa.[6] Bogged down in a hostile and alien world, the descendants of these Africans live lives of disconnectedness and dis-ease. For the characters in this novel, their disorders come most often from a loss of ancestral heritage and its spiritual potency. The loa of the town of Clayborne have, for the most part, "withdrawn in disgust, neglected, betrayed" (152); it is only in the marshes and beneath the Old Tree (planted in 1871 to honor the beginning of the Southwest Infirmary) that they still reside. In this community, born from the clay that their African forbears ate, it is the young people who have forgotten the ancestors. The loa "who danced and stomped unseen by those pretending not to know of spirit kinship" keep waiting for contact beyond a few, "weary and impatient with amnesia, neglect, and a bad press . . . , weary with so little to perform" (146). Velma, who is out of touch with the ancestors, is a social activist whose political burnout as a result of her fighting environmental destruction from multinational corporations, racism from the larger society, and sexism from her own men becomes too much for her to take. Ignoring the voice of the ancestors, Velma "pretends not to know" and in her confused state, succumbs to mental disease and attempts suicide.

In "Mechanisms of Disease: African American Women Writers, Social Pathologies, and the Limits of Medicine," Ann Folwell Stanford notes that *The Salt Eaters* "insists that understanding the connection between sick bodies and a sick world is crucial to the making of a workable vision equipped for urgent social change and global healing" (8). Resisting the separation of personal and political health encoded in allopathic medicine, this novel, like the others examined in this book, takes individual healing beyond personal well-being, so that healing also becomes a responsibility for those who have gone through the cure. The novel explores personal, community, and global dysfunction; however, Bambara does not present someone totally isolated from her community. The fact that her diseased protagonist Velma is a social activist, who is trying to link up all aspects of her life but is unable to do so without the help of the ancestors, is part of Bambara's design. One aim of Bambara's in writing the novel was "to investigate possible ways to bring our technicians of the sacred and our guerillas together" (Tate 31). As with Nellie, there is an opposition between Marxist theory, which is both Western and materialist, and the possibility of a kind of spiritual activism; and as will be evident in the final chapter on Jo Sinclair and Jewish cultural illness, Marx's own resistance toward any kind of spirituality in social protest might have been based in his uncomfortable position as a Jew in Germany. In contradistinction, Brodber's most recent work, *Louisiana*, describes how the spiritual activists gain strength from their political ancestors as they work together against oppression. In *The Salt Eaters*, it is evident that Velma, as a community worker, is not tapped into either the ancestors or the healers, to her own detriment. In her quest to change the unfair conditions she sees around her, she begins to withdraw from those who love her: her husband, Obie; her son; even her godmother, the elder Sophie Heywood, who is connected to the ancestors and to the tradition of activism (descended from the boardinghouse woman who helped fund Harpers Ferry). Velma is called a "crackpot" (100), but she really is a cracked pot. (To digress for a minute on a possible allusion in this text or within its African unconscious, there is a famous West African proverb, "Better the water spilt than the pot broken," referring to the loss of a child rather than the mother in childbirth.) In this case, the loss of this pot, if she remains broken, means the loss of a mother to her family, the repercussions of which we see in Tayo's struggles without his mother in Silko's *Ceremony* as well as in other African American novels like Walker's *The Third Life of Grange Copeland* and *Meridian*. But there would also be one less fighter for her causes and one less potential spiritualist to feed the ancestors (who, in turn, protect the community).

Through Velma's reliving of both childhood experiences and her adult life as a community worker under the guiding hands of the healer Minnie Ransom, as well as through the multivocal history presented by the other characters, the story of her breakdown unfolds. Velma believes she is connected to her community, but something remains missing. Under the influence of her godmother, Sophie, and the powerful presence of the Old Tree and its history, Velma, in a theoretical way, understands the necessity of being grounded in one's own traditions. She complains that her prayer partner Jamahl's solutions to dis-ease "always lay in someone else's culture: Tai Chi, TM, Reichian therapy, yoga. She argued that the truth was in one's own people and the key was to be centered in the best of one's own traditions" (169). Yet Velma does not listen to her own advice. She focuses solely on battling the needed fight against oppression, but, like Nellie in *Jane and Louisa*, she loses her own center. Ironically, Velma's commitment to her community leaves her little time to balance either her life or theirs with "underlying relational networks that give structure to whole of a person's life" (Sow 3).

As with other chosen healers like Minnie Ransom, who heals her, Velma, as a child, is visited by the ancestral mud mothers, but is frightened by their powerful force: "Ten or more women with mud hair, storing yams in gourds, and pebbles in cracked calabash. . . . Stepping out of the mouth of the cave, they tried to climb out of the specked glass [of the mirror], talk to her, tell her what must be done all over again" (255). Although the mud mothers in the cave reflect, on some level, any primordial women-centered world, Bambara's use of the yam (originating in Africa) and the calabash denotes a cultural specificity that clearly situates these mothers as African. Velma does not listen to these women as they come before her in visions; at first she is afraid, and later, too busy. The novel makes clear that, although the powers from the ancestors come to Velma through these mud mothers, she resists their call. She does seek out the marshes to commune with the loa, but she is unable to link this desire to these earlier visions or to her political work when she returns: "Feeling the healer's hands on her, she remembered that the marsh visit had failed to inform her days and nights, it had failed to inform her mind, the minute she got up from that tree. Whatever had occurred, stayed behind" (172). Like Avey Johnson in Marshall's *Praisesong*, who forgot the story of the Ibos until her healing journey to and cleansing bath in Carriocou, it is only once the healer touches Velma that she begins to retrieve the connections she had lost. What is interesting about this text is that, unlike the assimilated Avey, whom we expect to have these problems, Velma is intellectually aware of who she is and what she must do. Yet without the spiritual help, she cannot continue and accept her place as one of the healers of the community.

As Velma descends into despair, she becomes more guarded, more alienated from her family and community. Despite her commitments to them, she refuses their support, as she exhibits all the signs of personal/community unbalance that Sow details. Her breakdown is metonomized in the incident when, at her sister's house, she bites "right through her juice glass . . . spitting splattered teeth in a rusty can whose ragged lid cut her lips (140); moreover, Velma constantly asks her friends, "[when is it] appropriate to commit suicide?" (215). Her godmother, Sophie Heywood, despairs that despite their "eating salt" together, somehow she has not protected Velma; dialectically, in this case, the salt works as a linkage overcoming pain and bitterness. Sophie's view is that the influences from outside have distracted Velma and the others like her: "[Sophie] had been listening for years to the starchy explanations from the quacks who called themselves guidance counselors, social workers, analysts, therapists, whose views had more to do with their own habit of illusion than anything rooted in the natural, the real" (147). Disgusted with the conventional healers she calls quacks and leaving her place as one of the elders who guides the healing at the Southwest Infirmary, Sophie attempts to work through what is wrong with this godchild by herself. As in Granny Tucker's relationship with Nellie, Sophie has tried to teach Velma the ways of the ancestors, but Velma has been too distracted to learn. Sophie understands Velma's place in trying to bring together both the guerillas and the "technicians of the sacred"; however, she cannot comprehend why Velma has not listened to the ancestors and does not accept her own role as potential healer of the community. Still, Sophie has faith that Velma will finally accept her call: "[Others] might have faith in a science that only filled people's lives with useless structures, senseless clutter. But she knew better. . . . And in time Velma would find her way back to the roots of life. And in doing so, be a model" (147).

The Southwest Infirmary, the site of Velma's healing, is integral to Bambara's overall design in the novel. The novel not only poses a dis-eased culture and society, but also intimates that the very methods of healing are diseased; for this community specifically, conventional biomedical models are not enough. As identified throughout Sandra Harding's extensive work *The "Racial" Economy of Science*, the relationship between Black people in the United States and the science establishment has been, for the most part, antagonistic.[7] According to an editorial reprinted in *The Black Scholar*, "the reality of racism has excluded most of us from the pursuit of science. Regarded as degraded beings, prisoners of undisciplined emotions and suitable only for manual labor, black people have for generations been barred from white institutions of scientific training" (Harding 456). This institutionalized racism, connected to a general lack of cultural understanding, helped to amplify misgivings toward the medical establishment in African American communities as well as indigenous societies, as evidenced in Silko's *Ceremony* and Hulme's *the bone people*. Symptomatic of these feelings are the suspicious community voices in *The Salt Eaters*. In one telling example, two older women on the bus to Clayborne reflect a paranoia that has a strong cultural base. The first woman, Gracie, says that her son-in-law, who works at a hospital, told her that "those doctors don't know what they are doing playing around with viruses and germs and things. Will kill us all" (69). The two women's final judgment that the people should "tie [the doctors] up with their own stethoscopes" clearly defines their lack of faith in the societally prescribed "healer": in this novel, the doctors are not healers, they, like the others, need to be healed.

The portrait of Dr. Julius Meadows, a "real" doctor, is integral to the context of healing in the novel. Like the bourgeois, mulatto-class Dr. Foster in *Song of Solomon*, Meadows is light-skinned and alienated from his community; however, unlike this doctor, whose position does not change throughout the novel or even after his death, Meadow is healed in the course of *The Salt Eaters*. His own healing process and reintegration into the community are posed as a counterpoint to the healing of Velma, the community activist. We are first introduced to the doctor during the healing, when he and others from the medical establishment are invited to watch the incorporation of traditional healing, through the aid of Minnie Ransom and the twelve elders of the Master's Mind, within the context of the Southwest Infirmary. Although not all the visitors from the conventional hospitals take seriously the event that takes place before them—one calling the young bandaged woman on a stool, guided by the hands of the older woman standing up, a "comedy" (16)—they are not the least threatened by what they are seeing, but rather are mostly impatient. However, this is not so for Meadows, who recites the Hippocratic oath to himself like a protection from a curse, while he witnesses the healing at the Southwest Infirmary. On one hand, he envisions the healer, Minnie, and Velma in some kind of out-of-body collusion, and on the other, he calls upon his imported gods of medicine— Apollo, Aesculapius, Hygeia and Panacea—to save him from this travesty of science. Meanwhile, the loa that he fails to sense are watching him, "nudging each other, puffing on cigars and rearing back on their heels" (55). Cora Rider, one of the Master's Mind, hears him and call his recitations a "blasphemous prayer" (108). For Cora, and for others in this community, Meadows is not a symbol of African American success, but rather a collaborator who has bought into a culture that has oppressed him.

In the characterization of Meadow, we witness a doctor who not only is unable to cure his community, but is also not a very good doctor, even in the Western sense. He describes himself thus: "His presence or absence mattered to no one, not even to his patients" (58). Moreover, he suffers from all sorts of psychological disabilities, relating to his tenuous position in society and his own feelings of self-hate. He cannot fit comfortably into the role of doctor/scientist as prescribed by the dominant culture, yet he resists fiercely those tendencies he has to connect to another, ancient reality, signified in the healing: "Reviewing the Hippocratic oath after all this time, it was peculiar, a compulsion. He wanted to call them out, dialogue with those beings behind the names, know the gods he'd given allegiance to. . . . Seemed primitive" (122). Unknowingly tapping into the loa who are watching him, Meadows calls up Hippocrates and the others as ancestors, but there is no process by which they can answer him. And in a relevant way, Meadows perceives this desire to connect to his collective past as "primitive," some failing in himself to take on the "logic" of science.[8] For Meadows, the opposition between his "educated" city mind and his rejected "country self" is untenable: He cannot mediate, thus his emotional dis-ease. Unable to witness the completion of the healing, which he finds so threatening, Meadows manages to escape out the door into a space beyond the limitations of his perceptions, and there he begins a healing ritual that changes his life. He walks through the community, and his interactions force him to confront the aspects of himself he has rejected and that have contributed to his inability to be the healer he hoped he would be.

As Meadows wanders through African American sections of the town of Clayborne, like "a late arrival at one of the obligatory cocktail parties" (177), he begins to reassess his life, one that appears for the most part, unlived. He hears the word "suppah" and daydreams about a family he never had, and he understands painfully his inability to connect with the people he passes by. He tries to walk through this part of town unnoticed, but his physical presence makes him visible, "a putty-colored three toed sloth," as he recites the nickname given to him by his stepfather (177). In a reversal of the story of Ellison's invisible man (invisible because of his visibility), Meadows's light skin and uncomfortable behavior makes him clearly "visible" to those around him: "They were studying him. By now they knew he was not a honkey. . . . Now the grain of his skin would be coming into view, like a 35mm blowup. He was never clearer to himself than when Black people examined him this way, suspicious" (186). This interaction brings into stark relief his loneliness and longing, but it also exposes his arrogance, based in his color and class privilege. As he walks, Meadows, like Nellie's Aunt Becca, makes judgments on "these people," calling one a "welfare man," a recurring trope within the context of intrarace prejudice.

As his condescension mirrors that of those who trained him in his field, making Black people invisible, Meadows thinks patronizingly about another: He had him pegged. He didn't have to look in his face. "He never looked at the faces anyway" (183). Of course, the irony of this statement is that the man, Hull, whom Meadows felt he had "pegged" and his friend, Thurston, are the ones who perform his ritual initiation and integration into the community. A confrontation, which begins with Meadows stepping on Thurston's foot, ends by the two taking him under their wing to go get a beer. As he walks with them, Meadows thinks: "Whatever happened, he wasn't stumbling aimlessly around the streets anymore, at loose ends, alone" (190). For Meadows, this is the beginning of a personal healing rite in which he comes to realize that he is no longer isolated and alone, but he must travel further to be able to embrace the profession he entered and to perceive it as part of his commitment to heal others and the community.

In linking Meadows's attitudes toward the Black community with the fact that he matters little to his patients, Bambara illustrates Meadows's inability to be a true doctor. Furthermore, only through a process of ritual readmittance to this representational African American community can he be healed and a healer in an African holistic concept of health. Rather, it is in the portrait of Minnie Ransom and project at the Southwest Infirmary that Bambara's design for a new healing model unfolds. Minnie clearly is the healer of Velma, but she is indirectly responsible for Meadows's transformation as well; her presence in the healing sends him on his unknowing quest to be (re)integrated into the community. At the beginning of the healing (which is not going well), Minnie becomes distracted by Meadows calling forth his Greek idols, and she comments to her own spirit guide, Old Wife, that she'd have loved to have a "tete-à-tete over tea with Dr. Meadows, who would, I'm sure, be more interested in learning about the ancient wisdoms, the real, the actual, the sho-nuff original folk stuff behind them Greek imposters he's calling up and they're already there. Right there in the treatment room if he'd only see" (55).

In the design of the Southwest Infirmary, however, Bambara resists the oppositions encoded in Minnie's stark judgment of the beginnings of a Western medical tradition. Chiseled on the archway over the entrance of the Southwest Infirmary is the statement "HEALTH IS YOUR RIGHT" (114), and within it doors are traditional healers and doctors working together.[9] Although the visitors from the medical establishment are worried by the "blatant lack of discipline," the Infirmary has an excellent reputation in "radical medical circles" (10). Its history is also important to the design of the novel, alluding to its representation of the Penn Center and its training of the midwives as part of its community development (Lee 176). The Infirmary was established by the Free Coloureds of Clayborne in 1871, and the loa still reside in the Old Tree planted to honor its beginning. The plan of development of the Infirmary at its inception included a fusion of "Western medicine and traditional arts" (106), politics and health, the spiritual and the scientific. Its past, according to the administrator, Doc Serge, is another fusion of healing traditions, African and Native American. Doc Serge (not a "real" doctor) appears at first similar to the charlatan Dr. Buzzard in Naylor's *Mama Day*; however, even as a con man, he uses his skills to assuage the suspicions of visitors by telling them about the "courage and resourcefulness of the old bonesetters, the old medicine show people, the grannies and midwives, the root men, the conjure women, the obeah folks . . . who'd helped the Southwest Community Infirmary defend itself and build itself through the years" (107). In its present configuration, conventional medical treatments are integrated into the traditional healings, administered by Minnie Ransom and the twelve elders of the Master's Mind.

In this novel, the elders, both men and women, lead the healing in their role as the Master's Mind. The social role of the healers, in this sense, are, according to Sow, "that of any authority responsible for defending the community" (89). The twelve of the Master's Mind reflect the twelve chapters of the novel, and Velma's godmother, Sophie Heywood, is included in the group. Through the work of Minnie Ransom and the Master's Mind, as well as those ancestors like Old Wife and Cleotus the Hermit, diseased individuals are brought back into a more harmonic relationship with the community. Although in the novel there is a balance of male and female healers on the ancestral level as well as in the infirmary, it is often the older women healers who lead the way for the young female activists to (re)connect with their cultural heritage. Most significant of the healers is Minnie Ransom who customarily performs the laying on of hands in the Southwestern Infirmary. Minnie is described as "the fabled healer of the district, her bright red flouncy dress drawn in at the waist with two different strips of kenti [sic]) cloth" (3). In addition to this Ghanaian cloth, she also wears "a minor fortune" of African-styled silver and gold bangles and a hot-pink headtie.

In the methods she uses, Minnie is a healer in an African context, as identified by Sow and Makinde. As a defender of the community, she feeds the loa under the Old Tree, planted as a gift to generations to come (145). As healer, she is a vital part of her community. Moreover, like Naylor's Mama Day, Minnie focuses a great deal of attention on specific female disorders: "Miss Ransom known to calm fretful babies with a smile or a pinch of the thigh, known to cool out nervous wives who bled all the time and couldn't stand still. . . . " (113). However, unlike those of Mama Day or Pilate in Morrison's *Song of Solomon*, Minnie's healing practices do not include obeah. Her abilities do include major illnesses, and she is "known to dissolve hard lumps in the body that the doctors at the country hospital called cancers" (113), linking her to the Maori spiritual healer in Hulme's *the bone people*. From physical illness to what is called psychological trauma, Minnie tries to heal the whole person and restore balance in the community.

In "Psychic Healing," Daniel Benor describes Minnie's state during the healing, identifying Melville J. Herskovits's understanding of revelation as a basic tenet of African healing practices (241): "[The healer enters] a state of altered consciousness when [she] is healing . . . , a sense of being one with the healee and with the 'All'" (174). Finally, as a liaison to the ancestors and as Velma's spirit mother, Minnie performs her role as female diviner, as described by Washington in "Cultural Transmission and Female Diviners in Gullah Slave Society": "The guide was usually a highly respected, powerful elderly woman called the 'spiritual mother.' In African societies she would be called a diviner. Divination was the process of unmasking private drives, sin and vices, which interfere with the flow of society. On the plantation the diviner might also serve as medicinal healer, midwife, or prophetess. Spiritual mothers directed and guided seekers through their symbolic travels into the wilderness or world of the dead" (5). The spirit mother guides the diseased person to the ancestors and also takes them through their past pains and alienation, a process that most of the protagonists in the novels discussed in this book must go through, in one way or another, to be culturally healed. Within this African-based cosmology, there would be no separation of spirit guide/medicinal healer as Washington posits, since the aim is to restore balance in the whole person.

The fictional Minnie reflects the lives of identified traditional healers in the United States and the Caribbean. In Minne's re-creation, Bambara fits into Valerie Lee's supposition that contemporary African American women writers are "resuscitating the representation of the granny . . . and thereby creating complementary, but alternatives literary texts to the grannies' lived texts," which are often disregarded in historical accounts (1–2). As Lee notes, the role of the female traditional healer has become a major theme in contemporary writings; one recent example is Gayl Jones's *The Healing*, which centers on the faith healer Harlan Jane Eagleton. Like Eagleton and other healers who function in a postcolonial and/or Eurocentric society, Minnie is chosen for her profession outside of her own volition, and it takes time for her to finally accept her gift.[10] This contrasts sharply with the traditional healer within an African context; in that case, there would already be a cultural understanding of the role, and often that role would be inherited. Minnie's travels to fulfill her potential as healer come through her own spirit guide, Karen Wilder, Old Wife. Old Wife is "the teller of tales no one would sit still to hear anymore" (52), but Minnie, perceived as "batty" by her family and community, does listen and learn. Often chosen healers in a hostile environment will be considered mad, but this is a different pattern than that of the woman, as in Gilman's "The Yellow Wallpaper," Rhys's *Wide Sargasso Sea*, or Gayl Jones's *Eva's Man*, who is driven insane by her social situation; rather, Minnie's role is similar to that of the shaman, who is often perceived as disturbed and apart from society, but then later functions within it as a healer, once the gift is accepted. Like Ona in Flora Nwapa's *The Lake Goddess*, Minnie embraces her calling, receiving her instructions from the Source: "Minnie was told to clear the path that lead up to the cliffs, set the trees, erect a fountain and build the chapel in The Mind. And going there—the cooling dark, the candles, the altar—she saw the gift and knew, for at least that instant, where the telling came from" (53). Her altar, as described here, is similar to the settings of Yoruba shrines from New York to Cuba and Brazil in Diaspora religious ceremonies designed for communing with the ancestors. And like Nellie's Aunt Alice, Old Wife, after her death, is an ancestral presence who stays on as spirit guide to Minnie's healing, although this ostensibly serious relationship is often tempered by a humorous repartee. Throughout, their dialogue is the interweaving of Christianity with this African-based religion and the loa who inhabit the place. When Old Wife tells Minnie decisively that she "don't traffic" in what might be called the magical realm, Minnie retorts: "You do too. Fess up, what you hauling round in that gris gris sack of yours?" (50). Admitting to the *gris gris* sack (a Senegalese/patois term for a protective talisman), Old Wife still states firmly she is not a "haint" as Minnie calls her; rather, she is a "servant of the Lord" (62). And, in an act intended to demystify the notion of the solemnness of traditional healing and spirit possession, Bambara has the two elders—one alive, one dead—playing a sort of the dozens on each other because the healing is not going well. The use of humor in healing also reflect Native American practices, like that of the healer Betonie in Silko's *Ceremony*.

Minnie is surprised that what should be a routine laying on of hands is so difficult. Minnie asks Velma over and over again whether she wants to be well, whether she is willing to work for her health, listen to the voices of the ancestors that she, for so long, has ignored. Minnie complains to Old Wife that somehow the younger women, although descended from the "women-charged culture of Dahomey" (221), have lost their connection to the ancestors: "What is happening to the daughters of the Yam? Seems like they just don't know how to draw up the powers from the deep like before" (44). Audre Lorde also envisions a Dahomean woman warrior culture in her biomythography *Zami*, based in the Caribbean; however, in this community, the women have forgotten not only this historical source of their power, but also their responsibility in engaging the community in reestablishing the ritual. Eleanor Traylor comments: "As the community must engage its history in order to decipher the meaning of its own rituals, so the individual self must engage its history in order to be well" (60). The concept of wellness here reflects the African worldview identified in these two chapters, as well as a recurrent trope used by Black women writers. Velma, as both a member of the community and an individual in it, must balance personal and community his/herstory, through the acknowledgment of the ancestors, in order to be whole.

Velma's disaffectedness and resistance to the cure also epitomize a community that is used to being unwell. Here Bambara reconfigures individual and cultural illness, and demonstrates that these disorders are not easily dislodged: "So used to being unwhole and unwell, one forgot what it was to walk upright and see clearly, breathe easily, think better than one was programmed to believe" (107). This concept that cultures themselves can be ill reflects both Freud's and Ozaeta's comments, cited at the beginning of this book. In this case, Bambara relates the toll taken on African Americans in the United States because of the history of slavery, racism, and prejudice in a larger world sick from disorders that range from domestic violence to cultural hatred to environmental disasters. Strands from the interwoven, complicated plot connect the damage being done to all peoples by the destruction of the environment; however, Bambara explores specific examples of environmental racism. In the Fred Holt bus driver section, we see the driver Fred as a man "brimming over with rage and pain and loss" (80) who, at times, reacts aggressively and often speaks violently against the women in his life.[11] Fred is also, however, a necessary recorder of disasters done to the earth. In the surreal bus ride, Fred recounts the words of his friend Porter who, before dying as the result of a violent assault by a female assailant wielding knitting needles, was already half dead from a "wasting disease" from the atomic test blasts in Yucca flats (80). Fred and his friend Porter are subject to, and discuss, a myriad of socially constructed diseases. Porter philosophically tells him that here one can be minding one's own business when "some asshole expert releases radioactive fumes in the air and wipes you out in your chair reading the funnies. . . . [W]e are dying of overexposure to some kind of wasting shit—the radioactive crap, asbestos, noise, smog, lies" (79). In Bambara's encircling notion of health, lies are as destructive as radioactive waste.

Pertinently, it is in the bus ride section that we are introduced to the Seven Sisters, comprised of women of color in the Americas, including Velma's sister Palma. These women form a contrapuntal discourse to Fred's raging, anguished thoughts. They are taking the bus to Clayborne to rest and so that Palma can see her disturbed sister, after taking part in a major historical protest at the nuclear site in Barnwell, South Carolina.[12] Unlike Fred, they are activists who do something about the human disasters they witness around them; their interactions also present a model for women working across ethnic lines and cultural barriers. More-over, for readers aware of the testing of atomic weapons on sacred Native American land, the inclusion of Nilda, the sister of the Corn, links this novel to Tayo's trip into the uranium mines in Silko's *Ceremony*. This reinforces Bambara's focus on environmental racism to *Ceremony*'s central metaphor concerning the atom bomb.

After the bus trip, the women enter Clayborne, and Palma takes them to the Avocado Pit Cafe to wait while she goes to find out about her sister. The Avocado Pit Cafe is the site of both the opposition to, and the potential for, a healing community. Discussion in the Avocado Pit ranges from these Seven Sisters and their protest dreams to the nuclear engineers who are playing board games of threatened destruction, as well as the government informer listening to all the wrong conversations. Most relevant is the waiter, Campbell's board game, "Disposal": an educational board game for the nuclear age, including "fix cards" with which experts "conduct a study proving that the defective parts were neither vital nor even necessary to plant operations" (209). In Shakespearean style, Bambara places representation of all the conflicting views affecting the human condition in her cafe, and ultimately, the configuration of people in the Avocado Pit Cafe reflects the novel's resistance to single-issue answers. It is significant that Bambara does not pose a binary opposition between social activism and spiritual quest, African traditions and other ways of spiritual healing. As Brodber also demonstrates in her novels, the ancestors' help is needed to heal the community in sociocultural ways, and whatever else one gains strength from must also be grounded in one's own cultural heritage. I am inclined to agree with Keith Byerman that it is through one's folk heritage (in this case, an African-based culture) that individual and community can move toward wholeness; however, Byerman has missed the point when he states that this can happen by excluding other "ideological systems such as feminism . . . and environmentalism" (39). As recent work on ecofeminism has shown, it is precisely through a blending of these concerns, with a foregrounding in one's own culture, that the much needed activists can unite with the medicine people to help cure the affliction of disconnectedness.[13]

In the midst of the cafe is the conversation of two friends and activists, Jan and Ruby, who relate the issues of environmental racism to the healing of Velma, which is taking place at the same time. Through their talk, we understand the intrigue around the reenactment of a slave insurrection, organized for the carnival to retrieve a lost part of their history of resistance, as well as learning more of Velma's involvement in underground activity concerning her work at Transchemical. This company not only illegally transports radioactive waste, but also poisons its workers and the air everyone in Clayborne breathes. As Ruby notes wryly about this inferno of petrochemicals, "If the fumes are anything to go by, . . . Dante didn't tell the half of it" (207). Although they are worried about the health and welfare of their friend Velma, neither Jan nor Ruby acts on her feelings; nor is either aware of Velma's attempted suicide, thus emphasizing the lack of community interaction, even in the most intimate groups of political activists and women friends. However, it is at this point in the novel, unbeknownst to them, that the healing takes a mystical turn that will affect them all.

Through Minnie's guiding hands, Velma begins to heal as she (re)works her past. Her breakthrough comes when she realizes that she has chosen her own cure: "Thought she knew how to build resistance, make the journey to the center of the circle . . . , stay centered in the best of her people's traditions and not be available to madness, not go under. . . . But amnesia had set in anyway" (258). Velma tightens Minnie's shawl around her, as she centers herself. Like Marshall's Avey Johnson, in *Praisesong*, who reconnects with her great-aunt's story of the Ibos at the Beg Pardon for the ancestors, Velma begins to accept the mud mothers and her place in passing on the traditions; her knowledge has come "tumbling out of the mirror, naked and tatooed with serrated teeth . . . peeping out at her from the mud heavy hanks of the ancient mothers' hair" (259). For Bambara, as for Brodber and Hulme, it is the meeting with the ancestors that brings both the individual and, indirectly, the community back to health. Through her acceptance of her gift, Velma takes on the role for which she has been chosen: a potential healer. With Minnie's divination and the help of the ancestor Old Wife, Velma moves toward wellness, away from the affliction of disconnectedness, knowing that being well has its responsibilities. Minnie tells her: "The source of health is never outside, sweetheart. What will you do when you are well?" (220).

Of course, in the dialectical nature of *The Salt Eaters*, reflecting African cosmology, the source of health is both inside and outside, particularly in terms of the relationship of the individual to the community and the individual's role in helping her community. With Minnie's help, Velma's disease is cured this time by her looking inward toward her own ancestors and family as well as her moving outward to inform her activism with this knowledge: "Velma would remember it as the moment she started back toward life, the moment when the healer's hand had touched some vital spot" (278). Through the healing process, the conflict "in the underlying relational networks that give structure to the whole of a person's life" (Sow 3) is resolved and balance is restored. For the true sense of healing in an African context to be achieved, Minnie has to heal all that Velma comes with.[14] Here the novel takes what Abdul Jan Mohammed calls a counterhegemonic utopian turn, since Velma's healing affects all the others.[15] First of all, her healing affects her life with her husband, Obie, who has traveled on a parallel route during the healing. By the end of the novel, he is ready for her to join forces and truly be partners, breaking down the barriers between Black men and Black women, often forefronted in certain criticism of Black women writers' texts. As he walks up the steps to the hospital, Obie "[s]aluted the future, gold splashing in his eyes" (292). In another example, Fred Holt, who has been extremely agitated, violent and sick throughout the novel, wanders into the last minutes of the healing while looking for a doctor. But the minute he enters the healing room, he calms down, influenced by Minnie's presence: "The longer he looked at the two women, especially the classy old broad, the better he felt" (270).

Profoundly, the healing has both personal and geological effects, symbolized by the storm in the Avocado Pit Cafe. At the moment of the healing, the sky breaks open and the names of different African deities are called forth, most forcefully that of Ogun, the Yoruba god of thunder (248). At this exact moment, the loa return in the minds of the inhabitants, while Legba stands at the gate, and Isis lifts her veil. Moreover, in what one might call Bambara's own act of divination, the tremors from the healing are transformed into a flash forward. Campbell, the philosopher-waiter, recalls his visitation by the Dahomean deity: "But in the months ahead he would remember . . . that lightning had flashed lighting up the purple, smeared sky just as it came to him. Damballah" (245). All the people touched by the powerful thunder and lightning that will affect their lives hereafter ask one another: "When did it begin for you?" (246). Despite grounding in African-based traditions, this moment also includes the visions of the Seven Sisters, broadening out the healing moment to other oppressed cultures. Each of the Sisters, from the Chicana and the Caribbean sisters to the Chinese Mai, represent suppressed cultural traditions in the Americas, which could add to the health of the land. But in the end of the novel, it is Nilda, the Native American, on whom Bambara focuses. As she sits in the pouring rain, she is (re)visioning other systems of healings, as she returns to the hills and listens to "the tongue of the sacred cactus. . . . In the hills, becoming available to the spirits summoned to regenerate the life of the world" (249). As the next chapter on Silko demonstrates, the concept of healing the world is directly connected to the tongue and the tale.

Most relevant to the design of *Healing Narratives* is the conversion and healing of Meadows, the doctor. This may also be the most utopian of the visions presented in the novel. In his flash forward, Meadows says that sitting on the stoop with Thurston and Hull was where it began for him. At the moment of the first "rumble of thunder," listening to them speak about the health hazards and awful conditions at the Transchemical plant, Meadows had "taken time out to vow to give the Hippocratic oath some political meaning in his life" (281). Furthermore, and this is related to Bambara's overall vision of healing the medical establishment and charging it with its responsibility to the community, Meadows "understood that industrial arrogance and heedless technology was first and foremost a medical issue, a health issue, his domain" (281). But his flash forward does not stop there. He invigorates his practice, gaining a reputation for being concerned with the medical profession's "obligations" to the public, and finally returns to take a position at the Southwest Infirmary, working hand in hand with the traditional healers and integrating himself into the community (282). Through Velma's healing and the transformations of the other characters in the novel, Bambara takes us to the "probable realms of impossibility beyond the limits of scientific certainty" (246). However, with the conversion of Meadows, biotechnical medicine is not rejected but rather decentered, "placing it and all of its specialties and technologies in a broader context of healers and factors that affect health" (Stanford 23). This structure in the novel allows for new possibilities, new alliances—importantly, that of science and the traditional healing arts.

In the last few pages of the novel, we return to Velma's godmother, Sophie Haywood, one of the Master's Mind and a custodian of the culture. When she realizes that Velma will pull through, she thinks that finally "the girl at last will be ready for training. She'd waited a long time for the godchild's gift to unfold" (293). At the same time, Minnie's hands slide off Velma's shoulder as Velma begins to rise, sure of herself, happy, healed—at least for the moment. As Velma accepts her gift of life and healing, she stands up, bringing to mind the kumbla image from *Jane and Louisa:* "Velma, rising on steady legs, throws off the shawl that drops down on the stool a burst cocoon" (295). However, this utopian ending is tempered by Bambara's caveat: In her own flash forward, Velma reflects back on this day, understanding that being well and taking on her role as healer is hard work: "And years hence she would laugh remembering she thought *that* was an ordeal" (278).

In *The Salt Eaters*, Bambara, as diviner-healer, guides her readers through breakdown and healing. Through the oral medicine of this wellness narrative, Bambara tells us that the "natural response to stress and crisis is not breakdown and capitulation, but transformation and renewal" ("Salvation" 47). In this novel, Bambara presents to us, as readers, a way to begin our own process of transformation as her authorial narrator comments during the storm: "One would tap the brain for any knowledge of initiation rites lying dormant there, recognizing that life depended on it, that initiation was the beginning of transformation and that the ecology of the self, the tribe, the species, the earth depended on just that" (247). The movement toward health is linked to a turning inward and outward, to recovering lost parts of ourselves, to the ritual of transformation, not only for individuals, but for the earth itself. When Bambara calls for an "ecology of the self," she is both returning to the source of health as part of a balance among self, community, and the earth, and expanding notions of political activism and spiritual growth as part of a healing act. *The Salt Eaters*, as part of this transformational process, explores the necessary relationship between personal health, cultural affiliation, political activism, and spiritual growth; moreover, it opens a door for the scientists to commune with the healers to fight for a healthy planet. Bambara's wellness narrative is a ritual of radical change, and it (re)creates an audience with the ancestors as part of a continuum of being.

Part Two

Indigenous

Curative

Methods

3

The Novel

as Chant

Leslie Marmon
Silko's *Ceremony*
as Ceremonial
Healing

The devastation of indigenous people's lives
in many parts of the world also reflected a demise of their ability
to pass on centuries old knowledge of their culture and ways of
healing. "Indigenous Curative Methods" examines two writers
whose wellness narratives attempt to revive and reconstruct healing ceremonies of their respective groups: Native American in
the United States, particularly Laguna Pueblo, and Maori. Both
novels transform a specific kind of healing ceremony and a larger
prophecy to cure cultural illness in their groups specifically, but
for their oppressors and the ailing planet as well. In her first novel,
Ceremony (1977), Leslie Marmon Silko's design best reflects a
response to Deena Metzger's comment that we suffer from "global fatigue and despair, from cultural self-loathing, [and] from
national suicides." From the degradation of the indigenous people
of this hemisphere to the consequences of the atom bomb, the
novel unequivocally links the relationship between individual
illness and a diseased world. In a world made of stories, Leslie
Marmon Silko, a "mixed-blood" Laguna Pueblo, (re)creates a tale/
legend/novel that demonstrates that stories are more than stories, that they can both hurt and heal. Silko, in the pattern and
tradition of medicine women, takes us as readers on a journey

into her wellness narrative, so that we, too, can be part of the healing ceremony. In this role, Silko identifies herself as the conduit of Ts'its'tsi'nako (Thought Woman), who is "sitting in her room/ thinking of a story now/ I'm telling you the story/ she is thinking" (1).[1] Just as Alice Walker evokes herself as a medium for her ancestors and the spirits who informed the writing of *The Color Purple*, Silko also perceives herself as conduit of stories that are derived from a spiritual base. In this case, Silko, within context of her own Laguna Pueblo culture, functions explicitly as healer, as she relates Thought Woman's story, and the novel itself progresses as a chant to cure our collective dis-ease.

Silko opens her novel *Ceremony* with a word ceremony, which points us to the significance of her tale, stating that stories are "all we have to fight off/ illness and death" (2). This chapter examines Silko's re-creation of a Navajo chantway in the structure of the novel and the Native American healing traditions that bring back an individual and a community to health by the overthrow of the witchery. Through a discussion of the healing of the protagonist, Tayo, Silko revitalizes a traditional legend for a contemporary time. Although Silko moves beyond employing a specific Amerindian healing tradition to re-create this legend, she remains true to the cultural imperatives of Native American nations to find new ways to tell immemorial stories afresh.[2]

In *Landmarks of Healing*, Susan Scarberry-Garcia begins her study of N. Scott Momaday's *House Made of Dawn*, by commenting that "contemporary Native American Literature is centrally concerned with the process of healing" (1). This trope of culturally/physically ill people and communities is addressed in such disparate texts as Lee Maracle's *Ravensong*, which deals with a flu epidemic, Linda Hogan's *Solar Storms*, exploring the relationship of physical/mental disease to the destruction of the natural world, to the more psychosocial aspects of cultural dis-ease in works like Paula Gunn Allen's *The Woman Who Owned the Shadows* and Michael Dorris's *Yellow Raft on Blue Water*. This is most explicitly rendered in what might be considered the gendered urtexts of healing, Momaday's *House Made of Dawn* and Silko's *Ceremony*. These works of healing oppressed indigenous peoples and formerly vanquished nations are culturally bound to specific tribal groups and regions, but also have trans-Amerindian vision, often including the rest of the Americas. This examination of *Ceremony* explores Amerindian healing traditions, although it focuses specifically on

Laguna Pueblo and Navajo practices, inscribed in the cross-cultural Native American communities in which Silko has lived. Despite the complexities of moving between and among various Native American traditions, a cursory discussion of some of the tenets of a trans–Native American worldview and its healing practices is pertinent here. Silko herself states, for example: "In the novel, I've tried to go beyond any specific kind of Laguna witchery or Navajo witchery, and to begin to see witchery as a metaphor for the destroyers, or the counterforce, that force which counters vitality and birth" (quoted in Swan, "Healing" 314). Silko's revisioning of the metaphors of colonizing destruction in the form of a legend that comes out of the orature reflects the Caribbean writers' desire to transform the English language as a vehicle through which to revitalize diseased communities. Like Brodber's linguistic affront to the master narrative of the colonists, Silko's integration of the verse sections of the novel also challenges the bourgeois construct of the novel, as she links Amerindian legends with the Euro-narrative of Tayo's tale. Moreover, like the African-based writers, Silko, in presenting a worldview that challenges Western "scientific" rationalism, compels us to comprehend the restorative discourse of traditional healing acts that have been effaced, for the most part, by European conquest.

One of the most deeply embedded concepts of trans–Native American healing is the notion that an individual illness is dialectically tied to the health of the community and the earth. This concept can be easily related to African-based concepts, although the focus shifts from the ancestors within the earth to a more integrated notion of the earth itself as ancestor. In "Healing the Witchery: Medicine in Silko's *Ceremony*," B. A. St. Andrews notes: "In Amerindian thought, illness is a manifestation of imbalance. . . . One isolated part cannot be healed; the whole must be healed" (87; 88). Medicine woman Dhyani Ywahoo, a Cherokee healer, reinforces this worldview, which is also identified by I. Sow in his exploration of health and illness in West Africa. Ywahoo presents her vision of healing in imagistic language that resonates in Tayo's tale in *Ceremony*: When asked by the editors of *Medicine Women, Curanderas, and Women Doctors* how she defines illness and health, Ywahoo responds:

> It's a thought form, and idea of discord that causes one to be ill. . . . One person can become lonely, feeling emotionally de-

prived. And if the family, the clan, and the nation, don't come quickly to see that person in the circle again and invite that person to realize the seed of thought that has given them the feeling of being without, then the anxiety, through the pulsing of the earth and the break in the continuity of family, nation, and clan consciousness, can bring about a famine or a drought. . . . In the Indian mind, everything is related. (Perrone, Stockel, and Krueger 61–62)

Within this inclusive concept of health and illness, we understand the implications of a dis-eased person for the community and the earth itself. St. Andrews further comments that we who have grown up in the confines of Western dominant culture (whatever our ethnic background) are "stuck in the dualisms of Cartesian thought, while Amerindian thought is based on circularity and interconnectedness" (89). St. Andrews, a humanities professor at the SUNY Health Science Center at Syracuse, notes that this mind/body split "has long presented a problem for physicians," and doctors are beginning to explores these conflicts, although they are restricted by the confines of their practice. Still, the worldview and linguistic structure of Eurocentric thought, which separates the whole into compartments and binary oppositions, is a difficult system to reform. Furthermore, it is in the domain of language and stories that the differences between integrated and compartmentalized views of healing are most clearly accentuated.

African philosopher and healer M. Akin Makinde identified the idea of oral medicine, so prevalent in African-based healing, as a conceptualization beyond the demarcations of biomedicine. As in African-based thought throughout the Diaspora, the knowledge that words evoke the thing meant and that words can both heal and hurt is integral to the worldview of Native American and Amerindian societies through the Americas. Momaday, in titling his book of critical essays *The Man Made of Words*, based on the legend of the arrow maker who survives through his use of words, goes beyond the notion of a metaphor for a writer, proposing that language and the stories we tell are our "realities lived and believed" (3). Native American cultures have legends of these "word" warriors that define reality throughout the orature. This concept of reality is made explicit in Gladys A. Reichert's study of Navajo religion, in which she identifies the power of the word and a deep "linguistic awareness," noting that it is "a cognizance almost lacking in our own society" (*Navaho Religion* 267). Moreover, she states that, for the Navajo, "saying a thing was true made it true" (289).[3] Specifically, this conception of the power of the word to create substance within the material world reflects some of the concepts of Afro-Jamaican Rastafarian culture explored in the first chapter; words are connected to an actuality inconceivable within Western consciousness.

In *The Sacred Hoop: Recovering the Feminine in American Indian Traditions*, Allen most explicitly asserts: "[Words] articulate reality—not 'psychological' or imagined reality, not emotive reality captured metaphorically in an attempt to fuse thought and feeling, but that reality where thought and feeling are one, where objective and subjective are one, where speaker and listener are one" (73). This innate resistance to the binary opposition that poses science against spirit reflects a worldview in which words are "filled with an intangible but very real power or force, for good or bad." Allen states: "*Sacred, power*, and *medicine* are related terms. Having power means being able to use this extra force without being harmed by it. This is a particular talent that human beings possess to a greater or lesser degree, and *medicine* is a term used for the personal force through which one possesses power" (72).

Beyond the obvious fact that this understanding of the word "medicine" incorporates much more of the human condition than does the biomedical model, Allen's conjoining of these three words evokes a reality that links healing with the sacred. This concept of situating the healing act within a sacred realm is further explored within the tenets of Maori healing. Furthermore, the words themselves incorporate the meaning of these healing acts, as Allen tells us: "Ceremonial literature is sacred; it has power" (73).

Allen is clearly speaking here of the long tradition of Native American ceremonial literatures and not the contemporary novel *Ceremony*. However, it is the novel's recreation of these ceremonies that gives it power. As Robert Bell notes in "Circular Design in *Ceremony*," the Red Antway ceremony that Silko revisions (he says "imitates," but that word seems inaccurate to me) recalls to us a "circle of identification [that] is completed in the sanctity of the words of the ceremony" (55). For Silko, this association with the ceremonial stories that brought forth *Ceremony* is paramount: "[The] ancient Pueblo depended upon collective memory through successive generations to maintain and transmit an entire culture, a world view complete with proven strategies for survival. . . . Whatever the event or the subject, the ancient people perceived the world and themselves within that world as part of an ancient continuous story composed of innumerable bundles of other stories" ("Landscape" 87).

Silko makes it clear that all the stories are important, from the family ones to the ceremonial, those stories of time immemorial. In thinking back to her childhood, Silko remembers: "From the time I could hear and understand language, I have been hearing all these stories, and actually I have been involved in this whole way of seeing what happened—it's some kind of story" (Silko quoted in Coltelli, *Winged Words* 144). This strength in stories is reinforced by what the old people say: "'If you can remember the stories, you will be all right" (Silko, "Language" 68). As in the Jewish acts of remembrance, for Silko, remembering includes taking her place as storyteller to retell both painful and healing stories of survival for the next generation, and this becomes her aim in the novel.

The act of producing *Ceremony* was also a ritual for Silko; she explains that "writing the novel was a ceremony for me to stay sane" (Fisher 20). Suffering stress in both her personal life and the life of her protagonist, Silko states: "So my character is very sick, and I was very sick when I was writing the novel. I was having migraine headaches all the time and horrible nausea that went on and on" (20). Silko's symptoms reflect those of Brodber as she wrote out her responses to the sociological writings of her fieldwork, as well as the character Nellie's illness in the novel itself. And like Brodber, Silko states that it was only through writing Tayo's cure that she herself became well: "So here I was in my novel working on my character everyday, and I was trying to figure out how some stay sane and some don't, and then I realized that the one thing that was keeping me going at all was the writing. And as Tayo got better, I felt better" (20). James Ruppert notes in "The Reader's Lessons in *Ceremony*" that when "the speaker begins by saying that the stories are the only way to fight off illness, evil and death, she is being quite literal" (79). The novel becomes an extension of the words of a curative chant, and it develops a discourse of healing. Silko's obvious association with the character Tayo, whose mixed heritage corresponds to Silko's and who is linked to the males in her family, beginning with her grandfather, further demarcates the power of words as a potential healing tool. Moreover, Tayo's healing ceremony affects us as readers, for as we participate in this ritual process, we feel better, just as Silko did, and like our protagonist, we gain cultural knowledge through this literary chant.

In examining Tayo's transition to health, Paula Gunn Allen identifies the overriding conflict in the novel as "a tale of two forces: the feminine life force of the universe and the mechanistic death force of the witchery" ("Feminine Landscape" 127). In *The Sacred Hoop* and in many interviews, Allen identifies "female-ness" as a "central cultural value" in Native American cultures. She states further in an interview with Annie Eysturoy: "The status of individual women ranges from abject dependency to complete and absolute autonomy. . . , but you find significant female deities and you find significant female rituals that are necessary to the ongoing life of the tribe" (Eysturoy 101). Scholars of early women's cultures, like Achterberg, have identified a linking of a valued role for women as citizens and leaders in their own right in direct relation to female deities; this is even true to a lesser extent in the Marianismo cultures in certain Latin American Catholic societies, as well as the Haitian three-headed Erzulie. It is most evident today in West African communities where female deities are part of the religious environment, like Uhamiri in Igbo society, and women function as ritual leaders and gain power in the community postmenopausally. For many Native American cultures, the focus on having a balance in nature, including a gender balance, is evident in Silko's choice of Tayo for a protagonist in a novel that focuses primarily on the healing and spiritual capabilities of women.

Throughout the novel, Tayo is treated by both male and female healers; this clearly reflects Silko's movement toward gender balance and wholeness, unlike the earlier companion novel, Momaday's *House Made of Dawn*, in which the process of the healing is from men to men; there is barely a Kiowa woman in the novel. In *Ceremony*, not only does Tayo connect to his own female attributes by his relationship with his spirit guide and lover Ts'eh, but as a potential healer, he begins to incorporate both aspects of his identity in the healing process, unlike the clearly masculinist focus of Western medicine. Moreover, judging from Silko's own comments about her sickness as she developed the character, it seems that Silko deeply identifies with her male protagonist. There is a gender transference here, as there is in the last novel examined in this study, Jo Sinclair's *Wasteland*, in which both novels have a male protagonist in some ways modeled on male relatives (Sinclair's, in this case, is much more direct, since her protagonist is modeled specifically on her brother, whereas Silko patterns Tayo on her father in a more general way, without the particulars of his life situation), yet the characters are also based on the authors' own personal experiences.[4] Furthermore, Silko, as storyteller in this wellness narrative, connects the female creator Thought Woman, who is thinking up the novel, to the young man Tayo, who acts it out.

Many critics of Silko's *Ceremony* have added to our understanding of this wellness narrative, particularly in relation to identifying certain ceremonies or noting its healing capabilities in general.[5] Carol Mitchell, for example, sees *Ceremony* as a curing ceremony (30); Kenneth Lincoln notes that Silko's novel is a "word ceremony," and that Silko "writes out of an old medicinal regard for word-spirits powerful enough to make things happen" (237). However, what is most intriguing in the novel is the way in which Silko re-creates these traditions, chantways, and tales to develop a model of healing, linking this novel cross-culturally to the other ethnic women writers examined in this book and strengthening the concept of the novel as a discourse for healing the culturally ill. This chapter adds to the dialogue on Silko's healing text by exploring the structure of the entire work as a wellness narrative: how the novel itself progresses as a chantway, a "way—appropriate of restoring equilibrium" (Sandner 56) for the characters in the story, ourselves as readers, and possibly the earth itself.

Although actual ceremonies are performed in the novel, the plot of *Ceremony* itself develops as a healing chant. Chantways are often specific healing ceremonies of the Navajo, but in terms of the novel *Ceremony*, Silko pulls from various kinds of chantways to develop her wellness narrative; this is similar to her creation of the legend of the witchery within the context of the novel, as well as Keri Hulme's revisioning of the Maori origination legend of the seven canoes in *the bone people*.

Donald Sandner's explorations of Navajo chantways, in his discussions with healer Denet Tsosi, are relevant to a discussion of the structure of Silko's novel. Sandner, a doctor who learned from and worked with Tsosi, charts what he classifies as discrete stages included in most healing chants. Although Sandner includes five different stages, the actual healing process may be divided into four sections—*purification*, *evocation*, *identification*, and *transformation*—that correspond to the four corners of the universe in Native American cosmology as well as to the four sections of Tayo's healing in the novel.[6] The first stage, purification, is represented in the first section of the novel, when Tayo is diagnosed by Old Grandma and purified by Old Ku'oosh, through the vomiting out the toxins of hate and prejudice, as is done by other characters in healing novels such as Marshall's *Praisesong*, and the drinking of the ritual tea. The second stage, evocation, coincides with Tayo's trip to Betonie, the unconventional Navajo healer. In this stage, where the gods are summoned and a traditional sand painting is prepared to visualize the healing, Tayo undergoes a chantway with Betonie. Furthermore, the sand painting that Betonie and his apprentice Bear Boy Shush compose to transform the power of the healing to Tayo evokes the larger ceremony to come. The third stage is identification, in which, according to the ritual, "the power has been transferred from the painting, and the patient is identified with the gods" (Sandner 60). This part of the novel's structure becomes a visual representation of Betonie's sand painting, as Tayo not only is identified with the gods, but meets Ts'eh to become part of an immemorial legend unfolding in the present time.[7] By the end of the novel, Tayo has been transformed from a dis-eased "Indian" to a healed being; the novel's conclusion mirrors the final stage, transformation, as Tayo's final sunwise chant replicates the last moments of the patient's healing chant: "At dawn, the closing songs are sung, the patient breathes in the rising sun, and the chant is over" (60).

It is evident that Silko's use of traditional healing chants is layered threefold in the novel: There are the specific chants and healing practices performed in the novel; there is the structure of the novel, which progresses like a chant; and finally, there is the novel itself, which functions as a ceremony, dedicated to Thought Woman, who is conceiving the story as Silko writes it. Tayo's specific healing is intertwined with all the types of healing rituals identified in *Ceremony*; according to Silko's rendition of this tale, Tayo's cure is tied to the earth itself. Since the protagonist's healing is connected to the reviving of the people and the land, the novel becomes larger than its plot; both *Ceremony* and Hulme's *the bone people* create novelistic visions in which the characters' healings are linked to a greater prophecy of the life of the culture.

The novel begins with a common trope in post-World War II Native American literature, that of the disturbed, dysfunctional, and often drunk war veteran, whose vision of the violence of war is complicated by his inability to function back in his life on the reservation or in the community. Like Abel in Momaday's *House Made of Dawn* or the Vietnam vet Henry Lamartine in Louise Erdrich's *Love Medicine*, Tayo returns from war to the reservation, suffering apparently from post-traumatic stress syndrome

(Western medical configuration); however, as the novel progresses, it is clear that this is not his only ailment. Moreover, as in the portrait of the conventional doctors in Bambara's *The Salt Eaters*, the medical-schooled V.A. doctors are unable (or unwilling) to help him. In his illness, Tayo is caught up in his memories of his cousin Rocky's death and the haunting look on the face of the dead Japanese soldier, who he believes to be his uncle Josiah—calling up a collective memory of the historic link between Amerindian and Asian people.[8] However, the army medics' only response is to force their drugs into him: "Their medicine drained memory out of his thin arms" (15). As Tayo learns through his healing ceremony, there is nothing that the doctors can give him to make him function or forget.

Susan Scarberry-Garcia, in "Memory as Medicine: The Power of Recollection in *Ceremony*," identifies the allopathic hospital that Tayo is sent to as a "negative symbol," and she states: "The Veteran Hospital, where Tayo goes for help, turns out to be a house of bad medicine, staffed with witch doctors" (21). Scarberry rightfully notes that the "white" doctors can do nothing for Tayo's disorder; even more relevantly, her tongue-in-cheek response about the doctors being "witch doctors" calls forth the powerful imagery with which Silko is working. As Tsitsi Dangarembga, in *Nervous Conditions*, calls the white colonialists "witches" who steal away the souls of the Africans, Silko also plays with the image of conventional medicine as another form of witchery. However, in this novel, white people are merely the tools of those who command the witchery. Still, any possible healing relationship between the patient and his doctors at the hospital is ruined, as Tayo describes his condition in potently symbolic terms: "For a long time he had been white smoke. He did not realize that until he left the hospital because white smoke had no consciousness of itself. It faded into the white world of their bed sheets and walls; it was sucked away by the words of the doctors who tried to talk to the invisible scattered smoke" (14–15).

Beyond the unambiguously negative white imagery, associated with the dominance of both Western culture and Western medicine, as well as reminding us of the hospital scene in Ellison's *Invisible Man*, can also be seen as Silko's reworking of a traditional disease found in many Native American cultures throughout the Southwest—*ghost sickness*.[9] The Pueblo Scalp Ceremony is one of the rituals used to free the returning warriors from this sickness brought on from the ghosts of the dead, a problem faced by Tayo and the other World War II vets; however, Comanche medicine woman Sanapia, during her interview with David E. Jones, talks of the resurgence of this sickness in terms of dealing with white society. Although Sanapia likens the symptoms to what "white" doctors call a stroke (68), the symptoms also correspond to Tayo's in the white hospital. He is immobile and perceives himself as ghostlike "white smoke," linking his cultural illness with the ghost of his brother and the dead Japanese soldier. The portrait of Indians who are stricken with ghost disease mirrors Tayo's emotional disorders: Evident in these victims were a "definitive attempt at emulative adaptation to white society which failed, the unendurable psychological state of cultural marginality, and an intense desire for reintegration with the more traditionally oriented group" (Jones 86). Because of his own position as a mixed-race person, Tayo is a prime candidate for this disorder, since he is marginalized (at least at the beginning) from both the white society forced on him in school and in the army, and his own Laguna Pueblo society, because of his personal history and his alienation from the family by his Auntie. The problem of the mixed-race person being isolated from the oppressed reference group has profound significance in both *Ceremony* and *the bone people*, as Kerewin also struggles to find her place in Maori society.

Tayo's Auntie is a complicated character in the novel, reminiscent of Nellie's Aunt Becca in *Jane and Louisa*. She takes Tayo in, despite his mother's scandal, yet she constantly tells Tayo that he is tainted by his mother's relations with white men. Furthermore, as the most assimilated character in the novel, Auntie becomes a symbol of the resistance to traditional modes of healing. The profound irony of her contradictions is reinforced by Silko's use of the concept of the feminine as a healing force. The portrayal of Auntie is in contradistinction to portraits of Uncle Josiah and Old Grandma, who tap into the traditional culture's focus on balance and restoration, realigning the forces of the feminine with the masculine, so valued in Western thought. Although a woman, Auntie is plainly unbalanced, sick because of her own feelings of self-hate and the denial of the feminine force in her life. Auntie distorts a positive storytelling tradition by constantly reminding Tayo of the sacrifices she has made for her "dead sister's half-breed child" (30), retelling the tale of his mother's infidelity, a story meant to renew his hurt and isolate him. Auntie makes sure that Tayo is always aware of his outsider status; in taking care of Tayo and his full-blooded cousin Rocky, Auntie keeps him "close enough to feel excluded" (69). Since historically most Native American societies identified inclusion into the culture through the knowledge of it rather than through genetics, this further demonstrates her Eurocentric ways of thinking. Moreover, when Old Grandma states plainly that the white doctors have done nothing for Tayo, and that he needs a medicine man, Auntie responds: "You know what people will say if we ask for a medicine man to help him. . . . They'll say, 'Don't do it. He's not full blood anyway'" (34). Through this telling scene, Silko compels us to realize the limitations of Auntie's ability to comprehend the depth of Tayo's disease because of her own dysfunction. Kenneth Lincoln, in *Native American Renaissance*, comments that, according to Edmund Carpenter, before we destroy a culture, "we mistranslate it" (226). Although born into her Laguna Pueblo culture, Auntie has been taught to "mistranslate" it, so she can be of no support or help in interpreting Tayo's disease (or her own). Auntie has learned the lessons of self-hate well, and even her desire to maintain order (keep the family together and keep them pure blooded) arises from a distorted Western sense of racial segregation, which is not part of Amerindian cosmology.

Luckily for Tayo, Old Grandma doesn't listen to her daughter. She takes control of the situation and sends for Old Ku'oosh; this begins the first part of Tayo's healing, corresponding to the first stage of a chantway—purification. In both African-based and Amerindian cultures, it is often the female elders who not only pass on the cultures, but have the power to ignore assimilative behaviors in later generations. Through Old Grandma, whose vision is clearer than Auntie's, we perceive that she recognizes Tayo as totally part of her family, and relevantly, that a medicine man can also be a healing practitioner for people of mixed heritage. She calls for Old Ku'oosh to begin Tayo's cure. Old Ku'oosh performs the purification rites of the Pueblo Scalp Ceremony, spreading the blue cornmeal and giving Tayo Indian tea to drink, but he can only go so far in the healing process, taking Tayo to the end of the first stage. He tells Tayo: "There are some things we can't cure like we used to . . . not since the white people came" (39). However, Old Ku'oosh does not give up there; he realizes, along with Old Grandma, that the whole community will never be well if Tayo and the others sent to war are not treated for their cultural illness.

Although he is unable to go any further than the first purification rites and diagnostic designs with Tayo, Old Ku'oosh helps Tayo along so that he can function. At the end of a ritual cleansing act, Tayo is purged. He seldom vomits anymore, and he is able to eat the blue cornmeal mush, made by Auntie as a small positive gesture, without cramping up. Still, Tayo's environment at home and in the community is dysfunctional, and his nights at the bar with the other Indian vets demarcate all the symptoms of their dis-ease. They drink the beer in big mouthfuls "like medicine": "Liquor was medicine for the anger that made them hurt, for the pain of the loss, medicine for tight bellies and choked-up throats" (41). As Laura Coltelli comments: "The sense of 'remembrance' of these drunken Indians as they tell of their squalid adventures, becomes a kind of obscene ritual" ("Re-enacting Myths" 176). As in much Native American literature and historical observations, the role of alcohol as a kind of imposed poison brought in by the white man to subdue and disrupt is evident here; however, as is the case in Hulme's *the bone people*, not all writers of indigenous cultures perceive drinking as abusive, despite how it might appear. Still, in this case, the categorical drunken remembrances and retellings of these horrific war stories actually increase the men's illness, as the liquor "medicine" hides any real possibility of recovery. In illustrating the concept of words' actualizing events in terms of the power to heal, this scene vividly presents the power of words to harm.

The obscene rituals in the bar are rooted in the stories of destruction in the war, the loss of land to the white people, and the pursuit of white women as revenge. Part of their collective cultural illness is replicated in their diseased words, which are repeated "like long medicine chants, the beer bottle pounding on the counter tops like drums" (44). Among these diseased vets is Emo, who is both a prime example of the culturally unwell and a symbol of the witchery, blending contemporary angst and traditional evil. Emo shares certain similarities to the male protagonists in Momaday's *House Made of Dawn* and James Welch's *Winter in the Blood*; however, unlike in these two works, which present a fuller and more sympathetic portrait of this character, Silko offers Tayo an alternative to Emo, and the women in the novel, even those used by the men, become part of the healing process as Tayo overcomes cultural illness. Early on in the novel, Emo is identified as a destructive element; he has disregard for his heritage and the earth. Emo shouts: "Look what is here for us. Look. Here's the Indians' mother earth! Old dried-up thing!" Tayo thinks to himself, but does not articulate, that this way of perceiving the earth is "all wrong" (25). Emo's curse on the drought-stricken land is linked to one of the first mythic tales included in verse form, which tells about how Our Mother, in punishing those who neglect her altar, takes away the rain clouds and leaves the people in drought (49–50). Here readers begin to understand that the Euro-narrative is tied to the moral verse legends. Moreover, it is evident that these stories reinforce the power of words to hurt, as well as mirroring the most developed of the verse tales in the novel—the central mythic story of the witch who creates "white people," the frightening tale that cannot be taken back (139–145).

Emo, diseased by the witchery, affects all the culturally un-well, but his illness has a most potent effect on Tayo, the main target for Emo's witchery. Emo's diseased storytelling has the strength to make Tayo sick, as Tayo fights off nausea as Emo talks (57); in some ways, this reflects many of the readers' responses to the diseased tale-telling within Silko's second novel, *Almanac of the Dead*. In a flashback, Tayo remembers Emo showing off the teeth of a Japanese soldier he killed. Emo's bragging brings back the memory of Rocky's death, as well as the dead Japanese soldier Tayo finds in the rain forest, on whose dead face he saw his uncle Josiah's face superimposed. In this scene, Tayo realizes that the force of Emo's words challenges any life-giving, curative possibili-ties, as Emo himself feeds off death: "Tayo could hear it in his voice when he talked about the killing—how Emo grew from each killing. Emo fed off each man he killed, and the higher the rank of the dead man, the higher it made Emo" (63). Tayo's only way of dealing with Emo's witchery within the dominant paradigm al-lowed to him is to kill off that which is creating death. Tayo stabs Emo because he "felt he would get well if he killed [Emo]" (65). Tayo's decision in this important scene foreshadows his choice at the end of the novel—to finish the story or to become engulfed with the witchery by finally killing Emo. However, at this point, all his attempt really does is to send Tayo back to the hospital and reinforce the witchery, since it doesn't stop Emo or their sickness at all. At the hospital, which does Tayo no good, the doctor reads to him about increasing violence by Indian vets after the war. When the army doctor asks if he agrees, Tayo shakes his head, and his response alerts us to the larger implications of his post-traumatic stress syndrome: "It's more than that. I can feel it. It's been going on for a long time" (55).

Tayo's statement makes it clear that this purification rite with Old Ku'oosh after his return to the reservation from the hospital is only the first stage in the healing ceremony. Although Tayo is no longer vomiting and can function at the bar without violence, he is still unwell. And within the context of the community, he is part of its larger illness. As Joan R. Saks Berman learned from her experiences working as a therapist in Native communities, the Navajo (as well as many other Native American groups) understand that "somatic illness is caused by external forces or being out of harmony because of having transgressed one of many taboos" (70). Through both the external forces of "white" domination and the taboos broken in the war as well as by their contemporary lifestyles, the men at the bar and in the community at large are ill. Old Grandma and Ku'oosh, reflecting the wisdom of male and female elders working together, lead Tayo to the next stage of the healing. The elders warn Old Grandma that Tayo "better get help pretty soon." Tayo is, at first, resistant, feeling that, because of his mixed-race status, the old men are picking on him. Thinking about the Scalp Ceremony, Tayo grudgingly comments that it isn't just him: "The other guys, they're still messed up too. That ceremony didn't help them" (111). However, Tayo finally relents and accept the advice of his grandmother and Old Ku'oosh. He goes to see old Betonie, the unconventional Navajo healer, which begins the second stage of the novel's chant: evocation.

Within traditional cultures, male and female healers play similar roles in the society, unlike the gender differential in Western medicine. Like Baba in *Jane and Louisa*, Cleotus the Hermit in *The Salt Eaters*, and especially, the *kaumatua* in *the bone people*, Betonie is an influential figure in the novel, since his presence points to some of Silko's major aims in the work: his position as a mixed-race person, his relationship to his own grandmother, and his ability to revision the healing ceremonies for contemporary malaise. Some of the most far-reaching characters in the novel—Betonie and Night Swan, for example—have mixed cultural heritage like Tayo and like Silko herself. In speaking of her mixed heritage, Silko notes that being part of a community and its "language" is more important than being "full blood": "That's where a person's identity has to come from, not from racial blood quantum levels" (Fisher 19). Through his understanding of Tayo's background and condition, Betonie is the right healer, but it takes Tayo time to see it. At first, Tayo only observes the trappings of what he calls "the leftover things the whites didn't want": "All Betonie owned in the world was in this room. What kind of healing power was in this?" (133). Tayo immediately links healing power with capital ownership, but as he wrestles with himself, he begins to question these conflicting value systems: Should he adhere to what the white doctors have told him about the so-called quacks like Betonie, or should he try to really listen to what the old man is telling him? However, Betonie quickly wins Tayo over as he answers each of Tayo's questions even before he articulates them.

In accepting Betonie as his healer, Tayo begins to decode his struggle with his biracial status. This presents for him a more flexible and healthy sense of identity.[10] As a character Tayo also displaces the binary opposition between native and nonnative cultures. Betonie explains to Tayo that he need not commit a sort of symbolic patricide on the white father whom he never met, nor does hating white people help foil the witchery. Rather, Betonie talks of the importance of changing the ceremonies to fit the realities of what has happened after the white people came, and he tells Tayo about his own Mexican grandmother, who taught him that "things that don't shift and grow are dead things" (133), reinforcing for readers the importance of Tayo's own grandmother. Betonie's mention of his Mexican grandmother reflects a third ethnic group in the Southwest, one that includes both Amerindian and European ancestry. Unlike many Chicano/a writers in the United States who see a mostly positive, albeit often nostalgic, relationship to their former homeland, for many Native American writers in general and Silko in particular, the relationship to Mexicans and Mexican Americans is more complicated, linked to trans-Amerindian connections, while resisting Catholicism and colonial Spain. In Rudolfo Anaya's *Bless Me, Ultima*, there is a connection to the Native American culture through Jason's "Indian" and Ultima's healing practices as a curandera; still, the healing is linked heavily to Catholicism and the Christian God/devil split. However, this linkage is what is often problematic to the Native American writers in the same geographic location. In Silko's early short story "Tony's Story," the Mexican American cop is an evil figure, representing the status quo. In both *Almanac* and *Gardens in the Dunes*, Mexicans are often portrayed as underhanded; in *Gardens*, for example, the character of Delena, the dog woman who steals Sister Salt and Candy's money, also appears to be corrupt. However, the story is complicated, since she steals the money to buy guns for an indigenous revolt in Mexico. In *Ceremony*, the Mexican cattle symbolized a kind of cross-breeding for strength and endurance, and significantly, the Mexican women, Betonie's grandmother and Night Swan, are important figures in Tayo's growth.

Betonie's vision prepares us for the central legend of the verse tales in the novel. This legend is the one Silko creates of the witch who invents "white people" (139–145), and is linked to Tayo's own struggle with the witchery at the conclusion of the Euro-narrative part of the novel. Betonie, in this evocation, is the first to identify Tayo as a part of the broader ceremony that structures Tayo's search and the novel itself, which will, if completed, thwart the witchery that has overtaken them and heal the community. As he interprets what Tayo is saying, through his visualization, Betonie translates the vision for Tayo. Betonie ominously tells Tayo that not only is he an "important part of the story," but that "they will try to stop you from completing the ceremony" (130–131). He compels Tayo not to let them stop him, for the consequences are no less than the destruction of the world. This section of the novel and the second stage of the chant both end with Betonie and the Bear Boy Shush making the traditional sand painting that delineates Tayo's disease, transfers to him its healing power, and demarcates his ceremony to come. Betonie specifically directs Tayo to the next stage of his healing—identification—through the design of the sand painting, as he tells Tayo what to look for: "Remember the stars. . . . I've seen them and I've seen the spotted cattle; I've seen a mountain and I've seen a woman" (160). It is this prophecy, similar to the one Hulme presents in *the bone people*, that links the protagonists' individual healing to the broader concerns of these wellness narratives.

Through Betonie's words, Tayo begins his journey to find his uncle Josiah's spotted cattle, a special Mexican breed, linking his uncle's important influence on his healing ceremony with the meeting with Ts'eh and the more mythic aspects of his quest. Still, before Tayo is completely ready for the third stage of the ceremony, identification, he must go through a personal purification rite. In the midst of the drunken rituals of the witchery that defines his life with his friends Harley and Leroy, Tayo dreams of Betonie's prophecy, and as he wakes up to the drunk carnage around him, he begins to vomit more than the alcohol—"all the past, all his life" (177)—reminding us of Avey's boat ride in Marshall's *Praisesong*. Tayo is reminded of the Scalp Ceremony that he wished he had performed for the dead Japanese soldier, but it is clear that this private rite has cleansed him. As he walks back to Laguna, leaving the drunks with the truck, Tayo is ready for the next part of the ceremony to begin: "There were transitions that had to be made in order to become whole again, in order to be the people our Mother would remember" (178). One of these transitions coincides with

the next section of the novel and third stage of the ceremony, identification. This identification with the gods is actualized when
Tayo meets Ts'eh and, therefore, enters into a new legend, based
in part on the Yellow Woman story.[11] This is one of the many legends of the Laguna Pueblo people that has structured their existence since time immemorial and entitles them to be remembered
by "our Mother."

At their first meeting, Tayo sees Ts'eh as a young woman, not
much older than he; however, for Tayo as well as the readers, Ts'eh
is immediately identified with the gods—because of what is and is
not said about her. Ts'eh is associated with the color yellow: She
wears a yellow skirt, works with yellow sandstones, and her eyes
are ocher (185). That association, along with the her rich sensual-
ity that she uses to heal Tayo, bring to mind the love relations of
Yellow Woman in the Ka't'sina stories. Furthermore, she never
tells Tayo her "ethnic" identity, calling herself a "Montano" and
giving him little knowledge of her real name, telling him to call
her Ts'eh, since her Indian name is so long (233). Ts'eh has deep
knowledge of the interrelationship of the earth to the plants and
living creatures (including humans), and she can control the winter weather with a shake of her blanket (218). According to Allen,
Ts'eh is linked to Thought Woman, Ts'its'tsi'nako (the two names
are converged), who is thinking the story Silko is writing and we
are reading. Allen states further: "Ts'eh is the matrix, the creative
and life-restoring power, and those who cooperate with her designs serve her, and through her, serve life" ("Feminine Landscape"
127). Although Tayo is helped along the chantway by different
healers, male and female, it is Ts'eh's part of the ceremony that
takes the healing to mythic dimensions. As he enters Ts'eh's world,
meeting the Hunter and seeing legendary Mount Taylor in the
background, Tayo begins to understand their strength and power,
even though he, despite the sand painting and the guidance of
Betonie, does not yet see his own place in the story. Tayo, however, does recognize Betonie's stars outside Ts'eh's cabin door and
intuits that Ts'eh will help him find Josiah's special spotted cattle.
As in the Yellow Woman tale, Tayo enters into a historic as well
as intimate relationship with Ts'eh, since Ts'eh's role is to initiate
him into this emerging legend, thus actualizing the third stage of
the healing ceremony. The power of Betonie's sand painting becomes a reality as Tayo enters into its vision, and he continues the
story through his education with Ts'eh.

This section of this wellness narrative, reflecting the stages of the healing chant, also is a turning point in the plot structure of the novel. Until this section, the legends and Laguna traditional stories are in verse, and separated in both content and form from the "realistic" plot. However, in this third stage of the healing ceremony, these two strands of narrative, Native American and Euro-American, blend together, and the entire novel takes on mythic proportions. Each scene during this section reinforces what Gloria Bird calls a "mythic mirror," which provides a relationship between the story and the world of legend (3). Allen identifies the rituals in this part of the novel as "connected with a ceremony of cosmic significance, for only a cosmic ceremony can simultaneously heal a wounded man, a stricken landscape, and a disorganized, discouraged society" (131). As in many traditional narratives, each experience that Tayo has during his time with Ts'eh strengthens his position as part of the legend and his resolve to complete the foretold ceremony. Ts'eh teaches him about the plants and reacquaints him with the old stories. She also affects Tayo in the most intimate way; he is reacquainted with himself, as lovemaking with Ts'eh rebuilds a body ravaged by alcohol and other abuses. In their first night together, everything is connected: Their sexual intimacy brings forth his dreams of Josiah's cattle as well as symbolic seeds of renewal as he wakes and can finally breathe deeply. As the sun rises, he takes the mare to the riverside, preparing to find the cattle, and he sees "the Ka't'sina approaching the river crossing" (189). Each of Ts'eh's actions has cosmic significance. She explains why she replants one flower "the color of the sky after a summer rain": "I'll take it from here and plant it in another place, a canyon where it hasn't rained in a while" (235). This statement precisely links Ts'eh to the verse tales of the drought, as well as to Thought Woman who controls all aspects of the health of the earth. Ts'eh's intervention in Tayo's life and his own experiences in this stage of the healing elevates him to ones told about in legends. In regard to the formulation of this identification stage of the healing chant, Swan describes Tayo as "sun man" ("Laguna Symbolic Geography" 238), and Coltelli notes that Tayo comes out of a Laguna legend, cited in Franz Boas's *Keresan Texts* ("Reenacting Myths" 173).

The interweaving of Laguna legends within Silko's Euronarrative details Tayo's transformation from a war-traumatized veteran with a cultural dis-ease to a hero in stories from time immemorial. As Swan states, Tayo is "likened to the cultural hero of the myth documenting the origins of the ritual, [and] encounters deities whose powers make a contribution to the power of the ceremony" ("Healing" 321). This growth is demonstrated most forcefully when Tayo, in his search for the spotted cattle, has a confrontation with two racist and owning-obsessed Texans. After his encounter with Ts'eh, he goes to seek out the cattle and thinks to himself: "Betonie's vision was a story he could feel happening—from the stars and the woman, the mountain and the cattle would come" (194). Soon after, he recognizes Mount Taylor and spots the cattle, which he realizes have been stolen by white people. In trying to free the cattle, he is discovered by the Texans, who accuse him of stealing and want to bring him to their form of justice. As the mythic dimension of the novel expands, Ts'eh sends a mountain lion to distract the Texans from taking Tayo to town and then sends the snow to protect the mountain lion. The bewitched Texans clearly have no understanding of the earth and their place in it; as they let Tayo go to chase down the illusive mountain lion, they demonstrate their inability to perceive the world in anything but capitalistic terms: "These goddamn Indians got to learn whose property this is" (211). On the other hand, Tayo begins to fully comprehend his place in the story and his relationship to the emerging legend, as he perceives these misguided white people as mere tools of the witchery. He acknowledges the "lie" perpetrated on him and his people, already recounted in the startling central verse-legend about the storyteller witch who created white people. Not only has he believed the lie that only brown people steal, but the reality that white people, too, have been subject to the witchery, further mirroring this legend of the invention of "white people" in the center of the novel. By accepting that the cattle were stolen, Tayo recognizes that the land, too, has been stolen, and he realizes that finding this special stock of cattle will fulfill the prophecy and help him to replenish the drought-stricken land. Tayo's clarity of vision further links him to his ancestry and his relation to time immemorial: "This night is a single night: and there has never been any other" (201).

When Tayo returns to the mountain retreat after his close call with the Texans, Ts'eh guides him to the fourth stage of his healing: transformation. Transformation occurs after the patient has gone through the rest of the ritual, reflecting a cleansing and a transition to health. But that is only the beginning, and as the protagonist, Velma, alerts us in her flash forward in Bambara's *The Salt Eaters*, living as a healthy person in an unhealthy world is also hard work. This section of the novel, reflecting the fourth stage of the healing ceremony, transformation, examines the hard work of living as a healthy person in a dis-eased society, for the better Tayo gets, the more the authorities perceived him as sick. With her visionary powers, Ts'eh warns Tayo, as Betonie has done, that the witchery will try to stop him from completing the ceremony. Ts'eh cautions him that she may not always be with him to counter the "destroyers": "The end of the story. They want to change it. They want it to end here, the way all their stories end, encircling slowly to choke the life away" (243). As in novels such as Welch's *Winter in the Blood*, the power of white cultural stories to destroy self and culture is evident here; relevantly, though, the strength of the female spirit figure intervenes. This is a character lacking in both Welch's and Momaday's early novels, although prevalent in their cultural traditions. As Tayo's spirit guide, Ts'eh prepares him for the battle ahead. As she presents to Tayo a way to complete the ceremony, Ts'eh alerts him that his friends may not be the ones to help him. The realistic aspect of this section is clearly overladen with the mythic, as Ts'eh places Tayo in the ensuing legend for the readers. She tells Tayo of the problems with the tribal leaders and their confused position within the ceremony: "They are trying to decide who you are" (244).

Throughout this final section, Tayo is told by Old Grandma and by his uncle Robert that Old Ku'oosh and the elders are waiting to hear from him, but when Robert comes to see Tayo, he tells him that other, more threatening people are also looking for him. As Ts'eh predicted, Tayo's move toward healing has the authorities frightened, and they call in the army doctors to take Tayo away again to that sterile place of whiteness, the V.A. hospital. Relevantly, the army doctors and their medicine are part of the disease and the witchery; another kind of medicine is needed to cure Tayo, the earth, and ironically, the medical profession. Tayo must avoid them, so he can make his shamanistic return to tell the elders what he knows. However, first he must complete the most dangerous part of the ceremony; his final transformation is dialectically connected to the worst effect of the witchery: the creation of the atom bomb, a moral concern of twentieth-century writers from Faulkner's Nobel Prize speech to Chaim Potok's *The Book of Lights* and Bambara's *The Salt Eaters*. As Tayo escapes from the vengeful Emo, his former friends, and the army doctors, he ironically hides in an uranium mine shaft. In the mine, Tayo recalls Old Grandma's remembrance of the flash of the bomb, reminding us of Porter, Fred Holt's friend who is dying of radiation poisoning in Bambara's text. As he touches the contradictory yellow ore, reinforcing images of Yellow Woman and Ts'eh as well as the destruction that humans can cause when they carelessly transform nature, Tayo cries from the "relief he felt at finally seeing the pattern, the way all the stories fit together—the old stories, the war stories, their stories—to become the story that was still being told" (258). At this point the balancing of the stories, both painful and healthful, take over the hateful stories that were choking his life from him. Tayo's final ordeal, however, is witnessing the death of his close friend Harley at the hands of Emo and not interfering with the witchery of which Emo is a part. Tayo realizes that in not giving in to the witchery and killing Emo, he has stopped his own victimization; he is no longer "a drunk Indian war veteran settling an old feud," renouncing what the army doctors all along assumed would be his end (265). Rather, in a waking dream during the completion of the ceremony, Tayo visualizes being taken home by the spirits of Josiah and Rocky, balance restored as Old Grandma holds him. As the transformation is actualized and the ceremony completed, what Sandner identifies as the fifth stage, release, when the patient is brought back to health, Tayo "crosses the river at sunrise," ending the sunwise cycle (267).

Kenneth Lincoln calls Tayo a "storied warrior" who helps "bring native life back into the balance" (250). As he moves from patient to healer, Tayo returns to tell the story of Ts'eh and his healing to Old Ku'oosh and the elders in the kiva, thus completing the ceremony and healing the community. However, the novel does not end with Tayo, it ends with the voice of Old Grandma, the only living person in Tayo's waking dream. Old Grandma tells Tayo—and the readers—that these stories are "immemorial"; with the ironic twist of the elderly, she states that she's not that excited about the goings-on anymore: "It seems like I already heard these stories before . . . only thing is, the names sound different" (273).

By the end of the novel, Tayo has reconnected to his culture and his land, and as a patient/healer, he completes the ceremony, and the witchery is "dead for now" (274). Swan notes that it is through women Tayo "earns his social identity as a yellow person, beloved by family and welcomed in the Kiva." She states further: "All of the female characters are associated with the supernatural being called Our Mother" (246). Swan may overstate this association, since one major female character, Auntie, remains throughout the novel opposed to the female life force, although in keeping with balance restored, she does grudgingly accepts Tayo at the end of the novel. And as in Toni Morrison's *Song of Solomon*, even the strong elder women like Pilate and Old Grandma cannot always save the children of the following generations. Laura, Tayo's mother, is linked to the woman in the "Arroyo story" as well as to Helen Jean, the sad, permed bar girl that Tayo and Harley pick up. These women, like Christine in Michael Dorris's *Yellow Raft on Blue Water*, suffer and often die young for squandering their place in the story, but as Swan notes, even these women are connected to Our Mother, and their place in the story is linked to Tayo's emotional growth. Through his meeting with Ts'eh, his understanding of the Arroyo story of the woman who leaves her child, and his evening with Night Swan, Tayo, like Jake in Sinclair's *Wasteland*, begins to forgive his mother for her weakness and for his own sense of emasculation as he accepts his place in his own culture. Night Swan is one of the first women to direct Tayo to his healing place. Though his sexual encounter with Night Swan, Tayo comes to understand that his "Mexican" eyes are not just evidence of his mother's shame, but finally of her love for him. Moreover, she tells Tayo that people who are afraid of change "blame us, the ones who look different" (104), but, like Betonie's grandmother, and Silko herself, Night Swan is part of a female life force that helps to heal Tayo, as well as one of those who acknowledge that change is necessary for living beings. Betonie's (unnamed) grandmother is linked through her ethnic identity to the Mexican Night Swan. Although we never actually meet Betonie's grandmother, she plays a profound role in shaping Tayo's views on his mixed identity, and her visions reflect Silko's main aims in the novel. Her comprehension that after the white people came, new ceremonies have to be invented is the governing motif of the novel. Following his grandmother's lead, Betonie not only changes the rituals in Tayo's own cure, but uses these changed ceremonies to place Tayo in the larger healing narrative. Significantly, Betonie's grandmother is reminiscent of the most important woman in Tayo's family life, his own grandmother, whose name symbolically is Old Grandma.

Old Grandma functions throughout the novel as a foil to the assimilative attitudes of Auntie and as a custodian of traditional culture and values, Old Grandma takes Tayo's healing out of the hands of both the "white" doctors and Auntie, as she involves Old Ku'oosh and eventually Betonie. Most significant are resonances of his grandmother's words as Tayo proceeds through the healing ceremony; through the remembrances of her stories and directions, as well as his memories of his childhood with his uncle Josiah,

Tayo learns to read the experiences he is trying so desperately to interpret. Old Grandma is the one living relative who aids Tayo in identifying with his Indianness, despite Auntie's reluctance to do so because he is mixed; moreover, Old Grandma is linked to a traditional worldview in which one is part of the tribe not because of biology but rather because of one's knowledge of the group. She passes on this knowledge to Tayo. As he thinks back to her scolding him and Rocky for not respecting the deer they killed (53–54) or remembers that she told him that "back in time immemorial" people were more connected to the earth and its animals (99), Tayo begins to decode the world around him: "Everywhere he looked, he saw a world made of stories, the long ago, time immemorial stories, as Old Grandma called them" (100). Reflecting Grandmother Spider, Old Grandma is a repository of the storytelling tradition, and Tayo gains strength through her tales and her support of him. Relevantly, Old Grandma is the first to know that something has changed for Tayo when he returns from Betonie's ceremony and being with Ts'eh. She tells him: "You're all right now, aren't you, sonny" (225). Tayo is indeed all right, moving from cultural illness to potential healer, and through his relationship with his grandmother, as well as the other women who have helped him, balance is restored. Furthermore, even the women who have been lost to him, particularly his mother Laura, are restored to a place in the story, as Tayo sees the pattern of their lives, their pains, and the possibilities for health. Finally, as in the African-based cultures in the first two chapters of this book, as well as the final chapter on Jewish culture, it is the reconnection with the maternal that is a most significant part of the healing process. Specifically, through Tayo's relationship with Ts'eh, replicated in his grandmother's stories and the verse sections of the novel, Silko also presents the important role of women as female spirit guides in the healing of the wounds of the earth.

As Betonie's grandmother prescribes, Silko moves from her role of recording the stories and traditions to reframing the rituals so as to heal the wounding of the earth. In the violent and momentous changes in our world, signified by the atom bomb, the old ceremonies need renewed strength. In his first meeting with Tayo, Betonie tells Tayo what he has learned from his grandmother, reflecting what appears also to be Silko's aim in writing the novel: "They think the ceremonies must be performed exactly as they always have been done. . . . But after the white people came, elements in this world began to shift; and it became necessary to change the ceremonies. I have made changes in the rituals. The people mistrust this greatly, but only this growth keeps the ceremonies strong" (132–133).

Both Silko and Hulme reformulate major legends to create ceremonies intended to heal contemporary cultures. In *Ceremony*, Silko changes the rituals in two obvious ways (there are others): First, she uses the bourgeois form of a novel for her healing chant, thus enlarging the interpersonal nature of the healing to reach a very large group of the unwell (us all). At the same time, she transforms this Euro-narrative construct to include the verse tales out of the orature, directing us to her reformulation of the legends. Second, Silko revisions earlier Laguna Pueblo and Navajo legends of witches, especially the story of the Gambler, to examine a part of the witchery hard to imagine before the Western age of technology, even though Silko implies that it was through the witches' story, told in the center of the novel, that this form of the witchery was conceived. In *Nervous Conditions*, Dangarembga actualizes a trope in much postcolonial fiction, that "white" people take on the form of witches in twisting the minds of those colonized to reject their heritage; however, in *Ceremony*, Silko disrupts this trope and (re)places both the power and responsibility back on the Amerindians, as she conceives this legend, the "invention" of white people and the destruction they bring. Silko displaces the role of those in the dominant culture as solely perpetrators of the witchery, but also includes them as victims. Moreover, Silko implies that it is only the inclusion of white people in the healing that will truly heal the planet, a view that is apparently challenged by the pessimistic vision of her second novel, *Almanac of the Dead*, although it is revisited in the portrait of Hattie in her most recent novel, *Gardens in the Dunes*.

In "Landscape, History and the Pueblo Imagination," Silko notes that for the Pueblo people, "Everything became a story" (87)—a way of interpreting the world, including the arrival of the first Europeans to the land. She states further in the essay that in telling these stories of the people's history, the narrator always has choices: The ancient Pueblo sought a communal truth, not an absolute one" (88). These statements help decode the legend Silko creates/relates in middle of the novel, moving away from the earlier, more well-known, stories she presents in verse.[12] As in Keri Hulme's revisioning of the Maori origination tale (about when they first came to New Zealand) in *the bone people*, Silko takes parts of different legends to develop a verse narrative of the invention of "white" people, as well as their most destructive invention—the atom bomb. Although there are many Native American stories concerning witchery, Silko links them with interpretations of the first Europeans coming to the continent and the making of the atom bomb, further linking Native American concepts of health to the healing of the planet. In Silko's revised legend, placed firmly in the center of the novel, one particularly foreboding witch, who comes with "a story" as his part of the witches' contest of telling of evil things, spins his tale of formerly unseen "*white skin people/ like the belly of a fish/ covered with hair*" (142). In inventing these people, bent on the destruction of the world, the witch focuses in on their most violent act to be. With uranium found in these hills:

> *They will lay the final pattern with these rocks*
> *they will lay it across the world*
> *and explode everything.* (144)

This tale has special significance in light of the novel's connections between the Japanese and the Native Americans, as well as Tayo's hiding in the old uranium mine to avoid Emo and the army doctors. In "Healing the Witchery," St. Andrews comments that Tayo's final confrontation with the witchery "happens in a symbolic place: where the ancient creation myths of the Keresan people intersect with the nuclear age" (92). However, this intersection in terms of healing the land also brings up what cannot be healed, since the devastation from the atomic explosions in testing and in actual use has left on the earth a scar of extreme magnitude. Silko asks of us: How do we heal after that? Toni Cade Bambara's asides concerning nuclear power and nuclear destruction in *The Salt Eaters* are made explicit in this novel; this kind of violence needs a stronger ceremony, one that must include the white people who have also been fooled by the witchery. Within the context of Keresan tradition, Silko directs us to some sort of balance by Tayo hiding in the mine; still, we are also made aware in the novel that the evil that Emo exemplifies is not dead, just gone to California. The caveat encoded in that bit of news is reinforced by the verse narrative of Fly and Hummingbird, which at this point mirrors the Euro-narrative of the novel. After they have finally done their work to restore both the rains and balance in the community, they are warned by Our Mother: "'Stay out of trouble/

from now on./ It isn't very easy/ to fix things up again" (268). Silko's vision here reflects the caveat at the end of *The Salt Eaters* that being healed is a fragile condition and that some damage can't be fixed, as Hulme's *the bone people* demonstrates.

By the conclusion of the novel, Tayo returns to old Ku'oosh and the elders in the kiva, telling his tale and relating his own healing to a healing of the community and the land itself. The old men query him on his shamanistic journey and his meeting with Ts'eh. Linking Tayo's human experience with the voice of time immemorial, the Euro-narrative of the novel is finally blended with the verse-legend sections, restoring balance, as the words of the old men speak through both narratives: "You have seen her/ We will be blessed again" (270). Tayo's story takes its place in the ancient tradition, and the legends are revivified so as to heal the dis-ease of this community and the land for now. However, the novel does not end there; there is a home scene with Old Grandma, Tayo, and Auntie, very much like the beginning of the novel, except that something profound has shifted the space of their lives. As Auntie gossips to (not about) Tayo concerning the death of Pinkie, we understand that something has changed in their relationship as well. Although the situation is not perfect, since there is no indication of Auntie giving up her assimilative posturing, Auntie has learned something, and she accepts Tayo as part of her own. Significantly, balance is restored as Tayo is reintegrated into the family. Most relevantly, the Euro-narrative ends with the voice of Old Grandma. With her provocative comment that she had heard all these stories before (only the names sound different), we join in with the humor in the phrase as well as realizing that the stories are part of time immemorial, this story included! It is the strength of the woman's voice—from Old Grandma to Ts'eh to Silko to Thought Woman—that guides the healing process, although it cannot be completed without the men, from Betonie and Josiah to Tayo himself, who balance the vision.

Throughout *Ceremony*, Silko intertwines women's roles in Laguna Pueblo communities with the importance of storytelling and restoring balance as the only deep way to heal both the individual and the community. In "Language and Literature from a Pueblo Indian Perspective," Silko states directly what the novel as a whole demarcates: "The stories are always bringing us together, keeping this whole together, keeping this family together, keeping this clan together. . . . Inherent in this belief is the feeling that one does not recover or get well by one's self, but it is together that we look after each other and take care of each other" ("Language" 59).

In *Ceremony*, Silko takes this "we," which implies a specific community, to the larger audience, so that we as readers, regardless of ethnic background, become part of the healing ritual of the novel. Like Tayo and the other characters, we have undergone a healing chant and are also there to ask Sunrise to "accept this offering" (275). However, Silko, as part of revisioning the ceremonies in the novel, does not leave us completely cured. Right before this offering, we are left with a caveat similar to Bambara's: The witchery is only "dead for now" (274). As the Jewish vow to "never forget" the horrors of the Holocaust exemplifies, it is the vigilance in remembering the stories and (re)enacting them that keeps the witchery at bay, since there is no context in which to totally eliminate the witchery; even stories of destruction have meaning. Silko, who has led us in this healing chant, named by Thought Woman, leaves us without cathartic release; our healing, like our earth, is fragile, and we must take this story only as a model of healing, not as a cure in itself.

4

Becoming

the

Instruments

of Change

Maori Healing
Visions in
Keri Hulme's
the bone people

In *The Healing Tongue*, Peter Beatson identifies Hulme, as well as novelists Witi Ihimaera and Patricia Grace, as examples of activist Maori writers who are attempting to cure their culture, both Maori and Pakeha (New Zealanders of European descent). Appropriating the image of the mutilated warrior in Apirana Taylor's short story "The Carver," Beatson explores these authors' attempt to heal the tongue that has been mutilated by the imposition of the English language and Eurocentric values (37). He comments: "Maori Art is born of trauma and of healing. It is the art of pain and of anger but it is also the art of renewal and growth" (2). The violence of losing one's language and culture under the yoke of colonialism and Euro-dominant culture is reflected in each chapter of this book, from the Caribbean to Native American indigenous groups and formerly enslaved

African Americans in the Diaspora, and even functions in relation to Jewish culture, a prime "other" within European society.
The colonial experience of the Maori in New Zealand, as well as
their counterparts, the Aborigines of Australia, was and often still
is extremely violent, and that violence is mirrored in the literature itself, most noticeably documented in Alan Duff's novel and
later film *Once Were Warriors*. The loss of Maoritanga, the term
for connection to Maori culture and community, is, as Beatson
comments, the basis for the wounded tongue, and the possibility
of writing as a way to begin a narrative of healing. As Witi Ihimaera
and D. S. Long note in their introduction to the first major anthology of Maori writings in English, *Into the World of Light*, the
writings of emergent Maori authors have been characterized as
part of a *"renaissance* of Maori art and culture." But the editors
state further: "It has been more than this—it has been a cultural
revolution" (3).

This concept of a cultural revolution reflects the other novels
examined in my book, in the attempt to reconstruct the language
of the colonial encounter and dominant ideology to become a discourse of healing. Like the other women writers explored here,
Hulme examines the diseases of her community through her
wellness text and has turned to its Maori roots for the substance
of the cure. In the forward to her first collection of short stories,
Te Kaihau/The Windeater, Hulme speaks of her aim to heal this
wounded tongue, replacing what Marlene Nourbese Philip calls
the tongue cut out by the foreign "anguish" of English. Furthermore,
Hulme exposes the hidden history, values, and cross-influences
behind New Zealand's English language and the multiple meanings of Maori words.[1] She notes that one would have to be a "brave
human" to say where all the influences came from, but clearly
discerns that "the word sets the whole thing up" (14). Hulme looks
beyond the integration of Maori words and structure within a
Pakeha form such as the novel to the way in which the Maori
concept of profane (English) and sacred (Maori) words link together
to form the possibility of an emergent and healthier discourse.
Hulme's vision is grounded in the traditional belief of Maori
women's ability to negate *tapu* (in Maori, what is forbidden in
both a secular and sacred sense, linguistically as well as literally).
In *the bone people*, Hulme adapts this role as she neutralizes both
the tapu of the characters within the context of the novel and
metaphorically uses the novel as a way to remove the tapu infringement caused by assimilation, rejection of Maori traditions,

and loss of Maoritanga. What makes her novel unique is that, in Hulme's aim to heal the community through her writing, she envisions a model of wellness for all New Zealanders, including those of European heritage.

the bone people concerns three main characters, a Maori man, a part-Maori woman, and a European child, who all go through interpersonal cures. Their movement toward health reflects the dis-ease and potential healing of New Zealand/Aotearoa (the Maori name for the island). Through a blending and acceptance of Western and Maori traditions, the novel explores what it means to be well, personally and culturally. This chapter examines Hulme's conjoining of gender and ethnicity in the process of healing, in terms of traditional Maori concepts of health, personal identity, and cultural illness, and analyzes each protagonist's moves toward health and their healing potential as "instruments of change" (4) for self and nation. From the Maori beliefs and healing practices to what critic Mark Williams sarcastically calls "semi-magical cures for cancer," *the bone people* displaces binary oppositions like traditional vs. Western, magic vs. science, and health vs. disease. Through this wellness narrative, Hulme appropriates the role of a Maori woman healer to negate tapu and creatively visualizes a world that proffers the potential for personal and community health within the context of the novel, as well as exposes a new way to perceive well-being for her readers.

Like Leslie Marmon Silko, Keri Hulme perceives her bicultural heritage as giving her special insight into the two cultures that are her ancestry, as well as informing all her writings. Her creative and critical fiction has been to examine how these two disparate cultures, the Maori and the Northern European, can come together to (re)form that shining land, New Zealand/Aotearoa. In her essay "Mauri: An Introduction to Bicultural Poetry in New Zealand," Hulme identifies herself as a "mongrel" and comments that a "dual heritage is both pain and advantage. It gives you insight into two worlds" (294). Hulme is one-eighth Maori, like her persona, the protagonist Kerewin Holmes, whose name is a variation on the author's. Although Hulme's grandfather was Maori, Kati Tahu, a South Island tribe with origins in the Takimu canoe, Hulme describes her lineage as matri/lineage: "[M]y mother's mother, my grandmother, and the sister next to her both married brothers who were South island Maori" (Peek 2). Hulme's focus on the matrilineal mix of Scot/Maori reflects her aim: to find a comfortable bicultural heritage for New Zealanders, and the importance of women in passing on these traditions. Two other personal facts inform the writing of *the bone people*: Her grandfather died of cancer of the lung (possibly linked his work shoveling coal for the railway), which may have influenced her conflicts with the Pakeha medical establishment, and even more significantly, one of her uncles, the youngest, was an adopted Pakeha boy. After her grandfather died, he gave his land to the three children, but the Maori courts fought the distribution of land to this youngest son. Hulme's own adolescence was affected by this experience, as well as by her witnessing of racist behavior toward her darker relatives. Hulme's cultural "fence-sitting," as she calls it, and her desire to create a counterhegemonic utopia so that people can envision a New Zealand that blends the best of both cultures, resonates in the language of her writing, from her poetry and short stories to the lyrical prose of *the bone people*.

One specific anecdote from Hulme's adolescence clearly illustrates both the pain and the advantage of her bilingual heritage. A high school teacher, in responding to Hulme's dense writing style, criticized her essay by saying, "'You use far too many adjectives, you make your writing far too rich, it must be the Maori side of you coming out.'" Rather than being discouraged by this racist comment, Hulme resisted this put-down by telling herself, "Fine, if the Maori side means to be too rich and too adjectival, I shall continue being so" (Peek 5). Although this is said with humor, the implications are profound: It exposes the other side of the Pakeha romantization of the Maori.[2] It also illustrates the importance of language used once again as both a negative identifier and a healing tool. The next chapter on Sinclair/Seid expands this concept of language as a negative identifier in terms of Jewish self-hate, but here Hulme overturns this denigration as she uses her Maori English to challenge the literary conventions of the novel brought to New Zealand with the colonizers.

According to Miriama Evans in "The Politics of Maori Literature," Maori readers are "besieged from early childhood with literature patterned by the often unintelligible symbols of another culture" (359). Writers like Patricia Grace, Witi Ihimaera, and Hulme all work to transform in their own way this English language, developed by the colonizers who have mistranslated their own Maori words and culture. From her own bicultural perspective, Hulme, in particular, tries to build a new language that is inclusive. Revisiting language is linked to the cultural healing of the protagonists and the readers, so it is necessary to comprehend

both the hidden language and healing practices within a culturally specific context. Integral to the motif of healing in *the bone
people* are Maori concepts of health in relation to a Western biomedical system, as well as women role's in the spiritual and familial component of wellness. According to M. H. Durie in "A
Maori Perspective on Health," traditional Maori healing practices
focus on the four basic components of the person: the spiritual *(te
taha wairua)*; the psychic *(te taha hinegaro)*; the bodily *(te taha
tinana)*; and the familial *(te taha whanau)*. Unlike the binary opposition of mind/body, these four components are interrelated to
produce a healthy person. What separates this system (as well as
other systems of traditional healing examined throughout this
book) from the biomedical model is the importance of both the
spiritual component and the familial. For the Maori, the spiritual/
wairua is "the most basic and essential requirement for health.
Without a spiritual awareness, the individual is considered to be
lacking in wellbeing and more prone to disability." Moreover, the
person whose "first thoughts are only for himself [sic]" would be
considered "unhealthy" (Durie 484). As evoked in the context of
the novel, an individual who might appear physically healthy could
not be truly well isolated from his/her family and community.
The concept of Maori healing is a holistic one, reflecting the indigenous base of cultural healing, illustrated by Silko's *Ceremony*.
As evoked in the context of both novels, an individual who might
appear physically healthy could not be truly well if isolated from
his/her family and community. Healing, within an indigenous
culture, is "viewed as an inter-related phenomenon rather than a
inter-personal one" (Durie 484), in which health means a balance
between the individual and the community. However, within this
integrated approach to healing the whole, Silko places special
emphasis on the individual and community relation to the earth
in *Ceremony*, while Hulme places her own emphasis on the kinship and community based notion of health and wellness in the
fourth component of health: family/whanau. Witi Ihimaera's 1974
novel, *Whanau*, centers on this concept, as he presents a tale of an
extended family coming together to find the eldest village member, symbolizing the strength of whanau within rural Maori communities. Hulme expands on this formation of whanau in her novel,
the bone people, by bringing into this communal concept of a familial health another kind of family, which includes a Pakeha
young boy and an unrelated, bicultural, apparently asexual woman
cut off from her own family members, both Maori and Pakeha.

Hulme's literary reenactment of the concept of whanau reflects the way women writers are creating healing visions, as well as the imaging that is often practiced by traditional healers. According to Jeanne Achterberg, the practice of women healers in creating a healing vision is "likely to reflect a broad sense of healing that aspires to the wholeness or harmony within the self, the family, and the global community" (4). Achterberg also notes that this approach to health is "antithetical to the cosmological structure that binds the Western world" (3), while other cultures "more adequately reflect the positive characteristics of the feminine aspects of healing" (2). In *Woman as Healer*, Achterberg specifically cites Native American societies in the United States as her example, illustrated by *Ceremony*, among other works; however, many other indigenous cultures throughout the world, including the Maori, historically have had special roles for women in the act of imagining a healthy body, mind, self, family, and community.

Integral to Maori healing, and almost totally ignored by the somatic treatment of disease, is what might be called the social component: the pivotal relationship of cultural awareness and personal well-being. Disease, according to Maori healers, is linked to this loss of Maoritanga. Furthermore, the breakdown of cultural traditions and identity through assimilation into Westernized society has led the Maori as individuals and as a culture to be ill: "Mental illness in the Maori is often seen to result from a movement away from the age-old traditions and the loss of Maori 'spirituality' . . . and healing [is] a process of bringing back the lost spirituality and the emphasis on the 'Maoriness' of the individual" (Sachdev, "Mana" 968). The process of healing is done not only by the *tohunga* (traditional healer), but also by the *kaumatua/kuia* (male/female elder), who uses the knowledge of Maori culture to bring the unhealthy person back into the community and health.[3] As Beatson notes in *The Healing Tongue*, the link with the ancestors and "the cultural values embodied in those forebears" is encoded in the relationship between the young person and "his or her grandparent, most usually the grandmother. It was with the jawbone of his grandmother that the demigod Maui pulled Aotearoa to the surface of consciousness" (50). The role of the grandmother within Maori culture is powerful both mythically and literally. As in both African-based and Native American societies, the grandmother (in an extended, not strictly biological sense of the word) plays an important role in the healing of the dysfunctional and dis-eased individual. It is the "kaumatua, usually the kuia, [who acts] as transmitter of the cultural genetic code" (Beatson 53), and guides people in this significant aspect of their move toward wellness. As in other traditional societies as well as in the novels discussed here, older women play a critical role in passing on the culture to future generations and in fighting disease through maintaining heritage.

A particularly unique aspect of Maori healing and spirituality is the concept of "tapu." In "God, Man and Universe: A Maori View," Maori Marsden states: "Tapu is the sacred state or condition of a person or thing placed under the patronage of the gods" (196). Moreover, a secondary meaning of a tapu object is as something that is unclean or forbidden: "The condition of tapu is transmitted by contact or association and a person can be contaminated and polluted by it" (197). In *"Mana, Tapu, Noa*: Maori Cultural Constructs with Medical and Psycho-Social Relevance," Perminder S. Sachdev examines the aspects of tapu related to illness: In precolonial times, "infringement of tapu restriction was the most common cause attributed to illness . . . and removal of tapu was, and to a degree still is, practiced by the Maori for this purpose" (963). The belief that illness is connected to "wrong living" (Parsons 217) and the breaking of tapu is still present in Maori cosmology, and tapu infringement must be dealt with by the elders for the offending person to return to the family and community. What is particularly germane to this discussion, especially in regard to *the bone people*, is women's especial role in "negating or neutralizing tapu" (Sachdev, "Mana" 962). Within the context of this worldview, women do not have as high a quality of *mana* (personal spiritual force) as men do, but they have the significant function of being able to neutralize tapu infringement and, therefore, help lead the ill back to health. Hulme comments on this aspect of women's ability in her own essay on Maori spirituality, "Myth, Omen, Ghost and Dream." She states wryly that women are usually considered *noa* (ordinary), but that this in fact has its positive side—"its ability to disperse dangerous tapu" (36). Hulme, aware of this aspect of Maori culture, accepts her own role by adapting the notion of women's ability to negate tapu, as she literally neutralizes the tapu of the characters within the context of the novel and metaphorically uses the novel as a way to break the tapu infringement caused by assimilation, rejection of Maori traditions, and loss of Maoritanga. Hulme takes this component of Maori spiritual life as a metaphor for the presentation of healing and women's curative domain in the novel.

In *the bone people*, Hulme's act of healing with words links the aims of the Maori writer to heal the wounded tongue with the role of Maori women whose duty is to negate dangerous tapu—in this case, a kind of linguistic tapu brought on by the colonizer culture. Hulme takes her roles as woman writer and cultural worker one step further. She creates a healing narrative that examines the cultural illness of characters who reflect the ethnic demographics of New Zealand. The three protagonists are Kerewin Holmes, a part-Maori woman (in the United States, as she notes, she would be an octaroon); Joe Gillayley, a Maori man; and his foster son, Simon, a young silent boy of European/Pakeha descent whom Joe found washed ashore, orphaned after a shipwreck. As we learn in the opening prologue, these three characters take on mythic dimensions because they "were nothing more than people, by themselves . . . but all together, they have become the heart and muscles and mind of something perilous and new, something strange and growing and great. Together all together, they are the instruments of change" (4). The language of this opening recalls the language of science and medicine, surgical instruments, but at the same time, it resists the body/mind split so pervasive in Western culture. The novel takes the reader on a perilous journey through disease and toward health, as the characters come together and pull apart; violate and are violated by physical abuse and emotional isolation; and suffer from the lack of cultural connection. For Joe, who abuses his son and has internalized self-hate in relation to his Maoriness, for Simon who suffers from this abuse as well as post-traumatic stress syndrome from the shipwreck and from being left stranded on a beach; and for Kerewin, who is alienated from herself and her Maori community and may also be dying of cancer, the healing process is one that they cannot go through alone. Hulme's revisioning of whanau, through a linguistic healing, articulates the story of these protagonists as instruments of change. Like the tricephalous that Kerewin sculpts, each of the three characters is necessary for the healing process to begin in the novel—and metaphorically in the nation as well.

Most critical responses to *the bone people* focus mainly on the character of Kerewin and her role in the novel, but Hulme presents, rather, an integrated structure in her text, reflecting the double helix that forms the base of Maori spiritual life as well as a nonlinear design prominent in women's literature. Not only do many Pakeha critics stop short of exploring the familial aspect of the novel's structure in re-creating whanau and the cultural implications of the character's diseases, they often resist what Alejo Carpentier termed "magical realism" of the work, a significant aspect of Maori culture in general. In one essay reevaluating the novel, Mark Williams, who apparently has read little about traditional healing in his native New Zealand, skeptically asks: "Is the reader meant to respond to the sections on Maori religious belief or semi-magical cures for cancer with the same 'willing suspension of disbelief' with which he or she is evidently meant to respond to the realistic sections?" (86). In another example, Carmel Gaffney comments in "Making the Net Whole: Design in Keri Hulme's *The Bone People*," that Joe's experiences in finding the mauriora "seem at the time disconnected from the main concerns of the novel" (296). She goes on to say that each of the transformations at the end of the novel, especially Kerewin's "miraculous" cure, "fails to convince the reader" (297). Gaffney's assumption that the "reader" has the same cultural understanding as Gaffney herself not only leaves out Maori readers and others with knowledge of alternative worldviews, but is also linked to Williams's culture-bound question. Although Williams clearly asks his question rhetorically, assuming that the answer is no, informed readers realize that the novel's articulate response is a resounding yes! The ending of *the bone people* is utopian in a counterhegemonic sense, like the ending of Bambara's *The Salt Eaters*, yet this vision does not contradict the realistic aspects of the text, as Williams suggests.[4] What these critics apparently miss is the critique of biomedicine and limits of scientific rationalism encoded in the work, as well as the significance of an expanded worldview, including both the Maori and Pakeha visions of what realism is. To comprehend this wellness narrative in its fullest sense, the reader must be able to accept the alternative reality put forth through Hulme's feminist revisioning of Maori culture and healing. A reader who interprets this wellness text solely within a Western context will in fact be confused by the resistance to the binary oppositions portrayed in the work.

Each novel considered so far has dealt with a disjuncture between the medical profession and the potential healing of the culturally ill. In each case, from Brodber's doctor, Nellie, and Bambara's Meadows, who cannot heal within the limited context of Western medicine, to Tayo, whose experiences in the hospital only add to his disease, medical practitioners have failed the communities they have theoretically aimed to serve. Although Sinclair's *Wasteland* complicates this trope, since psychiatry, albeit born out of Jewish healing traditions, is the method for Jake's healing, *the bone people* is probably the most sustained attack on the failure of the medical system to heal the whole person. As in Ellison's *Invisible Man* and Silko's *Ceremony*, the hospital itself becomes a symbol of "whiteness" not merely in terms of cleanliness, as aimed, but rather as a frightening and hostile environment. The title of Ruth Bleier's essay "Lab Coat or Klansman's Sheet" reflects all the fear felt by many on the margins of the dominant culture upon entering the hospital.[5] Sally Morgan opens her novel *My Place*, which deals with a mixed, "passing" family trying to accept its Aboriginal heritage, with the young character Sally hating the smells and "dust-free window sills" of the hospital where she must go to visit her dysfunctional World War II veteran father, making her feel like "a grubby five-year-old in an alien environment" (15). As in *My Place*, our first glimpse of alienation caused by the hospital and the limitations of the medical establishment to cure the whole person comes through a young person, in this case, the Pakeha Simon's experiences. Simon has a pathological fear of doctors and hospitals, possibly stemming from his birth father's heroin addiction and the needles connected to it. Nor are the doctors able to do anything for Simon's extreme nightmares, except to give him trichoral to sleep. Joe, on the other hand, appears to understand the basis of Simon's problem, but he is uncomfortable with what he sees as the answer. As he explains Simon's fears to Kerewin, Joe tells her of Simon's bad dreams and comments that if he were a "proper Maori" he'd "take him to people who'd know what to do, to keep off ghosts in dreams. . . . See? Bloody superstitious Nga Bush? Get the Maori a bad name, eh?" (61). What is of particular concern here is that Joe, unlike Auntie in *Ceremony*, who cites Tayo's mixed blood to explain the reasons that traditional medicine won't work for him, doesn't even address the fact of Simon's European heritage. However, like Auntie, he is worried about what people will think. Joe, who is suffering from emotional dis-ease associated with assimilation, is caught in the binary opposition that calls one approach to health "science" and the other "superstition." On one hand, he believes that there are Maori tohunga who could help Simon, and on the other, he is too embarrassed about being perceived "bush" to do anything about it. Although Simon is Pakeha, Joe shows no hesitation in acknowledging that this type of healing might work for someone of European ancestry. Rather, his fear of being thought ignorant by the dominant culture keeps him from attempting to help his foster son by moving beyond the limitations of Western medicine—in this case, psychiatry (205). The failure of psychiatry to acknowledge the cultural complexity of a boy like Simon, whose lineage is British but whose cultural environment is Maori, is linked here to issues discussed in the next chapter as well as to the psychiatrists' own sense of superiority toward and Joe's rejection of the healing practices within Maori society.

Joe's inability to help Simon is directly related to his own self-hate and cultural illness. In a Western sense, Joe is, for the most part, healthy: He is physically strong and has no somatic illnesses; although he drinks too much, he is functional—that is, he goes to work.[6] However, if we examine Joe within a Maori concept of health, we find a different answer. In the Maori sense, Joe is extremely unwell. He is ashamed of his culture, he is isolated from his extended family, and his thoughts are only for himself, an individualist notion inscribed in Western culture. According to Durie, "the individual whose first thoughts are for himself, his personal ambitions, or his own body is considered unhealthy, even though his body maybe the epitome of fitness" (484). Just as with other urban protagonists in contemporary Maori fiction, Joe admits to Kerewin that "the Maoritanga has got lost in the way I live" (62), and therefore, he suffers from cultural disease.[7] Joe realizes the waste he has made of his life: "I'd worked hard, pakeha fashion, for nearly six solid years, making money for a home. And one thing I never made was a home" (324). It is not enough for Joe to succeed Pakeha-style as an individual, because it has not given him a life; rather, his emotional dis-ease erupts in a most extreme way, in violence. This is the first instance in these five novels in which the main protagonist suffering from dis-ease is also a perpetrator of violence against others, although novels like Alan Duff's *Once Were Warriors,* as well as Alice Walker's *The Third Life of Grange Copeland* and N. Scott Momaday's *House Made of Dawn,* explore the trend of violence toward women and children by men who are oppressed.

Joe's physical abuse of Simon is connected to a matrix of cultural factors that affect his emotional health. Finding Simon on the beach, Joe resuscitates him and literally brings him back to life: "He has got that of me, I suppose. My breath. . . . " (85). Joe's comment resonates with the formal greeting *Tihe mauriora* (I salute the breathe of life in you) and the birth of the deity Maui, yet the evocation does not imply any commitment to live up to the familial/spiritual implication of this ritual greeting. True, Joe's breath revives Simon, but he is unable to give Simon much more. He still grieves for his wife and son, who died of influenza soon after Simon came to live with them, and in some irrational way, he partly blames Simon for being the one left alive. Separated from his Maori customs, Joe is unable to deal with Simon's trauma (from his childhood amid heroin, the loss of his parents, and the shipwreck itself); nor does Joe look for support from his extended family. Joe is isolated from them because of his abusive behavior and because he has alienated himself from their strictures and their love—exhibiting, in a Maori context, extremely unhealthy behavior, in opposition to I. Sow's African concept of what a healthy personality is. After finding Simon beaten, Joe's cousin Piri warns him: "You've turned sour, Joe. You're bent. You've got all the resources of family in the world, and you won't let us help" (132). Joe is sick, and his inability to help Simon by accepting his family's involvement also functions in his refusal to help himself. Caught between his lack of faith in his family and his embarrassment about Maori cures, Joe does nothing but continue to hammer on his child.

At first Joe's behavior seems anomalous, as we witness the loving nature of most of his family members, especially the elders Marama and Wherahiko, who are attempting to maintain a whanau that includes both Joe and his Pakeha son. But as we learn more of Joe's background, we recognize the social constructs behind his illness, including his internalizing of the Pakeha culture that perceives Maori traditions and healing practices as inferior. Part of Joe's turmoil arises from the conflict between his grandparents, who, according to the family component of Maori health, are crucial in creating a healthy child. Joe's grandmother tries to raise Joe in Maori fashion, even though this antagonizes his grandfather, whom Joe describes as one who was respected in the church but not by the people, and who avoided any involvement with the *marae*, the Maori cultural meeting house and religious center. Rather than fulfilling his role as kaumatua (male elder) for his community's children, the grandfather takes on the values and judgments of the colonizing culture and mutilates the Maori traditions that could help Joe become a healthy adult. All the self-hate associated with assimilation (physical appearance and behavior) is passed on to Joe from his grandfather, despite his grandmother's adherence to Maoritanga. Joe comments: "I think he was ashamed of my Nana and her Maoriness. . . . I think he took it out on me for being dark, for speaking Maori first, all sorts of things" (227). Still, like Granny Tucker in *Jane and Louisa* and Old Grandma in *Cer-*

emony, Joe's grandmother fights her husband for Joe's spiritual life, attempting to fulfill her role in Maori society. Evident also in the grandmother's role is her knowledge of traditional healing practices. When Joe was young, he had "something like polio," and his grandmother cured him: "Nana was a great one for traditional medicine and avoiding Pakeha doctors. . . . As far as she was concerned, the old ways and the old treatments were best, even for new diseases" (228). Unlike many others of his generation, Joe recovers without any physical evidence of the polio. As in the case of the Aboriginal grandmother, Nan, in Morgan's *My Place*, who is able to help her daughter recover from polio through traditional methods but refuses to tell her granddaughter how she did it, Joe's grandmother's skills are lost, not passed on to the later generations because of the fear of appearing "bush." Moreover, even though Joe's grandmother cures him of the residual symptoms of the polio, she is unable to protect him against the emotional disease of internal colonization from which he suffers later. Unlike Tayo, who benefits from his grandmother's support and guidance throughout his disease and healing, Joe suffers the death of his grandmother when he is sixteen, leaving him without that essential link to whanau and Maoritanga as he sets out, Pakeha style, to make it on his own. Joe remembers his grandmother with a combination of awe and admiration; nevertheless, beaten and berated by his grandfather, Joe is caught in the middle and ironically ends up passing on a very different tradition: that of abuse. As Maryanne Dever has observed in her essay "Violence as *Lingua Franca*: Keri Hulme's *The Bone People*": "This disjunction between past and present, cultural past and personal present, is seen as being in some way responsible for the sense of emptiness that invades both Kerewin and Joe" (29).

Joe's sense of emptiness, his isolation, and his violent dis-ease is much more evident in the opening sections of the novel than are Kerewin's. In fact, Joe and Simon both think that Kerewin will be the one to heal their family, to save them (153). Because of his memories of a grandmother who healed him as well as his positive relationship with his first wife, Hana, Joe sees Kerewin as a woman who will come in, take over, heal the wounds that result from his violent acts, and make him and Simon into a family. In this way, her perceived role as a healer to cure cultural illness is similar to that of Debby, Jake's lesbian sister in the final novel examined in this book, Jo Sinclair's *Wasteland*. In *Wasteland*, Debby is the only person who keeps her dysfunctional family together, but to do this, she has to overcome her own cultural illness. Likewise, Kerewin must go through this process to be healed and to become a healer herself; however, unlike Debby who has undergone a cultural healing process before the novel begins, in *the bone people*, Kerewin is presented as both a healer and one of the diseased. Like Joe, Kerewin is suffering from personal and cultural illness, although her symptoms are not as overt. Even though she is the catalyst for change, a careful reading of the work demonstrates that Kerewin also needs to be healed both by the other two protagonists and through her (re)connection to Maori culture. Kerewin tells Joe, "By blood, flesh, and inheritance, I am but an eighth Maori, by heart, spirit, and inclination, I feel all Maori. Or . . . I used to. Now the best part of me has got lost in the way I live" (62). In this case, as in Tayo's experience in *Ceremony*, the concept of cultural identity is not solely biologically based.

Kerewin is extremely articulate; in fact, much of the early part of the novel is controlled by Kerewin's voice. But her overabundance of words hides feelings, and Kerewin uses this narrative technique to resist any attempts at intimacy. As in other cultures examined in this book, words have the power to hurt as well as heal; in this case, moreover, the use of words actually keeps Kerewin from dealing with her own dis-ease. Simon notes that she speaks too much, and Joe, who identifies with her in some ways, states: "She is lonely. She drinks like I do to keep away the ghosts. She's an outsider, like me. And then sometimes, she seems inhuman" (101). This inhuman quality in Kerewin is linked to her ability to use words as a shield against human interaction, particularly sexuality. Joe, who wants her as a lover, tries to understand her resistance to intimacy through a Maori worldview. He comments that perhaps her lack of sexual desire comes from her position as an artist, since in Maori custom there is a tapu restriction on sex during the period the artist is working on a sacred carving. Despite this admission, he thinks to himself that he'll convince her to love him in a more conventional way, rejecting the Maori traditions he just identified. Joe's response also reinforces the fact that, although Joe has knowledge of his culture, his assimilative lifestyle and attitudes take precedence over his understanding of Maoritanga.

Kerewin is not only isolated affectively from this loss of Maoritanga and physically through her dislocation from her own body, but she is also alienated in terms of whanau. Although we never find out the reason within the context of the novel, Kerewin has broken her bond with her Maori kin, because of an undisclosed argument in which she indelibly hurt them with "words and memories" (167). When she returns to Moerangi, the site of her family's seaside cottages and named a healing place (90), she despairs: "They were the only people who knew me, knew anything of me, and they kept loving me until I broke it. . . . Cut off from the roots, sick and adrift" (167). Kerewin identifies her isolation as a sickness, comprehended in the Maori sense; however, she is physically ill as well. She has a stomach tumor, which is at least cursorily diagnosed as cancer. Like Nellie's throat tumor, which begins to appear when she deals with her experiences with racism in the United States, Kerewin's tumor causes pain in relationship to any interaction with the family that bring up her sense of loss of whanau and Maoritanga. Unlike Nellie's, Kerewin's tumor does not dissolve when the incident is over. It remains, producing a nagging dull pain, and the sharper pains from this hard lump in her stomach are extreme and violent when they happen. Still she does nothing to treat her disease. She neither seeks medical help nor uses alternative herbal treatment, despite her knowledge of traditional medicine (61). The inclusion of her therapeutic capabilities indicates that Kerewin could be more connected to her role as a Maori woman healer, if she could address her own cultural illness. In addition to her knowledge of herbal remedies, she understands the relationship between physical health and emotional well-being, though she is unable to work out that balance in her own life. Her search for some kind of balance takes her to explore other cultures, like Velma in *The Salt Eaters*, but in both cases, the association of other spiritual remedies is empty without some reconnection to one's own cultural traditions. Kerewin tries aikido because she sees it a way to "reconcile" her world, but all she learns is the physical aspects and loses the "spiritual development" (199–200). Ironically, as an artist, Kerewin is associated with the sacred spaces of the Maori; those who practiced the art of carving were perceived to "call on the unseen forces of the world" (Simmons 24). Yet Kerewin finds no sustenance from her art or medicinal knowledge, nor is she able to give anything back to her family or community, which identifies her as unhealthy within a Maori context as is Joe. Of course, Kerewin is also seen as unhealthy in a Western sense, because of her possibly malignant stomach tumor, but as the novel progresses, this limited view is challenged as well.

Nevertheless, in her early dealings with Joe and Simon,

Kerewin often functions as healer. When she first meets Simon, she performs a commonplace curative act: She takes a splinter out of his foot (19). Although at first she identifies Simon as "one of the maimed, the contaminating" (17), she still gives him the attention that he needs. Throughout the novel, her conflicting views of Simon as victim and as the purveyor of contamination affect her healing capabilities with him. She helps Simon physically with herbal concoctions and emotionally as intermediary with Joe, but in each incident she pulls back, due to the breakdown in her own emotional health. Kerewin, who has been perceived by both Joe and Simon as the person to make it "all work out fine" (153), is separated from her own therapeutic qualities by her own dysfunctions, based in her horror of intimacy on any level. When Simon gets a fish hook stuck in his thumb, Kerewin illogically refuses to help Joe remove the hook, because of her fear of being involved in their life (220). Despite her inability to help them at critical moments, Kerewin still promises to be their personal healer. Kerewin and Joe tell his extended family: "We just decided that if Himi [Simon] ever needs a hiding again, Joe will have to wait till I agree to it" (287). However, Kerewin cannot make good on her promise; she cannot guide them toward health, because she is also unwell. She realizes this fact when she parts company with Simon and Joe after the sea trip to Moerangi. She despairs: "You're wounded, soul, too hurt to heal" (261).

If, as Maryanne Dever states, that violence represents a "an extreme or perverse form of the *lingua franca* of the novel" (31), certainly the scene in which Joe gives Simon the final beating is the most powerful articulation of this language. When Kerewin receives the agreed-upon phone call from Joe to stop the abuse, she fuels Joe's anger rather than abating it—making it possible for the violence to continue and, thereby, turning her role as healer into that of destroyer. In this way, Kerewin abnegates her responsibility to Simon and Joe, most importantly rejecting the sense of recreated whanau that the three were attempting to build. In using her words as weapons, Kerewin replicates the violent slapping of Joe's hands: "She can't touch [Simon] physically so she is beating him with her voice. What she says drums through his head, resounding in waves as though his head was hollow, and the words bounce back from one side to smash against the other. . . . 'She hopes his father knocks him sillier than he is now'" (307).

Later, when she visits the comatose Simon in the hospital, Kerewin recognizes her role in the near murder of a six-year-old child. While she despairs, the pain in her stomach intensifies. This reinforces Hulme's sense that the bodily functions are intrinsically connected to what is going on in the mind: In a short story called "Hooks and Feelers," the mother feels a hard lump in her breast after going through the trauma of crushing her son's hand in the car door (*Te Kaihau* 77–89). Although Kerewin initially appeared to be the catalyst for healing Joe and Simon, her rejection of whanau, as well as her repudiation of her position as artist, renders her unable to fulfill her role as healer.

This chapter, "The Lightning Struck Tower," includes the most violent scene in the novel; however, the title, taken from a card in the Tarot deck, has connotations of healing.[8] All the major sections in the novel are titled with reference to the diseases and healing potential of the characters, from "The Sea Round," which refers to the healing site of Moerangi, to a concluding section, "Feldapart Sinews, Breaken Bones," that recounts each character's move from extreme affliction to wholeness. According to *The Book of Tarot*, the lightning-struck tower is "an environment built on superficial knowledge [which] is struck down by a momentary flash of truth and insight. From this flash of truth, the false values are realized and understood." A further statement reflects Hulme's aims in the novel, as the card discloses: "Traumatic change that will eventually bring positive growth and new awareness" (Gerrulskis-Estes 45). Like the Tarot card that inscribes rebirth in destruction, elements of the final scenes between Joe and Kerewin before Joe goes to jail evoke their potential to be instruments of change. Developments in "The Lightning-Struck Tower" reveal the healing potential for Joe, Simon, and Kerewin, despite the apparent destruction of their familial relationship. First, Kerewin begins to acknowledge her own resistance to her healing capabilities. After the disastrous phone call, Kerewin evokes a distorted kind of personal tapu on thinking about what she did: "IF ONLY is the tapu phrase/ If only I had/ If only I hadn't" (310).

Hulme's evocation of the concept of tapu leads us to speculate how she is using this notion in the novel. On one level, she uses the term to mean exactly what she defines it as in her glossary: "Tapu—can mean forbidden in a secular sense" (499). According to Maori beliefs, tapu infringement can come from wrong living. Clearly, Joe's lifestyle would be classified as that. Although the abuse of Simon would not be considered tapu in a sacred sense, it is forbidden in general. However, Kerewin's use of the term "tapu" to stop herself from thinking about her own "wrong living" is problematic. By refusing to deal with her part in Simon's near-fatal beating, considering "if only" a tapu phrase, Kerewin perverts the meaning of tapu and doesn't explore the aspects of the past that could help the future. However, in contradistinction to Kerewin's initial actions, Hulme appears to be metaphorically evoking some of the implications of tapu infringement and women's ability to negate tapu at this point in the novel. Her protagonist, Kerewin, at this juncture takes on her role as Maori healer, just as Hulme does in the novel. Kerewin begins to take responsibility for her own actions before she meets with Joe, who is going to jail. She pronounces to herself: "The tapu on 'if only' is hereby lifted, soul" (325). Through her privileged position as a Maori woman, Kerewin begins to neutralize a personal tapu infringement in her own life, which later affects Joe and Simon. In her role of neutralizing tapu, Kerewin begins to truly talk to Joe, and each of them gains self-awareness concerning their lives and Simon. They start to pick through past patterns, but can only go so far alone; there is still no community or whanau support to help break these abusive and unhealthy behaviors. In their final moments together, Kerewin supports Joe fully, and Joe takes what Kerewin can give him, acknowledging her difference. Joe's acceptance of Kerewin outside a conventional male-female relationship reflects a theme in some of the novels explored here, that tolerance for the other is part of a healthy individual and culture. In *Wasteland*, for example, Jake's coming to terms with his own Jewish identity is linked to his learning to accept his sister's lesbianism. It is evident from Joe's comments that he no longer wants to force Kerewin into being his lover or wife, but will accept her totally as friend, healer, and artist.

Significantly, because of the sacred position of carvers in Maori spiritual life, it is Kerewin's role as sculptor that presents for us the most powerful potential for change, identified in the prologue of the novel. As in Roger Mais's *Black Lightning*, in which the protagonist, Jake, creates a sculpture of Samson to embody his pain and suffering, Kerewin returns to her art one last time to recreate the lost family; she manages to sculpt a tricephalous of the three of them. Unlike the sculpture in the Mais novel, which evokes the protagonist, Jake's no-way-out situation and actually strikes him blind like his model, Samson, Kerewin's tricephalous portends a healing. After Simon's beating, Joe sees the sculpture:

> The hair of their heads is entwined at the top in a series of
> spirals. Simon's hair curves back from his neck to link

Kerewin and Joe to him. . . . Round and round, and with each circumambulating, the faces become more alive.

Aue! She saw us as a whole, as a set. And soon we'll be parted forever. (Not forever, not forever, not forever.) (315)

The tricephalous is the strongest harbinger of a future among the three and what they represent. In the novel, visual art reflects Hulme's own aims in writing a cure for her bicultural community. Moreover, in addition to the importance of carving in Maori society, the heads in the tricephalous are linked by the double spiral, a Maori spiritual sign associated with the unseen forces in life. In an act intended to destroy the tower that signified her alienation, Kerewin burns down her home; ironically, this act fires the clay sculpture, thus strengthening it. In metonymic symbolism, the tricephalous reflects rebirth through destruction (the Tarot's sign) and the possibility for these three to function as the instruments of change for a new and healthier life.

However, the sculpture as it stands only signifies the potential for change; as in the other works examined here, the characters, along with the readers, must go through the process of healing. In the last section of the novel, "Feldapart Sinews, Breaken Bones," the firing of the tricephalous is a metonym for the transformation of the characters. In each case, the protagonists are strengthened and healed in a blending of traditional and Western medicine, but always in relation to a Maori presence. The broken bones of these "bone people" start to heal as each moves toward wellness, family, and community as identified in the Maori concepts of health. This healing, similar to the ones in *Jane and Louisa* and *Ceremony*, is inclusive of both Maori and Pakeha. Here Hulme most clearly envisions Aotearoa; as woman and author, she begins her job of neutralizing the tapu on New Zealand society.

This concluding section is divided into three parts, with Joe's story first, then Simon's, and finally Kerewin's. The first journey, Joe's return to his Maori past, is crucial to an understanding of the novel's vision of healing. This journey is the most explicit in terms of Hulme's aim to conjoin future health with a Maori past, since it presents for the reader details of the prophecy, alluded to in the prologue, of healing the fractured landscape of New Zealand/ Aotearoa. By taking an almost suicidal leap off a cliff to reach the ancestral lands, Joe meets a kaumatua, an elder (who like his female counterpart, the kuia, is both healer and the custodian of the culture). The kaumatua finds Joe on the beach and tells him: "You are a sick man, a broken man, but now it is time for you to heal, to be whole" (355). Besides the physical healing he performs on Joe, the kaumatua begins the cure of the other three components of Joe's health within a Maori context: the spiritual, the psychic, and the familial. As Joe's body heals, the kaumatua explains the prophecy to Joe and Joe's important role in fulfilling it.

Like Betonie's grandmother in *Ceremony*, it is the kaumatua's grandmother whose healing capabilities include the foresight to hold on to the prophecy for a new shining land. The grandmother contains the knowledge of the prophecy, passed on to her grandson, who acts on it. In fact, at this point, the two novels run a parallel course, incorporating the mythical aspects of each culture's healing traditions into their wellness narratives. As kuia, the grandmother takes on her role to maintain and pass on the Maori customs and healing traditions, when the others were "husks, aping the European manners and customs, Maori on the outside, with none of the heart left" (359). The kaumatua explains that without her perseverance, there would be no guardian for the *mauriora* (life principle; talisman of the little god), and the prophecy would be "just one more piece of lost knowledge Another legend. One more of the old people's dreaming lies" (359). In his grandmother's footsteps, the kaumatua has continued to guard the special mauriora, waiting for the family of three to bring the prophecy to fruition.

The kaumatua's prophecy, passed down by his grandmother, involves a broken man, a stranger, and a digger. Joe is easily identified as the broken man of the prophecy by the physical injury incurred by his leap. Joe's dialogue with the kaumatua also directs us to Simon as the stranger and to Kerewin as the digger. Their discussion of the prophecy imbues with sacred meaning an earlier scene, apparently tangential, in which the three visit Kerewin's ancestral home and site of healing, Moerangi. Kerewin hears voices from a Maori pendant she finds on the beach, telling her to "dig" (254). At first, despite his desire to believe, Joe is skeptical about the kaumatua's tale, much as Tayo first responds to Betonie in *Ceremony*. Slowly, as he gains respect for the old man's knowledge, Joe begins to accept the prophecy. Through the kaumatua's words, Joe connects the wasteland of his own life to the destruction of Maori life under colonialism. The kaumatua recites the breakdown of the culture: "I was taught that it was the old people's belief that this country, and our people, are different and special. That something very great had aligned itself with some of us, had given itself to us. But we changed. We ceased to nurture the land. We fought among ourselves. We were overcome by those white people in their hordes. We were broken and diminished. We forgot what we could have been, that Aotearoa was the shining land" (364).

As in indigenous cultures elsewhere, the imposition of European hegemony has broken a relationship to the land and its healing attributes. This is evidenced in Maori literature, from novels about the first intervention with both the emotional and physical disease like Ihimaera's *The Matriarch* to the violence of the mutilated warrior in the writings of Apirana Taylor, noted at the beginning of this chapter. In each culture examined in this book, there were always some, often the elders and women of the families, who retained aspects of this heritage and struggled to pass it on to skeptical new generations. As his grandmother revealed to him, the kaumatua introduces Joe to the mauriora housed in the living waters, and through these learning experiences, Joe begins to heal, grow, and accept his role in fulfilling the prophecy. He gains self-knowledge relevant not only to his personal life, but also to his role in healing the culture. He finally accepts his foster son as a gift and realizes that Kerewin can be part of his family without taking on the role of wife and sexual partner, presenting for him a way to be a healthy individual within a Maori context. After the death of the kaumatua, Joe begins to settle the affairs of the elder and returns to the carving he once did as a young man, making *rahui* (sacred boundary markers) of all those he loves. The earth itself responds to Joe's actions, as an earthquake destroys the pool that housed the mauriora. At first it appears to Joe to be a "nightmare," and he loses hope, but then he realizes that it is a signal for him to continue. In the noisy evening air, he sees the talisman: "Settled on a broken-backed rock, balanced on the crack as though it had grown there. It looks very black or very green, and from the piercing, the hole in the centre, light like a glowworm, aboriginal light" (384). Heartened by the life force in the mauriora, Joe sets off to situate this talisman in a new home as part of the process of healing, hoping that Kerewin will be there to meet him.

At this point in the novel, Hulme moves from recreating the Maori traditions and worldview for the reader, to creating a new vision for New Zealand/Aotearoa, similar to Silko's revisioning of Laguna Pueblo legends in *Ceremony*. In "The Reawakening of the Gods: Realism and the Supernatural in Silko and Hulme," Thomas E. Benediktsson comments on both authors' construction of "alternate version of traditional myths" and states further: "To heal her characters through a recovery of Maori spirituality, Hulme, like Silko, must create an alternative narrative of Maori culture" (130). In Maori cosmology, each of the original canoes that came to New Zealand represents both a whanau and a mauriora; however, in Hulme's revisioning, the canoe and this mauriora represent all of New Zealand/Aotearoa. When the kaumatua tells Joe how his grandmother had the courage and foresight to preserve this aspect of the past, he intones: "How do you weigh the value of this country's soul?" (370). The elder follows this comment with some advice for Joe, again reflecting the words of the Navajo healer, Betonie, as well as those of Night Swan: "Everything changes, even that which supposes itself to be unalterable. All we can do is look after the precious matters which are our heritage" (371). On one level, the kaumatua gives Joe the courage to take on the responsibility to preserve the mauriora. On another level, these words speak for the author and her aims in the novel: Hulme begins to negate the tapu on her fragmented and dis-eased society, identifying these figures as instruments of change for a new world. Like the kaumatua and his grandmother, Hulme accepts the changes in the country, transforms traditional concepts like that of tapu, and adapts them as a metaphors for what needs to preserved. Most evident in this section is that the healing can only be achieved if the whole of New Zealand is included. Benediktsson comments that the "ideological project of the novels [*Ceremony* and *the bone people*] is not to overturn the white culture but to transform it" (131). Although it is true that both novels acknowledge the theoretical necessity of including white people in their wellness narratives, Hulme goes one step further by including the young Simon as a active participant in the healing process.

The healing of Simon in this section of the book is most significant for the inclusiveness of the novel. Not only is he Pakeha and a stranger (coming onto the shores as his forebears did a century before), but he is blond and pale. Through his healing, Hulme integrates Western/Maori medicine, a coming together of Pakeha/Maori oppositions for following generations. But his character also embodies what is problematic about the historic relationship between the two cultures and what is perceived by Hulme as the violence that appears endemic to the colonizing culture. As a child and a victim of abuse, Simon is mostly acted upon, but there are a few indications in the novel that, as a product of Western society, Simon must undergo changes to exorcise the violence associated with European dominance.[9] Joe tells Kerewin that he thinks there was a pattern of abuse in Simon's life before he picked Simon up in the surf (328). Moreover, Joe laments to Kerewin: "There is a vicious streak in him, Kere, and I'm frightened it might be bred in him" (107). There is evidence that Simon was abused in his former life, because of the bruises and scars Joe finds on him.

The short story "A Drift in a Dream," in Hulme's collection *Te Kaihau*, may shed some light on Simon's behavior and history. It presents a tale similar to Simon's, articulating the death of his mother as well as the violence and drug abuse of his father before the shipwreck. Still, another level of meaning in the term "bred in him" is an identification with a cultural heritage based on domination, reflecting the "European Tribe" and its streak of violence, conqueror mentality, and sense of supremacy against those perceived as "others" that Caryl Phillps defines in both his critical work *The European Tribe*, and his novel *The Nature of Blood*.[10]

Still, Hulme, in her healing rite, does not set up a binary opposition between Pakeha and Maori; neither does she deny the violence that existed in precolonial Maori society. Instead, Hulme portrays a six-year-old Pakeha who is more open to the alternative reality presented in the novel than Pakeha adults would be. In fact, there is evidence that he is intuitively connected to a Maori worldview. Simon makes "music hutches" that frighten Joe because of the sculptures' connection to unseen, he sees auras around people, and finally he is visited by a Maori ancestor:

> He wonders if Kerewin knows about the little brown man with blue lines across his face who seemed to sleep in the floor. Not on it, the floor looks like it's not hard for him, he just lay down and went halfway through it. Then he became aware that Simon was staring at him, and grinned at him, and said something in a soft indistinct guttural voice.
> It was Maori. (176–177)

As a young boy who had grown up within Maori culture, he accepts that part of his heritage, reflecting the view in many indigenous societies that identification with the tribe is connected more to the understanding of the culture and behavior than to straight lineage, despite the importance of whanau. In this way, Hulme suggests that one's relation to one's culture is not necessarily biologically based, emphasizing the concept of assent/descent that is raised in the introduction and explored most fully in the next chapter on Jewish identity and Sinclair's *Wasteland*.

Still, with no role models and no real way to be included in the culture because of Joe's separation from his family, Simon finds himself unable to integrate the disparate aspects of his personality in any cohesive way. Because of the anger of the rest of Joe's family's at his constant abuse, Simon distrusts them, aligning himself with the abuser—a well-known pattern. Joe is cognizant of how his abuse is affecting Simon, for he tells Kerewin: "The child heals, at least his body heals; but then, and each time after, he becomes both more diffident and more unruly . . . and the worst part is that he still loves me" (175). Western medicine and drugs can help heal Simon's young boy's body, but it can't cure his cultural disease or that of his father. When the final beating comes, it is the medical establishment that helps heal the breaks in his body, but complete healing must be done in community—in this case, within a Maori context and with his Maori family. These, however, are exactly the people from whom the police and the doctors want to keep him away.

This trope of Western medicine mistranslating traditional cultures and concepts of health has been evident throughout my examination of these novels. Furthermore, Patricia Grace's most recent novel, *Baby No-Eyes*, describes a most extreme example of a conventional medical disregard of Maori traditions and culture. When Te Paania is almost killed in a car accident caused by her husband, the child in her womb dies and the doctors take out the eyes to save for medical research, but the family wants the baby back to bury her within the Maori tradition. The attitudes of the doctors toward them lead her family members to say: "They think they can experiment on us brown people" and "Get eyes for other people's babies" (84).

In the case of Simon, the doctors do not investigate what has happened; rather, they see all his Maori family members as guilty, imposing their view and rejecting the elders, Marama and Wherahiko, who want to take him home. It is only another "stranger" Pakeha who listens to Simon at all. Dr. Sinclair Fayden, whose name is linked to Simon's self-identified name, Clare, realizes that the hospital can or will do nothing more for Simon. So in opposition to his colleagues, Sinclair encourages Simon to escape (398–402). Although not developed in the way that Meadows is in *The Salt Eaters*, Sinclair Fayden represents a possibility that some doctors can listen, yet as in the other works, the medical establishment is often resistant to commonsense solutions or alternative modes of healing. Still, Hulme does not reject Pakeha presence or the treatments that fix Simon's body, but true healing comes with uniting Western medicine with Maori concepts of health, including family, community, and spirituality.

The final chapter of the novel, "The Woman at the Wellspring of Death," most challenges Western medical structures. From the first sharp pains of Kerewin's apparent stomach cancer after seeing her brother at Moerangi to her increased suffering after the final beating of Simon, we perceive a correlation between her physical disorder and her emotional dysfunction. During their last days together before Joe goes to jail and she leaves to die, she describes her feelings, reflecting the progress of cancerous cells: "She lies stiffly still, night after night, her mind focused in fear on the thing that has invaded her. The wide spreading cells that grow and grow. . . . She feels no remorse. All her feelings are dulled these days, as though life is already going, slowly leaking out and ebbing away" (317).

As she prepares to succumb to death, she goes to a doctor for sleeping pills. Trained to treat only the somatic aspects of her disease, the doctor "speaks to her as if she were an excited idiot child" when she explains that she is not "interested" in surgery or other medical procedures for the "cancer" (414). Kerewin identifies her problems with the medical establishment in further conversation with a cancer specialist. Although Kerewin links her physical disorder to her own "mental discontent" (415), the specialist coolly refuses to discuss this possibility further. Kerewin responds to the "brisk" woman, mirroring the trope that runs through the novels examined in this collection: "Medicine is in a queer state of ignorance. It knows a lot, enough to be aware that it is ignorant, but practitioners are loath to admit that ignorance to patients. And there is no holistic treatment" (416). All the works examined in this book identify a need to include the cultural aspect of illness and healing in order to become well. Kerewin recognizes that what she needs is a holistic cure; however, there is no Minnie Ransom to help her dissolve the hard lump in her stomach. Because she can find no model in the medical establishment, and because she is alienated from the cultural source of her health, Kerewin has decided to let herself "decay piece by piece" (420).

In small narrative thrusts, Hulme graphically evokes Kerewin's decomposition with descriptions of her sagging flesh, eczematous hands, and skeletal body, evocative of Nellie's symptoms in *Jane and Louisa*. Interestingly, both Nellie and Kerewin have healing skills (one a doctor, the other connected to alternative therapies), yet these skills are useless without an understanding of the cultural component of their own illness. Moreover, without the advice and relationship to a traditional healer, Kerewin's only companions are the pills, from laetrile and vitamins to painkillers and a hallucinogen (417). However, once we accept the Maori spirituality of the novel, Kerewin is not alone. As she lies on her bed, waiting to die, she is visited by a moth—representing the ancestors—who evokes the memory of Joe, Simon, and her family.[11] As she lets go of her anger and self-hate, a voice directs her to what she loves.[12] Through this dreamlike encounter, she echoes the words of the prologue: "I'm the link and life between them. We're chance we three, we're the beginning free" (424). At this moment, the process of healing has begun for Kerewin. What happens next may be read as drug-induced, but regardless of how we posit the visitation from the spiritual healer, it also works as a metonym for Hulme's breaking down of the binary oppositions of race and gender, as well as spiritual/allopathic healing. The voice that asks her "What do you love?" is seen at first by Kerewin as "a small dark person," resembling the Maori elder who visited Simon. When Kerewin gets a good look, however, she sees "a thin wiry person of indeterminate age. Of indeterminate sex. Of indeterminate race" (424). Like the characters of Tayo and Jake's lesbian sister, Debby, in Sinclair's *Wasteland*, Kerewin has struggled with both the polarities of her biracial heritage and her sexual identity. Therefore, this spiritual healer's androgynous identity reinforces Kerewin's acceptance of herself, as the visitor's thick, red potion, what Mark Williams calls a "semi-magical" cure, helps Kerewin along in the healing process: "The thing that had blocked her gut and sucked her vitality is gone" (425). Kerewin had already begun the healing process by letting go of the anger and despair. However, to take her place as potential healer, she must reconnect with her whanau and with the Maori community. The formal welcoming greetings she hears from her Maori ancestors in her waking dreams direct her to what she should do next.

Kerewin's move to "dig" up Simon's history through the excavation of the boat that brought him, as well as her decision to rebuild the old cultural meeting house, the marae at Moerangi, is her contribution to the prophecy of the kaumatua's grandmother. The "commensalism" that Kerewin envisions for herself, Joe, and Simon creates a healthy alternative for the ostensibly oppositional cultures of Maori and Pakeha (383). Hulme clearly resists a binary opposition of Maori good/Pakeha bad in the character of Kerewin, who pulls experience from various cultures, but Hulme neverthe-less privileges Maori inheritance for all people on the island.[13] Within Maori heritage is the spirit that has been withdrawn. With-out this spirit, identified in the mauriora, there can be no shining land.

As Kerewin returns to the healing site of Moerangi to rebuild the marae wrecked through disuse, she dreams of touching an old marae that springs back into life as "strangely clad people, with golden eyes, brown skin" welcome her. This incident is reminis-cent of the moment in *Jane and Louisa* when Nellie, through her dream journey with Aunt Alice, is reconnected with all her kin: "They touch and caress with excited yet gentle hands and she feels herself dissolving piece by piece with each touch. She diminishes to bones, and the bones sink into the earth. . . . The land is clothed in beauty and the people sing" (428). In this dream vision, Kerewin turns into bones, welcomed to the marae by the bone people, evok-ing those ancestors described by the kaumatua and inscribed in the title of the novel. The rebuilding of the marae is part of the healing process, since it relates to the concepts of Maori health, especially the whanau and the wairua (spiritual). Beatson notes that this act in the novel reflects the actual act of regeneration for Maori culture: "The central literary symbol of rebuilding used by Maori writers (once again mirroring actual social events) is that of the resurrection of the meeting house" (56).[14]

A significant aspect of the healing process is that of turning personal cure into community action. In *The Salt Eaters*, Velma take her place as a cultural healer; in *Ceremony*, Tayo returns to tell his story to the elders; and in the next chapter on *Wasteland*, Jake's accepts his role as the youngest son in the Passover Seder and chooses to fight to help victims in the Holocaust. In *the bone people*, Kerewin's move to rebuild the marae is a very explicit act intended to heal the community, and she does it with the help of those Maori who earlier did not accept her because she was Pakeha-looking. This act of rebuilding the marae, coupled with Joe's situ-ating of the mauriora, signifies a rebirth that is "both a personal healing for Joe and Kerewin and a symbolic renewal of the collec-tive power of Maoridom" (Beatson 53). With the inclusion of Simon in this rebirth, however, Hulme's vision of the shining land resists polarities by opening the marae and Maori traditions to a new gen-eration of Pakeha, those who do not assume moral, cultural, and "scientific" superiority. The main body of the novel ends with this image of rebuilding and reconstruction, a move toward personal, familial, and community health. Each of the three, those instruments of change, has gone through a transition: By accepting the spirit that has been withdrawn and integrating Maori traditions into their lives, they exemplify both the healed and the healer. However, Hulme does not leave us there; she locks in this vision with a celebration of whanau, with both Joe's and Kerewin's families, in an epilogue that conceptualizes Abdul Jan Mohammed's theory of a counterhegemonic utopia, reinforcing the view that an utopian vision can work as a way to prepare us for a healthier society. Through the reuniting of the three, the ending of anger between Joe and his family, and the end of isolation for Kerewin, the four concepts of Maori health have been restored. Furthermore, in the circular structure that often defines women's narratives and parallels the ending of *Ceremony*, Hulme closes the novel with "TE MUTANGA—RANEI TE TAKE" (the end—or the beginning, 445).

Still, if this ending—or beginning—marks a seachange for "sea people" (126), encoded in this move toward collective health is a caveat, often linked to these restorative endings. Human life is fragile, and some abuse can never be totally healed. The singing Simon, who loves music, has lost part of his hearing, a loss that Joe laments when he sees Simon straining to hear the high notes of Kerewin's guitar: "'What have I done? I've taken away his music. . .' / 'O, not all of it' Kerewin responds" (443). As this interchange signifies, healing is a process, connected to all aspects of one's personal and collective life: there is no binary opposition of ill/well.

In "Healing the Planet/Healing Ourselves," Deena Metzger notes the personal effects of the "cultural self-loathing" I address at the beginning of this book: "As we hold the world pain in our own physical bodies so the body politic comes to live out our physical illnesses" (199). As a healing narrative, *the bone people* links child abuse and physical/emotional diseases with the body politic of oppressed cultures, and it poses a way to respond. In a culturally specific manner, Hulme takes the Maori traditions she grew up with (and away from) and recreates them as a new model for healing the self and community. As a Maori woman writer, she takes on her role in neutralizing linguistic tapu to mend, metaphorically, the dis-ease that has affected Maori and Pakeha since the first fateful encounter. The vision in *the bone people* challenges the binary oppositions that are the basis of resistance to an understanding of alternative ways of knowing; moreover, it evokes the possibility of familial and community wellness that does not rest on the superiority of one culture group, one way of thinking, one way of responding to cultural illness. Hulme's wellness narrative does not "cure" New Zealand society or the medical establishment within the system, but it does begin to bring back the words of the mutilated tongue. In healing the wounded tongue of the first encounter, Hulme aims to include all members of her society in this process as she says "*Tihe mauriora!* (I salute the breath of life in you)" (163), guiding us as readers to also become instruments of change.

Part Three

Cultural

Linkages

5

When the

Psychiatrist

Is Part of

the Cure

Healing the "Sick
Jewish Soul" in
Jo Sinclair/Ruth Seid's
Wasteland

René Ozaeta and Sigmund Freud have
stated, each in his own way, that not only can one be culturally
ill, but that cultures themselves can be ill. The focus of this chapter
on Jewish identity and culture is reflected in Theodore Reik's reference to Freud's allusion to "nations whose past history has been
full of suffering." In his study *Jewish Wit*, Reik states explicitly
what Freud merely alludes to: "It is clear that Freud's side glance
rests on the Jewish people" (231). Freud's inability to take this
next step in cultural illness is linked to his own conflicts with
his ethnic/racial/religious identity, and is pertinent to this final
chapter on *Wasteland* by Jo Sinclair (Ruth Seid).

At first glance, this chapter may appear outside the purview
of this book, since it deals with psychoanalysis, clearly within a
Western model of medicine, and the chapter concerns a work by a

Jewish writer. Jews, who have long been perceived as a social minority, have also been linked to European culture and Western traditions. However, Jewish culture, as Gregory Jay points out in "The End of 'American' Literature: Toward Multicultural Practice," can be seen as a unique example of cultural otherness, since European Jewish thought has remained part of Eurocentric practice, yet the people themselves have always been the prime "Other" within that context. Therefore, this chapter is intended as a bridge from the earlier chapters, exploring the role of traditional healing in curing the culturally ill. Psychiatry, although stripped of its cultural markers, may be an aspect of conventional medicine connected to what Grossinger suggests is necessary to contain "exactly those things indigenous to us." Since, within the structure put forth by the writers examined here, in both African-based and indigenous cultures, no individual can be healed in isolation from family and community, we need a process of healing for the cross/ multi/transcultural environment that our world has become. Thus, the examination of Jewish cultural illness and the potential for healing within the same structures that made this group "sick" is paramount to a revisioning of what it means to be well for the larger global community. This chapter examines Jo Sinclair's first novel, *Wasteland*, to investigate cultural illness in relation to the fractured psyche, as well as the role of psychoanalysis in healing the "sick Jewish soul" (Josef Praeger, quoted in Gilman 297). Furthermore, this chapter investigates the role of women in the cultural healing, based in the matrifocality of Jewish lineage and descent, especially dealing with the complexities of the Diaspora.

For the purposes of this exploration, Jews are identified as a culture/ethnic group with a collective memory and history, apart from national affiliation and not linked solely to religious beliefs. This concept of identity is inclusive of the notions of descent and assent (that is, "I call myself a Jew") that are explored in the introduction to this book. According to David Theo Goldberg, who developed this terminology in his introduction to the collection *Jewish Identity*, Jews as a group "raise in an especially acute way the general question of what it means for one to have an identity, to identify with a culture, and to be identified in terms of cultural membership" (3). Cultural markers for Jewish people are mitigated by each society in which Jews live, and Jewish identity is both self-referential and demarcated by the reference group, also the dominant culture. Early U.S. definitions of Jewish identity most often included some notions of race and blood. Jewish immigrant writers such as Abraham Cahan and Anzia Yezierska, and even assimilated (and at times "passing") authors such as Fannie Hurst, identified Jews as a race. In *Salome of the Tenements*, Yezierska takes the notion of the difference of race and blood between the Anglo-American and the Jew to chart the breakdown of the most intimate attempts at assimilation through marriage. Present-day definitions often denote being Jewish in terms of religion.[1] However, in *How the Jews Became White Folks*, Karen Brodkin details what she sees as a move from race to ethnicity through both historical document and the anecdotal history of her own family, although she still sees most Jews as a kind of subgroup of white Europeans.[2] Still, as Brodkin notes, ethnicity replaces the notions of race, which were "associated with biology, eugenics, and other forms of scientific racism," while "'ethnicity' emphasized cultural attributes in contrast to biological ones" (189; note 1). The term "ethnicity" is more precise, since it keeps in line with ancient and precolonial ideas of group identification in relationship to shared values, traditions, religion, lineage, and/or language. Jews have been nationless until recently, and that relationship is still complicated in the Diaspora; therefore, Jewish identity remains a complex figuration in the modern world of nationalities, linked to a kind of citizenship in whatever place in the Diaspora Jews live. However, since Jews have generally functioned as Other in the Western world, as works of Shakespeare, Dickens, George Eliot, Ernest Hemingway, and Djuna Barnes point out, this tenuous relationship has repeatedly been shot through with feelings of self-hate in reference to the dominant culture.

Although popular at the time of publication, Sinclair's *Wasteland* (1946) was not reissued until 1987, and there is still little critical discussion of the novel. Written in the aftermath of the Holocaust, this wellness narrative is Sinclair's attempt to free Jewish identity from self-hate while articulating a desire for assimilation through a quest for universal acceptance. The novel reflects contradictions that still exist in the levels of discomfort in Jewish contemporary life. *Wasteland* exemplifies the conflicted position of American Jews in the Holocaust era and the psychological toll of Otherness, since it is the story of a young Jewish man (John Brown, né Jake Braunowitz) detailing the wasteland of his family's lives to his (Gentile) psychiatrist. It also details the ambivalent position of women within Jewish culture, while examining their significant role as cultural healers in passing on traditions even in assimilated homes. This chapter examines the concept of cultural illness in terms of the breakdown of Diaspora Jewish families and communities in the United States, and it explores the inherent possibilities and contradictions of psychoanalysis as a healing discourse as signified in *Wasteland*. Although psychoanalytic theory has often been separated from the issues surrounding ethnic identity, the intersection of ethnicity and health in this novel calls for an interweaving of these theoretical positions in the use of psychoanalysis, Freud's "talking cure," as another version of Makinde's oral medicines for curing the culturally ill.

To ground this discussion of healing within a cultural context, it is relevant to examine the relationship between Jewish culture/intellectual tradition and psychoanalysis, particularly in relation to its Jewish originators. The basis of psychoanalysis may be understood as connected to a Jewish ethos, what might be called a "folk" tradition, similar to the traditional cultures examined in the first four chapters: the history of Judaism dating back to an earlier, cultural model of "tribal" identity in which one's language, ethnic identity, and religious/healing traditions are inextricably linked.[3] However, as Adrienne Rich details in her poem "Yom Kippur 1984," this view has been complicated in our postmodern world, as she laments: "What Is a Jew in Solitude?" (75). The life of Diaspora American Jewish communities, isolated individual Jews in the modern age, has been fraught with the pressures of assimilation and prejudice, breaking down traditional bonds as well as its matrifocal emphasis on lineage and generational continuity, emphasized in each chapter of this book and reinforced by Rich's own work. Moreover, the specific confusion and self-hate of the originator of this "Jewish science," so to speak, diminishes the power of psychoanalysis as a tool to cure culture-based illnesses. This complication is examined here in the context of the evolution of a healing tradition, arising from a culture group despised by the reference group to whom the healers have directed their cure, before exploring the healing attributes of this same remedy to cure the "sick Jewish soul."

Historically from ancient times, Jewish culture has been tied to the word, the book, the discourse of human meaning. The basis of health, well-being, and a way to live has been examined in Talmudic study and everyday life through the act of questioning. As Rachel Naomi Remen comments in *Kitchen Table Wisdom: Stories that Heal*, although her medical school and the doctors in her family taught her answers, it was her grandfather, an Orthodox rabbi, who taught her how to question life through stories: "[These doctors] rewarded me for having the right answers. My grandfather had rewarded me for having the right questions" (xx). Although, as Remen documents, the discourse of science has been separated from the open questioning of the Talmud and everyday tales and parables of the kitchen table, it is not difficult to perceive this religious/cultural mode as being transcribed into the medical language of psychoanalysis and the narrative developed in the consulting room.

Although there has been much critical debate concerning the effect of Jewish culture on the beginnings of the psychoanalytic movement,[4] it is undeniable that the major figures at its inception were Jews. Dennis Klein states further in *Jewish Origins of the Psychoanalytic Movement*, that these psychiatrists' "Jewish self-conceptions must be regarded as the real, and not merely fabricated, origins of psychoanalysis" (xv). For Freud and his colleagues, the awareness of a reinvigorated anti-Semitism toward the Jews of Vienna affected their every relationship to the world in which they lived, especially after the hopeful words of the Enlightenment and the philo-Semitic promises of Franz Josef. According to Klein, these intellectuals could not "continue the self-deception" that the ideals of inclusion would be realized: "Rather, they renounced their assimilationist aspirations and examined the only free realm left to them, the inner life of the psyche" (14). For Freud and Otto Rank, among others, the move toward the individual psyche was a move toward the universality of all human consciousness without the restrictions imposed upon them as Jews, yet at the same time, they shared a belief that the "Jews were responsible for the fate of humanity in the twentieth century" (Klein 31). Relevantly, this view surfaces later in the century in Jewish critics like Irving Howe, who challenged Jewish writers to become more "universal" in telling their tales, again emphasizing the contradictions encoded in Jewish particularity versus Gentile universality.[5] The apparently irreconcilable contradiction encoded in these concepts—and illustrated in *Wasteland*—reveals these thinkers' belief that psychoanalysis as a Jewish healing method was of profound importance to humanity as well as manifesting their desire for acceptance, relinquishing the particularity of their Jewish experience. As Rothman and Isenberg point out in "Freud and Jewish Marginality," Freud saw psychoanalysis as a "universal doctrine which denies the reality of culture and of cultural differences" (47). According to the authors, Freud knew the "subversive" nature of psychoanalysis, and somewhat ironically aimed to "end marginality by undermining the bases of the dominant culture" (48). In attempting to dislodge the foundation of prejudice by subverting the restrictive base of the dominant culture, however, Freud also reinforced the discrimination inscribed in his own discourse by denying the cultural differences that exist.

This unyielding opposition at the core of psychoanalysis also reflects the inability of the marginalized Jew to move beyond this restriction in language—a condition that affects psychoanalytic discourse, rooted in narration, as well as novels like *Wasteland*. From Abraham Cahan's Yekl, who tries to break from all Jewish things, including his wife, to Philip Roth's Portnoy, whose cultural milieu keeps him from ever seeing himself as an American, "Jewish" language, especially the cadences of Yiddish, entrap these writers in this world they hope to escape. This question of language also reflects the other chapters in this book, since the "colonial" language is the one that inscribes their otherness (we can, quite easily, conceive of Jews as one of the earliest colonized cultures of the Christian West, being relegated to the "Judeo" prefix). Sander Gilman, in *Jewish Self-Hatred*, notes in this regard: "When those who are labeled as marginal are forced to function within the same discourse as that which labels them as different, conflict arises that may not be consciously noted by outsiders, for they are forced to speak using the polluted language which designates them as Other" (14). Ironically, Gilman goes on to state that psychoanalytic discourse was perceived as a "Jewish" language, "the Viennese answer to Hebrew as a cultural language" (297). What is profoundly puzzling about this double bind in relation to Freud is not only that he seems to have been unable to identify what was going on in his own subconscious in relation to his Jewish identity, but also that he was in fact defining a discourse that would leave him and his culture group still marginalized and diseased. And this complexity is revisited by Jewish male novelists from Ludwig Lewisohn to Philip Roth, as their characters try to talk through their conflicts with their own Jewishness by turning to psychoanalysis or by speaking to a psychiatrist who doesn't listen.

What appears to be played out as "case study" in the novel *Wasteland* is this inner conflict acted out by the creators of the psychoanalytic movement, linked to what these originators rejected as they rejected Jewish particularity—the role of women (from mother to *mama-loshn* [mother tongue]) as a signifier of that particularity. Although the passing on of the religion tradition was the domain of men, within Jewish communities (a matrilineal culture), the role of the women included inculcating the children into the culture as well as being the emotional and physical healers of the community. Although the position of women as healers in Jewish communities is not well documented, there is much anecdotal data regarding women's role as healers, especially in shtetl and immigrant Jewish communities in the United States, including the humorous rendering of the Jewish mother serving chicken soup as a remedy.[6] Joyce Antler, in *The Journey Home: Jewish Women and the American Century*, notes that, although Jewish women's "extraordinary devotion to their families has been the subject of much comic treatment, yet behind the criticism stands the reality of the Jewish mother's strength, nurturance, and competence" (xii). Part of Jewish women's significant role has been in reinforcing group identity, the passing on of tradition, and the generational continuity like that described in the African-based section of this book. As Sydney Stahn Weinberg observes in *The World of Our Mothers*, her response to Howe's gender-based study of Jewish culture, *World of Our Fathers*: "Women's preservation of the Sabbath Ceremony and the holidays celebrated chiefly in the home assumed an importance that it had lacked in Eastern Europe, where the synagogue was central to religion." She states further that the passing on of these traditions in this way "became a major rather than peripheral components of transmitting a sense of Jewish identification to the children" (140). The visual image of the mother lighting the Sabbath candles becomes a trope of comfort in the Diaspora Jewish home in memoirs and literature, as recounted in such diverse works as Anzia Yezierska's *Bread Givers* and Tunisian writer Albert Memmi's *Pillar of Salt*. As both Weinberg and Antler note about their studies of Jewish women, it is the memory of the grandmother or mother that is linked to a communal sense of Jewishness, despite the fact that the males in the family are more often connected to specific religious acts of Judaism. This separation of duties and the value system inherent in it is reinforced in relation to the health of family and community. Intellectual Judaism led to a kind of rejection of Jewishness and its "folk" traditions. Fannie Brandeis Nagel, whose doctor husband rejected the Jewish traditions of their families, throughout her life suffered what doctors called an unknown illness, yet she knew the problem, linking the spiritual emptiness in her family to her "miserable depression [of] body and soul" (Antler 5). This conflict between the men and women in the home, usually connected to Jewish culture in the United States, existed with the primary originator of the psychoanalytic movement and his desire to strip the psyche of its cultural markers. Freud's wife, Martha, when having guests on Friday night, told them, "You must know that on Friday evenings good Jewish women light candles for the approach of the Sabbath. But this monster—*unmensch*—will not allow it because he says that religion is a superstition" (Gay 153). Gay goes on to say that Martha never totally forgave Freud for separating her from her traditions, and it is evident that Freud himself tried to isolate his "Jewish science" from its earlier antecedents. This assimilative kind of scientific rationalism, arising from an Eurocentric intellectual Judaism, rejects the "folk" remedies, spiritual essence, and cultural nurturance of Jewish women. The loss of these healing stories sets off a dysfunctional dialectic, which often presents the mother figure as one who is so Jewish as to be embarrassing and, like Sophie in *Portnoy's Complaint*, makes her children sick.

Despite its own ambiguities and the rejection of earlier forms of oral medicines, psychoanalysis, like Jewish healing storytelling within communities and households, still holds promise in responding to the disease of self-hate and repairing the fractured psyche. In regard to the role of psychoanalysis as a tool to heal the "sick Jewish soul," I cursorily examine two sources identified by Gilman in his study, which further illustrate the relationship of psychoanalytic discourse to Jewishness in the novel. For example, Rafael Becker, a young Jewish doctor in post-World War I Germany, compared Jewish and non-Jewish patients in terms of mental illness. He found that increased psychopathology of what he calls "acculturated" Western Jews is not due to a "special proclivity"; rather, "the 'assimilated Jew' is diseased, self-hating, and thus self-destructive" precisely because of the attempt to assimilate (Gilman 295). Josef Praeger, in Martin Buber's well-known collection *The Jew*, also notes that in the attempt at assimilation, Jews must repress aspects of themselves that identify them as Jews. For both Becker and Praeger, this repression is no longer perceived as part of "the nature of the Jew," but as a sociopsychological construct. Through the lens of psychoanalysis, one can identify this dis-ease. Furthermore, Praeger emphasizes that the "articulation of one's Jewishness [is] the first step to a 'healing of the sick Jewish soul'" (Gilman 297), linking this view to the African-based and indigenous healing traditions examined in the rest of this book. What is articulated here is the relationship between the denial of aspects of the Jewish self and the cultural disease of attempted assimilation into a reference group that continues to perceive one as Other. The analyses by both authors are limited by their historical moment and its focus mostly on male patients, as well as an "essentialist" notion of Jewish identity, which we, in a postmodern age, tend to resist. Still, this sense of being culturally ill as a result of not dealing with one's Jewishness functions largely in Arthur Miller's 1994 play, *Broken Glass,* about an American Jewish family in the late 1930s. In the play, the wife becomes paralyzed through her family and community's refusal to confront the realities of the Holocaust, as well as her husband's own Jewish self-hate. Aspects of these studies and the initial contradictions in the origins of the psychoanalytic movement are replicated in Sinclair's *Wasteland,* written right after the Holocaust. This comprehension of cultural disease exposes another layer in the healing model proposed in this book.

Wasteland (1946) is Ruth Seid's first novel, written under the pseudonym Jo Sinclair. She chose the name when submitting her first short story for publication. In her autobiography, she comments about the change: "Yes, she would hang on to that pseudonym she had made up as one more 'being different' for that Ruth trapped in the ghetto" (*Seasons* 3). The novel won the Harper's Prize, which gave her a $10,000 award and the promise of publication. Some early critics of *Wasteland,* such as Richard Plant of *The New Republic,* complained that the work "appeared more of a case history than a novel" (84); however, it is precisely its simultaneous position as a case study and creative fiction that lays bare some of the difficulties as well as the possibilities of psychoanalysis as a cure for the culturally ill, blending the scientific with the storytelling tradition inherent in this form of narration. According to her biographer, Elisabeth Sandberg, Seid "had to be a writer to discover the soul of [her] people in order to reclaim them from all the types of poverty and prejudice" (4). Like the other women writers in this book, Seid hoped to heal her community through her wellness narrative. Furthermore, Seid told her prospective publisher at Harper why she wrote *Wasteland,* referring to the psychological disease she witnessed in her family and others in her culture: "I have been surrounded by wastelands most of my life" (Sandberg 5). For Seid, both the concept of psychoanalysis and the act of writing are healing tools with which to address the wastelands of the children of the immigrant Jews; nevertheless, the contradictions encoded in Sinclair's statements mirror profound questions raised in the novel: Why would a novelist who had anglicized and degendered her name write her first novel about a young man whose (re)naming embraces cultural identity and reaffirms Jewish self-esteem? Why isn't her awareness of the importance of naming enough for "Jo Sinclair" to return to her own name? To what extent is the healing of the "sick Jewish soul" instigated by the lesbian sister both a reaffirmation of women's role in the healing of Jewish culture and a rejection of it? These questions expose problems for the curative model based on traditional cultures presented by the other chapters of this study, but as is demonstrated in this chapter and in the conclusion, the exploration of these problems also expands the nature of the study by further complicating these models of ethnic identity and health.

The novel presents the shifting narrations of Jake and his (Gentile) psychiatrist, the third-person tales of his family, and the unnarrated healing presence of his sister Debby—a lesbian whose sense of Jewish "doubleness" is heightened by a sexual invisibility. Between the eclipsed narratives of Jake (who denies his heritage) and the psychiatrist (who is outside the culture) comes the sisterly guidance of Debby. She helps Jake articulate his own identity through his acceptance of her difference and her own revision of the Jewish woman's traditional role in preserving the culture. Jake Braunowitz, who calls himself John Brown, hates himself and his life with his family but is tied to them, despite the fact that it makes him sick. He lives in a personal and cultural netherworld, which he calls a "wasteland." Most pertinently, he perceives his familial traumas as affixed to his Jewish identity, an identity of which he is ashamed, and this formation structures the wasteland that isolates him from the dominant world outside. This theme is reflected in Sinclair's other works, in the pogrom survivors and broken-down community of *The Changelings* as well as the dysfunction family and Holocaust survivors in *Anna Teller*. On a personal level, Jake represents much of Jewish experience in America—a process of mediation between his own culture and the dominant one, coupled with a dialectical sense of doubleness and invisibility identified in much immigrant fiction, as Chametzky notes in "Immigrant Fiction as Cultural Mediation." However, as I explore in "Cultural Mediation and the Immigrant's Daughter: Anzia Yezierska's *Bread Givers*," this mediation is not always successful, as exemplified by this child of immigrants, Jake. On a cultural level, Jake's experiences reflect what Jacques Lacan calls the "alienated self"—a fictive unified self with which one identifies but that is actually something other, alien. One formation of this fictive, "unified self" is to deny Jewish "otherness" by renaming oneself as Gentile, rejecting traditions, and rebuffing connections to family and community. Jake, who "passes" (using this term most often identified with African American experience) as Gentile, begins to lose hold of this fictive self as the novel opens, and he finds himself both physically and emotionally ill.[7]

The profound ambivalence in the novel is heightened by the historical moment of writing. Sinclair wrote the novel in 1945, and it was published in 1946—after the Holocaust and, according to a Gallup poll, a peak year for U.S. anti-Semitism (Sandberg 61). Yet Sinclair comments that the novel is about Jews almost incidentally: "I wrote about Jews because I have known hundreds of them, and lived with them, and because I am a Jew" (Sandberg 5). Sinclair's simultaneous separation from and allegiance to Jewish experience (us vs. them) reflect the oppositions of particular and universal inherent in the psychoanalytic movement and govern the dialectical structure of the novel, reflecting part of the cultural illness that Sinclair and others suffer. The novel explores the exchange between Gentile and Jew in the most intimate way: through a depiction of the psychiatrist and the patient. The fact that Sinclair chose to make the psychiatrist "Gentile" also reflects some of the unresolved ambiguities in the novel, although it clearly illustrates the problems in cross-cultural psychiatry. Sinclair bases her protagonist, Jake, loosely on one of her brothers, Herman Seid, who was a press photographer. Like Silko, Sinclair develops the cultural illness in her community through a family member who is male, presenting a further layering of healing the culturally ill. In both *Ceremony* and *Wasteland*, the male protagonist is led to health through the women in the family, as well as by the healers—in this case, Jake's sister, Debby. Her memoir, *Seasons: Death and Transfiguration*, uncovers the character of the male protagonist as also rooted in the author's personal experiences, another similarity to Silko's *Ceremony*. In *Seasons*, Seid remembers herself as a self-defined "ghetto punk," who was taken in by a well-to-do older woman, Helen Buchman. Seid, at the time, found living with her own family unbearable and moved in with the Buchmans. Buchman realized when Seid moved in that Seid needed a psychiatrist desperately but would not go. Buchman was an assimilated Jew who was the love of Seid's life.[8] She becomes, for Seid, the same liaison to health that the character Debby (the lesbian) is for the brother Jake in *Wasteland*.[9] Buchman contacted a psychiatrist friend, acted as liaison to the dysfunctional Ruth, and helped her to become the writer Jo. Through the act of writing out her own cultural illness, Sinclair states, she begins to heal herself, like Brodber and Silko in their own writing processes. And like them, Sinclair understands this process not only as her own path to health, but also as a way to cure her community among others.

The novel revolves around the weekly meetings in the consulting room. Most of the narrative is Jake's story and that of his family members, told through Jake's limited perspective. The psychiatrist's "notes" on the case are also included. The use of these case notes adds a formal, "objective" structure to the novel and represents dialectically the actual relationship of patient to psychiatrist, which is also a fiction of a sort, as Eagleton points out. The structure of the novel becomes a metafiction that illustrates not only the fictive relationship between doctor and patient, but also the complexities that arise when aspects of ethnicity are entered into psychoanalytic discourse. Jake's problem is in some ways a textbook case of the breaking down of what Lacan calls "the armor of an ideal self," which is basically fictionalized, and in the development of a personality, inaugurates "the dialectic that will henceforth link the I to socially elaborated situations" (5). When this "armor" begins to break, the person becomes aware that the image one has of oneself is fictive; therefore, the sense of self shatters and the person becomes unable to function healthily in social situations. The specific problem for the protagonist, Jake, however, is that the shattering awareness of his fictive identity is twofold: The unified self with which he identifies is also a cultural Other; this self is a "Gentile" one, born from the dominant society and hostile to Jewish culture. For Jake, there is a double alienation: When his unified imaginary armor begins to break apart, Jake's carefully elaborated (false) relations to the social environment threaten to disintegrate, and he finds himself mired in a psychic wasteland. Although male writers like Philip Roth and Joseph Heller address this double consciousness in their writings, the focus is often humorous and self-parodying in posing the breakdown. This novel, in contradistinction, presents a double consciousness closer to W.E.B. Du Bois's notion of the internal conflict of the African versus the American, with all its in traumatic implications.

Jake's cultural illness, arising from his inability to reconcile this double consciousness, revolves around his inner wasteland in opposition to the person presented to the world. On the outside, to both his family and his co-workers, Jake (John Brown) is a very successful person. He is a photographer for a major newspaper and has risen far beyond his class and educational background. He has one life at work and another, grimmer one at home. He feels that he is a fake who will eventually be found out; he is "passing" for Gentile, and anyone from his past could give him away. He makes sure that no one at the paper knows he's a Jew, yet at the same time he reacts violently (but only inside) to what he hears about the Holocaust. Furthermore, his own feelings of self-hate (because of his shame and guilt) are complicated by his physical rage at the anti-Semites, making him ill: "The trouble was, whenever he heard somebody say 'dirty Jew' he thought immediately of his family. Sure, and of himself. Was he ashamed of being a Jew? It looked like it, didn't it! And yet every time he read about what was happening to Jews all over the world, he wanted to smash faces. . . . " (29).

Like the Jews of Vienna, Jake is angry at the increasing anti-Semitism he sees around him, yet is uncomfortable with his place as a Jew. Moreover, in his attempts to assimilate, Jake's acceptance of the dominant culture's image of him undercuts his justifiable anger. In his confused state, Jake hears what Gilman identifies as the "voice of the power group saying, under the skin you are really like them anyhow." Gilman adds that "the fragmentation of identity that results is the articulation of self-hatred" (3), identified in this book a disease.

Clearly, Jake's self-hatred is part of his cultural disease; his fictive unified self is disintegrating, and he can no longer function healthfully. Despite his fears of being exposed as a poor Jew, he still lives at home and helps supports the family he refuses to acknowledge whenever he meets one of them in a public place. His family is too Jewish, too dirty, too poor for his Gentile friends and co-workers at the paper. He is frightened of their Jewish difference, and his own move toward success is full of the denial of his background. He sees his father as a dirty old Jew who is responsible for their poverty, his sister Sarah and her family as the next generation wasteland, his sister Roz as a tramp, his brother Sig a loud-mouth failure, and even Debby, whom he loves, as strange and different. Most relevantly, it is the breakdown in the relationship with his mother that makes him the most ill. He perceives his mother as a weak woman about whom he feels both ashamed and guilty. It is his mother who keeps him "all tied up with shame" (20), and when he thinks of the way she acts and speaks in relation to his Gentile co-worker's mother, he experiences "a sick feeling" (105). In this way, Jake has not only isolated himself from the negative aspects of his Jewish experience, but has also become estranged from what was traditionally a major support in the Jewish communities through centuries of oppression, the women in his household. In "On Not Making It in America," Jules Zanger comments how "the frequency with which [the Jewish mother] is rejected by her son suggests that the denial of the mother has come to stand in the Jewish literary imagination for the rite of passage necessary for the male Jew to pass into mainstream American culture" (39). In turn, the rejection of one's Jewishness necessitates for the assimilated Jewish male a rejection of the mother, who has become, in America, the keeper of the mother tongue, Yiddish, and "the embodiment of the traditions" (Zanger 44).[10] Therefore, as Tia does with all her children in *Jane and Louisa*, the move to assimilation separates, in this case, specifically the male child from his most intimate female relation and her language, while also alienating him from the healing attributes of his cultural heritage.

To gain acceptance, Jake plays on his Gentile looks and changes his name from Jake to John, further anglicizing the change (Braunowitz to Brown) that Sig made earlier to help himself get a job. Ironically, despite the change, Sig later loses the job because he is Jewish (285). Jake writes down his newly created name on his job application—John Brown: "It was beautiful. It was as American-looking, as anonymous, as any name he could think of. . . . It was like Indians, or Plymouth Rock, it was like American history" (85). Ironically, the name Jake, which Jake gives up because he thinks it connects with exposing a hidden Jewish identity, was, in fact, an Americanization of the Yiddish name Yekl for earlier immigrants.[11] There are also two other ironies involved in this name change, reflecting Sinclair's aim to connect Jewish experience to hidden histories of other marginalized groups. Besides being an Anglo-Saxon name reminding Jake of "Indians," the name John Brown most likely reminds students of American history of the famous abolitionist, hardly a model for Jake's desire to assimilate, rather than of Plymouth Rock.

Dialectically, because of his construction of a Gentile identity, Jake feels isolated from his culture, sick and scared. He feels insignificant because of the loss of his name, and at the same time, he is terrified to be associated with being a Jew—to be named in that way is to be "trapped with that word, Jew" (70). Moreover, Jake is in constant fear that, even after eighteen years, through his language and behavior, he will be found out by his associates: "Things happen [and] you're still waiting for the roof to fall in.

You're still waiting every day for somebody to say, Hey, I hear you're a Yid. Hey I hear you're really Jakey the Yid" (94). According to Ellen Serlen Uffen, "the emergence of a wasteland in [Jake's] consciousness, tied to Jewish things, is to him solely a Jewish fact" (44). Unequivocally, the Jewish fact of Jake's wasteland is intricately tied to his fictive unified (Gentile) self, which is disintegrating. When his imaginary armor against his Jewishness begins to crack, he breaks down physically and emotionally and must seek help. His sister Debby, his healing agent, who has already undergone psychoanalysis to come to terms with her own cultural illness, introduces him to the doctor (Gentile and unnamed) and begins his sessions. Ironically, these sessions are on Saturday afternoons, the traditional Sabbath when observant Jews throughout the world rest and reflect.

In situating the weekly consultations on the Jewish Sabbath, Sinclair reveals Jake's conflict in resolving Jewish particularity with his desire to assimilate into what he perceives as a society free from the unhealthy wasteland of his family's lives. In Euro-American Christian culture, Saturday is the day to do things, while Sunday is the day to rest.[12] Jake is therefore once again caught between his desire to be like others and his guilt, arising from his diseased sense of Jewish self. Zanger comments specifically that in *Wasteland*, among other Jewish novels, the male protagonist, in giving up the "appearance" of his culture, also has to deny the traditions that have kept the culture alive, as well as the women in his household who continued these practices. Therefore, he is seen as an "apostate" by those in his group. Zanger states further: "Perhaps even more significantly, he frequently stands in this judgment of himself, which serves to further his alienation. . ." (43). This passage identifies the internal fracturing of identity and feeling of self-hate as the protagonist perceives himself through the eyes of his demanding yet potentially supportive community. In Sinclair's later novels, *The Changelings* and *Anna Teller*, the mother/grandmother figures are powerful women, connected to their culture, but they also create an incredible sense of guilt and shame in their disabled and assimilated sons. Jake's own judgment of himself, exposing cracks in his self-protecting armor, leads him to the psychiatrist, who ironically is part of the reference group that has set the preconditions for his group's disease.[13]

For Jake, the psychiatrist represents everything that is absent from his family. This nameless doctor is seen by Jake as almost larger than life. He is the quintessential "Gentile" in Jake's eyes, cool and detached but also gentle and anonymous. He comments in his notes that he is, for Jake, the "person of authority, symbol of the world" (239), reinforcing the trope from Yezierska to Roth that Jews are not part of this American world. It is important for Jake that the psychiatrist not be Jewish: "If you were a Jew maybe I couldn't tell you. It's all about Jewish stuff. . . . Maybe I couldn't talk about all of that to a Jew" (48). The fact that the doctor is not a Jew allows Jake the freedom to talk about his Jewish self-hate, but paradoxically, this comfortable otherness keeps the doctor from fully understanding Jake's narrative, a language informed by his Jewish mother, the community's mother tongue (Yiddish), and the culture's sacred traditions. The psychiatrist continually isolates Jake's Jewish identity from the problems he has with his family. By viewing Jewish identity solely in relation to religion, the doctor compartmentalizes Jake's life, acknowledging neither the hostile climate for Jews in America nor the unyielding cultural environment in even secular Jewish homes. Moreover, as the other examples in this book have demonstrated, one cannot be healed completely outside family and community.[14]

In marking out a place for the cultural component in psychoanalytic discourse, Wen-Shing Tseng and Jing Hsu note that intercultural analysis can be difficult for the practitioner "who does not appreciate cultural differences and who tends to interpret things only in terms of his [sic] own culture without being aware that other interpretations exist" (295). In the novel, the psychiatrist is trying to learn about the complexities of Jewish identity through Jake's distorted connection to his culture, but it is inconceivable for the doctor, an outsider and a member of the dominant culture, to comprehend how deep Jake's feelings about his Jewish identity run. In view of the goal of Freud and the other originators of the psychoanalytic movement to find a universal discourse of the mind, Jake's narrative illustrates what this psychoanalytic discourse, stripped of its necessary interpretive cultural markers, turns out to be. Furthermore, the psychiatrist's own language loses meaning for Jake, since "Jewish" signification has no place in the doctor's discourse. In relation to the concept of oral medicine embedded in each of these wellness narratives, the inability of the doctor to understand Jake's "Jewish" language, or to use a healing discourse that can be part of Jake's cure, poses the problems of psychoanalysis without its cultural components.

Although the doctor is presented throughout the novel as helpful in Jake's eyes, we as readers are aware that the doctor can only glimpse the fact that Jake's fractured identity is dialectically related to both his fictive "Gentile" self and the denial of his Jewishness. In his report, the doctor writes revealingly: "S feels deep shame arising from 'Jewishness.' Apparently, however, religion in itself means nothing to him" (44). Jake's complete association of Jewishness with his family's wasteland and the psychiatrist's inability to comprehend Jewish culture apart from a limited concept of religion are clearly articulated in one of the sessions. Jake relates a story about going with his "friends" into a restaurant where his brother sits with other Jews and his sister works as a waitress. Jake tells the doctor how he ignores both of them (250). This is the perfect "passing" scene, but the doctor interprets it merely as Jake's personal embarrassment about his sister Roz's actions and dress. For both Jake and the psychiatrist himself, the psychiatrist appears to be "cultureless" rather than part of an intercultural relationship; this strengthens the pressure on Jake to conform to a hegemonic standard, even in the consulting room. As Tseng and Hsu note, the transference between analyst and analysand often projects the "customary cultural image" of the therapist (296), in this case reflecting Jake's false, unified self. Moreover, this portrayal reinforces the notion of the psychiatrist as culturally neutral, when in fact, he represents the reference group that has, in many ways, defined the demarcations of Jake's disease.

Throughout the novel, the doctor dichotomizes personal, familial relations and Jake's feelings about his Jewishness (claiming that what Jake really feels is anger and guilt about his family, not his "religion"). However, it is evident from Jake's own narrative that these two aspects of his life cannot be divorced, reflecting the governing force of these wellness narratives that one cannot be healed in isolation. Can we separate the descriptions Jake gives us of his father as a dirty, stingy Jew from the dominant ideology that links those words together, as well as the immigrant experiences that circumscribe his family's life? Is it, as the psychiatrist suggests, merely that his father is dirty and stingy, not Jews as a whole (75)? Or rather, is it also that Jake's internalized prejudice helps him to see his father in just that way? Jake, in this way, reflects the real-life experience of Rachel Shilsky (aka Ruth McBride) in *The Color of Water*, who rejected all of Jewish culture and denied her own mother because of her selfish, sexually abusing father. In both cases, the dysfunctional father becomes a metonym for the child's internalized reaction to antagonism toward Jewish culture.

Sinclair compels us to examine the dynamics between doctor

and patient within this sociocultural milieu as well as the problems of a psychoanalytic discourse disassociated from its relevant cultural markers. It is in this regard that Sinclair presents Debby, Jake's lesbian sister, as the liaison between the psychiatrist and Jake. Debby, as culture bearer and through her own experience with psychoanalysis, allows Jake to deconstruct the imaginary Gentile self by bringing the necessary cultural markers to Jake's dialogue with the doctor. Despite the fact that no section in the novel is specifically narrated by her, Debby's "angled" presentation works to help fill in the gaps in Jake's story, what the psychiatrist misses. Deborah Brown, whom Sandberg considers as "the author fictionalized at age 29" (7), is clearly a privileged figure in the novel. Debby's connection to the author is identified by Seid's autobiographical statements, as well as her own (undefined) lesbianism. What is particularly revealing about the autobiographical impulses of the novel is that Seid's love and own liaison to the psychiatrist, Helen Buchman, was an assimilated Jew who always made sure Seid celebrated Christmas with the family. Yet the character Debby is represented as a Jew who has worked through her own cultural illness. Debby's role as the author's persona is most explicitly established by the scene in which Debby is telling Jake about a book she is reading. The plot she describes is that of *The Changelings* (which Sinclair would publish almost ten years later), about which Debby comments: "I'd like to have written it" (207). In *The Changelings*, two young girls, one Black, one Jewish, try to heal their dysfunctional neighborhoods, although Jules, the young Jewish man who guides their healing act, dies from a broken heart, because the Jews in his community reject the sense of social justice, the principle of *tikkun olam* (the repair of the world), that governs Jewish moral life.

Debby represents the healer in the novel; her healing is a cultural one, going beyond the family out to the community as well. As in Bambara's connection to other women of color in *The Salt Eaters*, for Sinclair, her sense of community contains other oppressed groups, especially African Americans. The relationship between Black and Jewish Americans, in all its complexities, is a trope that runs throughout Jewish American literature, including diverse works like Bernard Malamud's *The Tenants* to Lore Segal's *My First American* and the short stories of Grace Paley. This has been an especially vital issue for Sinclair, who grew up in Cleveland, whose short stories often have Black main characters, and whose novel *The Changelings* explores the issues of "white" flight from a neighborhood that includes Jews who have also suffered oppression. In *The Changelings* as well as in *Wasteland*, cultural self-loathing and perpetrating oppression is what makes communities sick, and in both cases, it is young women who take on the role of healer, since there is often a break in generational continuity because of the denigration of the position of mother/grandmother in the household. Although she is the youngest in the Braunowitz family, Debby is the one member of this dysfunctional household who tries desperately to keep it whole. Despite her problems in dealing with both gender and ethnic identity, Debby not only helps the lost people of her family, but extends her vision to oppressed others. Each member of her family, with the exception of her father (the shadowy figure of this novel), goes to Debby for help. Debby, as the youngest child, tries to heal the wounds of the other family members; ironically, she takes on the role of mother to Jake because their own mother, because of her Yiddish words and immigrant behavior, is not respected by the children. As in other cultures discussed in this book, the breakdown of this most intimate bond of mother and child presents a discontinuity in those traditions that have kept Jewish culture alive for centuries.

Debby convinces Jake to go the psychiatrist, and it is his admiration for her, as well as the breakdown of his fictive unified self, that opens the door to the consulting room for him. For Debby, psychiatry is a way of getting at the wastelands that have surrounded her world. As the scholars of the Torah examined it, in order to determine the way to live, the discourse in the consulting room presents for Debby another way of deciphering the words that can heal. However, despite his feelings of affection for Debby who is guiding his healing process, Jake also fears and is ashamed of this sister he loves. He knows that there is something wrong with her; she doesn't act like other women. She is his one connection to the good qualities of their family, and he's petrified that he is going to find out she's "bad" (a lesbian, a word he will not even utter). Evelyn Torton Beck states in the introduction to her collection, *Nice Jewish Girls: A Lesbian Anthology*, that according to Jewish law, Jewish lesbians "do not exist." She comments further that for those in the dominant group, one might accept a Jew or a lesbian, but to "claim" both identities was "exceeding the limits of what was permitted to the marginal" (xiii). This is evident in other writers like Adrienne Rich, Bonnie Zimmerman, and Ruth Geller, who in some ways found it easier to identify themselves as lesbians than to come out as Jews. Although Sinclair has only

discussed her lesbian identity in print recently in her later memoir *The Seasons*, her creative fiction explores both the healing capabilities and the uncomfortable place of this figure in Jewish
communities. For Jake, who is a self-hating and "passing" Jew,
Debby's double otherness is too much. Furthermore, he is discon-
certed about her other strangeness—why she writes stories about
Black people; his racism is clearly connected with his own self-
hate. Yet, dialectically, it is his desire to comprehend her (lesbian)
otherness that compels him to examine both his narrow vision
and his own feeling of being other. To help him along, Debby tells
him what the doctor aided her in understanding, despite the fact
that the relationship of Debby to the doctor is never articulated in
the novel. In this way, though, she works as a healing liaison by
bridging the gap between Jake and the doctor. Debby explains to
Jake how she was drawn to those who were in a ghetto, persecuted, like Blacks and Jews, by the "world." But through her analysis, she began to see that her pitying of others began first with
herself: "It was myself, I was pitying. After a while I knew I was
part of these people because they were part of the world" (155).
Through this Jewish form of healing discourse, developed as psychiatry, Debby works through her own cultural illness and is a
transformed into a healer. Like Tayo, she begins to understand the
cultural markers of her own and Jake's disease and can translate
them to Jake as part of this oral medicine. Furthermore, as the
women in the shtetl kept the lifeblood of the community going by
dealing with the Gentiles outside the Pale in their own languages,
Debby appropriates this role of the Eastern European Jewish woman
by taking the alien words of the Gentile psychiatrist to translate
them for herself and her brother. Here the woman works as cultural interpreter as well as culture bearer. Despite the tensions
encoded in psychoanalytic discourse, Debby begins to learn how
to be in the world in a positive way through therapy, and this is
what she shares with her brother in her role as healer and cultural
mediator. In that role, Debby persuades Jake to go to the doctor, so
that he can become part of the world too.

At this point in the novel, the tension of being Jewish versus
being "in the world" is explicitly exposed. For Debby and for Jake,
the particularity of Jewish culture and its strangeness is further
heightened by the desolation and poverty of their family. That Jewish fact, coupled with being poor in America, is what has kept
them from being in the world. It is relevant to note here that the
two children who "look" the most Gentile and have the greatest

possibility of passing are the ones most incapacitated by their relationship to their Jewishness. Rafael Becker notes that it is often
the most acculturated Jews who suffer the most self-hate, and it is
easier to assimilate if one does not "look" Jewish. Certainly lighter
skin and hair, as well as "Anglo" noses, made it possible for some
Jews to escape the Holocaust, perceived by the Nazis as Gentile
rather than Jewish. Although their position as the two youngest
in the family as well as the two who look the most "Gentile"
brings them together, Jake also feels that Debby betrayed him at
their family Passover Seder by metaphorically stealing the only
name he felt he had, and that name is connected to the Jewish
identity they are trying to regain.

Much of Jake's narrative in the consulting room revolves
around the family's Passovers, a holiday filled with the ritual of
naming. As a child, Jake associates this ceremony with what is
beautiful in his family and culture, but as he grows older and reacts against the "wasteland" of his family, he is also alienated from
this ritual that he loved, as well as from the mother who has sustained it. His memories are filled with the once comforting vision
of his mother setting the Passover table, whispering the "solemn
sounding prayers" for the lighting of the candles, as she did for all
the Friday-night Sabbaths of his life (37). Jake's role in the Passover Seder is a very important one, since he is the youngest son. In
Jewish tradition, the youngest son reads the Four Questions (beginning with "Why is this night different from all other nights?")
at the Passover feast. As a young boy, Jake is thrilled with this
ceremony, which presents the many possibilities for growth, and
is proud of his part in it. In one of his interior monologues, he
remembers: "And you know that for thousands of years Jewish
boys, the youngest present on those ancient, ageless, never-dying
evenings, have been playing this same part. No, you do not quite
understand, but you are happy in this moment because . . . you
feel you are a definite, named (in the Bible, named) part of this
holy thing" (58).

For Jake, who gives up his name for an assimilated one and
who feels nameless throughout the novel, this is a powerful scene.
But he loses even this name, as he decides that he will no longer
sit at the Passover table. His anger at his father's stinginess and
his embarrassment and guilt about his mother's "tearful, pleading
eyes" blend in his mind with what he sees as the "lie" in his family (65). Furthermore, he has internalized the outside view of his
culture, as he hears the chanted Hebrew "suddenly [as] an alien

language" (68). By linking the external view of this "alien" culture with his family's dysfunctions, Jake becomes repulsed by the
sacred language of his ancestors and disgusted with the Seder he
once loved.

At the prodding of the psychiatrist, Jake begins to confront
the basis of his anger at Debby through his memory of that specific Passover night. In perfect Freudian structure, his remembrance
of the occasion when Debby steals his name allows him to (re)gain
his Jewish identity and to accept his sister's otherness. It is also
evident in the following passage that, once again, the psychiatrist
misses the important context of Jake's statements:

> "Hell, we're dirty, we're low-down Jews . . . we're—failures, all
>   right! But we don't steal."
> "What did she steal from you?"
> "The questions. She took them away from me."
> "The what?" (197)

As informed readers, we know that Jake is speaking of the Four
Questions that the youngest son (no matter how old he is) speaks
at the Passover Seder. In a flashback, Jake remembers a Seder when
his brother Sig is out and he, refusing to be present at the ceremony, lies on his bed with his whiskey, listening to the family at
the table. Debby, the youngest child, since there are no males at the
table, reads the questions. Jake is horrified by what he considers
her betrayal. He is separated from this important role both in his
family and in Jewish history as well as isolated from his mother
and Debby, the two women who mean the most to him. This linguistic fracture leads to the loss of the last shred of his being named
in his culture and to the final construction of John Brown.

In the discussion with the doctor, Jake comes to terms with
his guilt at forcing Debby to take over his role in the family. However, the psychiatrist never addresses the cultural issues, but challenges Jake with models out of the status quo: "Who helped steal
her right to be a girl, a baby sister, the one to be protected, not to
protect?" (204). Debby, who has always been the strength of the
family, is perceived by both Jake and the doctor as "defeminized"
by her role of financial backbone and emotional supporter. A laying bare of this section (ex)poses the conflicts in the novel's vision
of ethnicity as well as of gender orientation. First of all, in opposition to Anglo-Christian society, Ashkenazic Jewish culture commonly perceived women as being responsible for worldly activities
so as to leave the men time for Torah study; therefore, Debby's

position would not be construed historically as unfeminine. More problematic in terms of the confines of patriarchal Judaism is the fact that Jake has disengaged himself from his spiritual responsibilities, leaving the religious rituals to the women. Second, the inference that the loss of manliness in the Jewish male as the reason for Debby's "homosexuality" designates lesbian culture and identity as a negation. Third, the whole concept of the emasculated Jewish male reinforces another damaging stereotype; this deep-rooted prejudice, in relation to the Jewish male's separation from his mother, includes a Christian belief during the Middle Ages that Jewish men menstruated (Efron 5).[15] The tensions encoded in the unconscious of this wellness text are revealed, since the novel aims to dispel stereotypes as well as to valorize Jewish identity and to privilege the lesbian character as healer.

For Jake, however, the psychoanalytic unmasking of his anger toward Debby is a way for him to start to accept Debby's otherness and consequently his own. He begins to acknowledge her difference as part of who she is; he is no longer is embarrassed by it: "Is it such a terrible way to be? Just because she isn't like most women?" (204). Jake has finally "recognized" his sister and tells the doctor: "I want every body to know she's wonderful" (205). Although her narrative voice is not heard in the novel, Debby's role as healer reflects Sinclair's authorial voice and leads Jake to break through the rigid structure of assumed Gentileness to (re)construct a Jewish identity, in a symbolic discourse in which he can truly participate. Jake's appreciation of Debby's nighttime discussions with him, her directions on how to function in the psychiatrist's office, and her almost palpable presence in that consulting room, create a curative space for Jake to accept who he is, following in her footsteps. In this way, Debby fulfills her role as culture bearer and cultural healer; moreover, Sinclair transforms the Jewish lesbian from a threat to society into a restorer of family and community. Jake learns from Debby, beyond the psychiatrist, how to name himself. When Jake drops the Christian "John" and (re)names himself (at least the first part of his original name), it is a major indication of this healing. However, the construction of this identity and his total acceptance of his otherness is marred by his (re)naming only his first name and by the fact that he never does tell his Gentile peers that he is Jewish.

One of the ways Jake begins to heal himself is by acknowledging his secret, "art" pictures, which to him are somehow Jewish-identified. Jake takes pictures unrelated to his professional work, particularly ones depicting interpersonal relations of other poor and oppressed people. Although he hides them away, he is unable not to shoot these scenes, as if that part of his psyche is reacting against its fictive constraints. Jake's photographs reveal his own belief in a visual as well as written discourse of the Other— something that links him to his Jewish marginality, no matter how hard he tries to escape. In this way, his hidden pictures reflect the problems of assimilated writers, and perhaps some of Sinclair's own contradictions in writing this novel. According to Sander Gilman's notion of a hidden "Jewish" language, when assimilated Jewish writers are faced with perceived "Jewish topics," anxiety surfaces: "Suddenly they are dealing with that category which they have successfully repressed through the very act of writing and which now draws this success into question" (20). When he remembers first telling Debby about these pictures (after his epiphany about her and the Passover questions), he comments that they are "queer" (interesting word choice) and done mainly for himself: "I always called them Jewish pictures when I was thinking about them. I don't know why. It was like they went with this house" (209). In linking these pictures with Jewishness, Jake at first fears that these pictures will jeopardize his Gentile status and success as a news photographer, since these other pictures could expose him as a Jew. However, this concept of the creative act being imbued with his cultural identity has a dialectic effect. Jake takes these art pictures to relieve him of his sickness, a nausea that he feels living his sham existence. When he finally acknowledges his photographs, Jake feels better; he begins to articulate the sustenance he receives from his culture as well as identify with Debby's writings. As with Kerewin's return to her sculpture in *the bone people*, the creative act is often linked to healing the cultural self. Moreover, this scene uncovers another significant aspect of healing cultural illness within this novel, a reaching out to other groups that are also suffering. Both Jake and Debby gain their artistic inspiration from expressing beauty in what the dominant culture might call the underclass, their own group and other marginalized people, especially Black Americans. Certainly, one of the most powerful features of the novel is its connection of Jake and Debby's personal, Jewish wastelands to other ghettos everywhere in the world, reflecting, one might say, a preparedness in Jewish culture to fight for social justice.[16]

In the process of cultural healing, Jake has moved away from his psychiatrist as "symbol of the world" (239); he has decided to face the world with his sister and become part of it without fear or self-hate. In an extremely symbolic gesture, brother and sister give blood together to aid the war effort and, of course, in this case, also to help millions of Jews in concentration camps. In giving blood, Jake fulfills his desire to "be like any guy in America," a universal impulse, since like other "real" Americans, he can give something of himself to this fight, while dialectically accepting his difference and its special relationship to this war (305). Through the ritual act of giving blood, Jake gains a sense of himself as doing something for the rest of the world. When Debby tells him why she gives blood, he first thinks that he is doing it not for "faraway, persecuted people" but "against wasteland" (306). But then as the blood is being drawn, he thinks back to her statement and realizes that other people's persecution is real for him: "And I give my blood for people like me, she had said. Any kind of segregation. Negroes, Jews. And my kind, too" (307). Besides linking his own feeling to his sister's lesbian identity, Jake moves beyond the notion of racial "blood" that limited opportunities for his immigrant forebears to the human blood that we all share. In a final gesture, Jake gives back to his sister his pride in his name, accepting his selfhood as a Jew: "He wanted to show her how he had written Jake Brown on his card" (307).

Ultimately, in an act that completes the circle of health and ends the psychoanalytic moment, Jake extends his creative impulses to taking pictures of his family, his pictures no longer secret. He even functions as an instrument of healing the wounds of the family; Debby no longer has to do this alone. Jake begins to take pictures of his sister Sarah and her children (the next generation of wasteland), giving her hope as well. Jake even forgives his father for their poverty and the old man's poverty of spirit. Most significantly, Jake reconnects to the mother he lost in his attempt to assimilate. He accepts her Yiddish and her painful history, by respecting and honoring the Sabbath table she has prepared for the family. Jake is once more integrated into the household; his family, in turn, is thrilled by his attention. Naming his family in his pictures helps him (re)construct his identity, and he begins the process of curing the family through the words and scenes of his culture. To finalize this vision, Jake takes a picture of the family's table, set by his mother with the special dishes for the Passover ceremony: "JEWISH HOLIDAY, TWENTIETH CENTURY, he thought. Or I could call it, THEY KEEP FAITH IN AMERICA, TOO" (343). In titling this photograph, Jake attempts to reconcile a conflict in American Jewish culture, which runs from the early immigrant writers to Philip Roth and others: how one can be both Jewish and American.

The novel ends, cyclically, at the Passover Seder. It is both Jake's birthday and the day he has enlisted in the army. This Passover festival is indeed a rebirth for Jake. He even refers to it in that way. He takes a shower and puts on his best clothes, calling it a "symbolic bathing and dressing" (342), a "mikvah"—although he does not name it. He prepares to sit at the table and read the questions. He has come to terms with his family and identity, and he is ready to become part of the world, to help his people and others suffering under Hitler's rule. He hears the words of the Seder as he has never done before, which links him to the Jewish collective memory and community through its healing language: "All over the world, wherever Jews were gathered for this holiday, the youngest son was ready to speak" (346). Moreover, the youngest nephew, Allen, will study Hebrew, so that the next year he can read questions in their sacred, ancient language (345). In this way, the novel ends on an extremely uplifting note. On one hand, Jake sees himself assimilated into the dominant culture, an American soldier who will fight for justice, and on the other, the family is together for Passover, linking both ancient Jewish traditions and a modern one: the psychoanalytic discourse that brought him to this point.

However, the apparent easiness of the solution to Jake's "Jewish problem" reflects the conflicts of Jewish identity and cultural illness addressed at the beginning of this chapter. Encoded in Jake's healing is the construction of a new form of self-identification, reflected in Sinclair's own experience, which still leads to the ultimate rejection of the Jewish self. This new sense of Jewish identity can be seen as another kind of assimilation, reminiscent of Freud and his group's move toward the universal inner realm of the mind through psychoanalysis. In the introduction to the reissued 1987 edition of *Wasteland*, Vivian Gornick comments on this aspect of the novel in an almost diffident way: "Jake must abandon his childhood grievance if he is to mature, and in a very real sense he must abandon his Jewishness as he has known it if he is to integrate his own experience. . . . The handwriting is on the wall" (n.p.). Uffen makes a similar point much more forcefully: "Is it right to believe that a man who despised himself and his family for being foreigners and Jews, is cured when he is able to see himself as an anonymous Everyman?" (49). Jake's acceptance of his Jewish identity leads him to abandon, on some level, his fictive, unified self, and to claim his otherness. Yet simultaneously, as Jake becomes one with his American identity, his healing ends by further subsuming his Jewish difference, Unlike the blending of cultures allegorized in the epilogue of *the bone people*, *Wasteland*'s uplifting ending encodes in it a potential for another kind of assimilation, which, in some ways, places Jake healed in the same position as he was diseased. In this way, the curative vision in the novel is not complete, further exposing the complications of psychoanalysis as a healing discourse in itself.

What healing model does *Wasteland* present to readers if the only true way to affirm Jewish identity also prescribes the future effacement of that same culture through assimilation? To what extent can a cure developed through the sole attention to the "inner realm of the psyche" help heal the fractured cultural self? How are the contradictions exposed in the origins of the psychoanalytic movement replayed in the novel? What does it mean when a novel concerned with women's healing role and the strength of renaming oneself as part of a cultural healing is written by a woman who never returned to her Jewish-identified name of Ruth Seid? These questions reflect the novel's ambiguities as well as present psychiatry as limited in its ability to heal cultural illness, despite its Jewish ethos. In attempting to comes to terms with the disease of Jewish self-hate, the linguistic cure, as Gilman so exhaustively details in *Jewish Self-Hatred*, becomes, in some ways, another manifestation of the disease. This is clearly discerned in Sinclair's own remarks, cited at the beginning in this chapter, concerning the reason she used Jews in this novel—because she's known "hundreds of them." In this statement, Sinclair seems to reject allegiance to this oppressed group, of which she is a member. In fact, the author at times borders on stereotyping Jews (as well as lesbians), while trying to find acceptance for them from her readers. Furthermore, for all her desires for her characters to become "part of the world," the text reveals an environment still uncomfortable for the particularity of Jews.

Wasteland ends without the clear direction found in the other books discussed in this study, leaving us with a sense that the tools of healing, stripped of cultural markers, cannot truly cure the individual, even the one from whose culture these tools have sprung. Embedded in the text's healing narrative is a "cure" for cultural dis-ease that is, ironically, also a cure for Jewish identity, leaving the tensions and neuroses encoded in Jewish mediation in the Diaspora intact. Aware of the historicity of both Freud's and

Seid's time—heightened moments of anti-Semitism—we can understand the apparently insurmountable task of resolving Jewish difference and being part of the world, as well as its ostensible solution found in the "inner realm of the mind." Still, as a wellness narrative, *Wasteland* adds another dimension to the understanding of cultural illness and healing. At the beginning of the twenty-first century, with its lens focused on multiplicity and cross/transcultural identities, the healing strategies based both in traditional societies and within the context of biomedicine and psychoanalysis may pose for us a way of curing dis-ease, but the language for this discourse is just in its formative stages.

Conclusion

Toward (W)Holistic
Healing

In the process of writing this book, I have presented papers and discussed the issues I have raised here with health professionals, traditional healers, and literary critics. Above all, one idea keeps surfacing, linked to Richard Grossinger's comment in *Planet Medicine*: "If visualizations and symbols are to work, they must contain within them exactly those things indigenous to us" (70). Grossinger's insight into what is "indigenous to us" and who "we" are in our complex cross/transcultural global society is one of the major questions that arise from this study. How does this kind of culture-specific healing model operate within a postmodern, cross/transcultural environment, as well as in relation to the realities of migration, hybridity and globalization.

The challenge is what if anything in this fragmented, clash-of-cultures world, which poses traditional knowledge in opposition to modern science, is indigenous to us as humans who inhabit this ailing planet. In this book, by posing these five respresentative novels together, I have tried to examine a cross-cultural approach to the kinds of wellness narratives that challenge conventional notions of health, typically isolated from culture. By presenting wellness narratives that attempt to integrate the concept of cultural illness/health into the cathartic aspects of the novel, these works aim to revision the social structures of our lives through a discourse that begins to reintegrate the cultural self into our concepts of identity in this fragmented, postmodern age. Through their writings, these authors are reconstructing the relationship between artist as healer and physician as healer, as identified by Sewell in the introduction and broken by the age of empirical science.

Still, as evidenced from the complexities of cultural illness in contemporary society, we can't just "go back" to earlier, utopian notions of health through traditional practices. Moreover, as these wellness narratives point out, there is no specific formula for cultural healing. Still, envisioning health in this manner may also function as a counterhegemonic tool to break down the self-hate that comes from prejudice and oppression as well as the limitations of binary thinking about culture and health. Although linking these works from such diverse cultures across the globe might seem a bit arbitrary, taken together these works present a discourse of healing that goes beyond the traditional healing traditions they honor as well as expanding out from the limitations of scientific rationalism that has restricted understanding of the ways culture affects our personal and community health. The innovative mode in which these novels address how culture fits into the other components of health is similar to the way creative writers first conceptualized the integration of the competing aspects of race/class/gender before the social critics and theorists fully recognized those linkages. For it is through the concept of oral medicine, a "writing cure," to paraphrase Freud, and the words of that process that we begin to reconnect.

The first two novels, *Jane and Louisa Will Soon Come Home* and *The Salt Eaters*, are wellness narratives based mainly in the traditional healing practices of the African Diaspora. Furthermore, they are linked an array of personal disorders and dysfunctions of those of African descent, first initiated by the trauma of the slave trade. In the next section, Silko's *Ceremony* also explores the direct connection of Native American healing systems to the health of her Laguna Pueblo community. However, unlike the African American writers, who, despite the fact that they probably have the ancestry of other ethnic groups, focus predominantly on their African heritage as the healing tool, Silko present her protagonist as a "mixed-race" person and examines the complicities of that position in cultural healing. Hulme's *the bone people* takes one step beyond Silko to attempt a blending of the apparently oppositional cultures of Maori and Pakeha to create a healing narrative that is inclusive of all the people of Aotearoa/New Zealand. Furthermore, Hulme challenges gender roles as well as ethnic identity, as she presents alternative ways of being a healthy individual within a changing society. Finally, the last work discussed, Sinclair's *Wasteland*, both reinforces and complicates the concept of cultural healing. The earliest of the novels examined here and the one most connected to Western medicine, *Wasteland* poses Freud's talking cure, psychoanalysis, as a healing tool to cure Jewish self-hate. Despite the ostensible curing of the protagonist, Jake, the unconscious of the text still raises questions of the disjuncture of this oral medicine (and in some ways, this is true of all dominant medical practices) from its traditional roots, the folkloric and religious Jewish healing traditions. However, in attempting to reconnect one's cultural tradition to the contemporary practices arising from it, this novel begins a response to one of the major challenges of my study: What do these healing discourses mean to a cross/multicultural society?

Although the discussion here does not answer this question explicitly, these novels taken together expose cross-cultural approaches to the healing of culturally ill individuals and oppressed communities in relation to our hybridized world. However, the models presented here resist the simplicities of a kind of cultural self-help book to open new avenues of healing discourses through the fluidity of the metaphoric language of literature. The investigation of each novelist's aim to heal her specific dis-eased community through the healing practices associated with her own group presents these works as sites of healing and links the discourse of the novel to the possibilities of breaking through the boundaries that have limited discussions of culture and health. By choosing such diverse cultures (from Maori to Jewish) associated only through their long histories of oppression, we return to the concept identified in the introduction of the book: that cultures themselves can be ill, leading us and, it is hoped, the medical establishment as well, to rethink the restricted assumptions that only individuals can be ill.

Finally, we return to the writer and his/her role in the healing of cultures/societies that are ill. For these writers envisioning a language from cultures formerly denied, the novels work dialectically as a healing discourse, one that might aid in a further integrated medical practice as it works toward curing the culturally ill. With the contemporary challenge to scientific rationalism and the emergence of a new, more inclusive paradigm for the health of our world, these wellness narratives by women writers reform, as art often does, the social constructs of our lives. Through the literary language of fiction, these works and others like them defy the binary oppositions that have plagued modern science and Western philosophy by constructing another way of knowing. At this historical moment, as illustrated in these texts, the healing arts can once again be in dialogue with the health professions to set an agenda for the twenty-first century. Rather than a rejection of the successes of conventional medicine or a reversal of history, nostalgic for an earlier, less complex traditional world, these works taken together constitute, if not a complete answer, then a way of rewording the question: how we can revitalize our often diseased lives and planet through a discourse of cultural healing.

Notes

Introduction

1. Although I am not totally satisfied with the opposition of Western/ traditional, it is the clearest differentiation I could find. Since Western medicine is noted for a scientific model that most doctors in the world (wherever they come from) follow, and because traditional is often the basis for alternative, so-called New Age, methods developed by those often trained in conventional medicine as well as a growing number of physicians who are looking into traditional healing practices, this apparent opposition—as other oppositions encoded in our language—resists the totality implied in these contrasting terms. One other clarification: I use the term "traditional" throughout the book to mean those healing systems of pre- and non-Western cultures, rather than in the meaning of conventional or dominant medical practice, and "alternative" for contemporary practices that combine several traditional healing strategies without necessarily understanding their cultural base.

2. For example, discussion of the determinants of what makes up African American culture in the United States and throughout the rest of the African Diaspora, both in relation to African survivalisms and dominant U.S. culture, have been hotly contested since Reconstruction.

3. Although in dominant usage, the word "spiritual" is overladen with Christian connotations and connected to this and other organized religion, I am using it here in a more inclusive way, in relation to that "other world" outside the realm of a scientific worldview.

4. Because of U.S. politics of ethnicity, the Spanish language has become a symbol of oppressed cultures; however, it is necessary to remember that the oppressed cultures are the Amerindian societies, who had been colonized and often vanquished by the Spanish. The *curanderas* are viewed not from within the domain of Spanish culture, but in their relation to the Amerindian societies, like the Mayan, from whose cultural traditions that Spanish term was derived. "Hispanic" cultures (again a U.S.-dominant term) will be discussed in relation to African-based (like Cuban or Puerto Rican) or indigenous (Mexican and southwestern United States). For further connections of the cultures explored here, see Kathleen Alcalá, *Spirits of the Ordinary*, on the relationship of crypto-Jews and Amerindians in Saltillo, Mexico.

5. For a fuller discussion of this issue, see, for example, Ruth Bleier's provocative essay "Lab Coat or Klansman's Sheet."

6. For an intriguing article that exposes certain similarities between women's visions (as a linked group) and African sensibilities (also

identified as a discrete group, including both male and female healers), see Sandra Harding, "The Curious Coincidence of Feminine and
African Moralities."

7. Many of the women healers (as well as men, like Grossinger), who
are examining alternative practice are Jewish, yet they explore healing methods from cultures throughout the world, excluding their
own. Perhaps this reflects the curious position of Jews as contribut-
ing to Eurocentric Western culture, but always marginal to it. In
addition to the chapter on Sinclair/Seid, see Leonard Glick, "Types
Distinct from Our Own: Franz Boas on Jewish Identity and Assimilation."

8. The relationship of literature to medicine has been developed in
medical humanities programs in universities throughout the United
States and other countries. However, the majority of these programs
reflect how literature can be used within hospitals and conventional
medical practice, rarely exploring traditional modes of healing and
its discourse. Still, for fertile interaction in examining the healing
arts in medicine, see the journal *Literature and Medicine*, as well as
the other works cited in this study.

9. See, for example, George Lamming, *The Pleasures of Exile*, and my
article "English is a Foreign Anguish: Caribbean Writers and the
Critique of the Colonial Canon."

1 *Reclaiming Residual Culture*

1. Both male and female West African writers, such as Chinua Achebe,
Flora Nwapa, Sembene Ousmane, Efua Sutherland, Ama Ata Aidoo,
and Kofi Awooner, have integrated aspects of their oral traditions
into their works to resist the colonial disease imposed on them and
to promote more culturally connected and healthier African communities. One recent example is Flora Nwapa's last novel, *The Lake
Goddess*, which details the life of a traditional healer coming from a
Westernized Christian home.

2. See, for example, Rhonda Cobham, "Getting Out of the Kumbla,"
and Yakemi Kemp, "Woman and Womanchild: Bonding and Selfhood
in Three West Indian Novels."

3. As I noted in the introduction to this book, the discourse of mind/
body split is inscribed in the language of science/medicine. Despite
the fact that Nellie has many somatic disorders, hers is identified as
a "mental" disease. It is to be hoped that new ways of perceiving the
self in health will also come with a new discourse.

4. William Wedenoja, in his essay "Mothering and the Practice of Balm
in Jamaica," focuses on the gender specifics of both the practice of
balm and obeah in Jamaica. Generally, but not always, balm healers
are women whereas obeah practitioners are male, as I discuss later
in this chapter.

5. In the meeting of poststructuralist with postcolonial, the thrust of
the power of words (what they mean; what they exclude in de-
constructive terms), as forces in a traditional worldview, may be developing now as an emergent concept to reconfigure language as health.

6. See Wilentz, "English Is a Foreign Anguish: Caribbean Writers and the Disruption of the Colonial Canon."

7. Wilson Harris, comments during graduate seminar, University of Texas, spring 1983.

8. Maureen Warner Lewis, in "Nkoyu: Spirit Messenger of the Kumina," notes the role of the African-based Kumina bands in responding to a "major defect" in the West Indian's consciousness by attempting to preserve a "sense of historical continuity through spiritual and cultural means." She states further: "One wonders at the sense of purpose that could be unleashed in the West Indian people [if] a sense of participation in a long historical process could be fostered" (77). See also A. Barrington Chevannes's discussion of the role of the Rastafarians in "The Repairer of the Breach: Reverend Claudius Henry and Jamaican Society."

9. Jamaican writer Michelle Cliff identifies the dual meaning of the abeng in the opening of her novel, *Abeng*: "*Abeng* is an African word meaning conch shell. The blowing of the conch called the slaves to the canefields in the West Indies. The *abeng* had another use: it was the instrument used by the Maroon armies to pass their messages and reach one another."

10. See, for example, the portrait of both parents in Marshall's *Brown Girl, Brownstones*, in terms of their ways of adapting to U.S. race relations, as well as the novel's treatment of conflict between the Afro-Caribbean and African American communities in New York.

11. For a discussion of the healing of Ella by the myalist in relation to the novel and to the disease of postcolonial societies, see Catherine Nelson-McDermott, "Myal-ing Criticism: Beyond Colonizing Dialectics."

12. Katon, Kleinman, and Rosen, in "Depression and Somatization," note that too often in response to a depressive disorder, "the patient's physical complaint is treated symptomatically, whereas the underlying disease is left untreated" (128). One specific physical manifestation the doctors note is "diabetic neuropathy" (129).

13. Caliban's famous line is: "You taught me language; and my profit on it/ Is, I know how to curse" (William Shakespeare, *The Tempest*).

14. The role of the female healer, whether alive or dead, is integral to the novel's structure. As Brinda Mehta notes in "The Shaman Woman, Resistance, and the Power of Transformation," in contemporary Caribbean women's fiction, these cultural figures are not used for "local color"(as in earlier Eurocentric writings) but instead are involved in a "more self-conscious examination or reevaluation of the literature's sociocultural and historical 'specificities'" (234).

15. Clarissa Zimra comments: "It is out of the silence of the maimed self that the female voice attempts her recovery of the happier past, which is, for the Caribbean, the only past that matters—Africa" (247). However, as the chapters in this book indicate, and Wilson Harris so forcefully states elsewhere, the recovering of the African aspects of heritage cannot be a denial of other influences, or a new, and equally harmful, hegemony may be imposed.

16. In addition to the works cited in this and the following chapter, see

Byron Foster, *Heart Drum: Spirit Possession the Garifuna Communities of Belize,* for examples of recorded and remembered experiences of African-based possession.

17. See Wilentz, "Civilizations Underneath: African Heritage as Cultural Discourse in Toni Morrison's *Song of Solomon.*" In addition to the anthropological studies, beginning with Herskovits, who examines the power of names in African-based communities, see John Edgar Wideman's *Damballah* for a fictionalized expression of this concept.

2 *A Laying On of Hands*

1. Some of the recent historical studies on African retentions are: Joseph Holloway, *Africanisms in American Culture;* Gwendolyn Hall, *Africans in Colonial Louisiana,* Daniel C. Littlefield, *Rice and Slaves;* Bernard Makhosezwe Magubane, *The Ties That Bind;* Ronald W. Walters, *Pan Africanism in the African Diaspora;* and Margaret Washington, *"A Peculiar People."*

2. *Praisesong for the Widow* is a major healing text that could easily have been included in this study; however, Bambara's *The Salt Eaters* focuses more fully on African-based traditional healing in relationship to medical practice. Moreover, as the two articles I cite demonstrate, Bambara's wellness narrative has not received the attention it deserves. Still, for my own exploration of Marshall's restorative text, see "Paule Marshall, *Praisesong for the Widow,*" *Binding Cultures* 99–115. Furthermore, to read Bambara's short discussion of *Praisesong* in terms of her own aims to heal her community, see her essay "Deep Sightings and Rescue Missions," in her posthumous work of the same title, 146–178.

3. The Penn Center, built in 1862 as an educational institute, has historically been a place where Black activists worked together for social change and brought in major figures for group discussions of pan-Africanism in the period ranging from the early years of the century to the time of the Civil Rights movement.

4. In the study *The Signifying Monkey,* Henry Louis Gates Jr. takes the figure of Esu-Elegba for the changeable quality of African literary discourse in the Americas; for two fictional versions of his role as cross-over figure, see Marshall's Joseph Lebert in *Praisesong* as well as Reed's Papa Labas in *Mumbo Jumbo.*

5. For a fuller discussion on women's role in maintaining cultural traditions in African societies and cultural preparedness in the Americas, see "Introduction," *Binding Cultures,* xi–xxxiii.

6. Salt and its effects is a common theme in the literature of many cultures, from this cautionary tale and the biblical story of Lot's wife to the salutary use of salt in reviving the zombified. Like other images associated with oppression, salt has both a metaphorical and a biological duality: Salt keeps us alive, but too much can also kill us. For a fuller discussion of salt in relation to a return to Africa as well as the Legend of the Flying Africans, see Wilentz, "If You Surrender to the Air."

7. See, for example, Krieger and Bassett, "The Health of Black Folk: Disease, Class, and Ideology in Science, in *"The Racial Economy of Science* (161–169). For a collection of fictional representations, see also *Trials, Tribulations, and Celebrations: African-American Perspectives on Health, Illness, Aging and Loss,* ed. Marian Gray Secundy.

8. As I have noted in the introduction and as shown in Stepan and Gilman's "Appropriating the Idioms of Science," the idioms of other modes of healing were termed "unscientific" in the discourse of medicine, thus causing a conflict for the African American doctor. The authors state: "Our argument is that from the mid-nineteenth century onward, scientific claims could only be rebutted by scientific discourse to which resisting groups stood in an especially disadvantaged and problematic position" (173).

9. Although in 1980, when this novel was published, this vision was somewhat utopian, much has changed in almost twenty years since. From Germany to Madagascar, various types of medical practices link traditional healing to conventional medicine, not only to use the scientific method to see whether these traditional practices work, but also as joint projects conducted with respect for both the doctor and the healer. Moreover, throughout the continent of Africa, these linkages are working much better than had the imposition of strictly conventional systems.

10. See, for example, the difficulties Lillian faces in her acceptance of her role as healer in Barbara B. Sims's "Facts in the Life History of a Black Mississippi-Louisiana Healer" as well as the many examples in Valerie Lee's *Granny Midwives and Black Women Writers.* For a Caribbean perspective, see the development of Sarita as a Garifuna *buyai* in Byron Foster's *Heart Drum* (19–34) and the discussion of "myalism" in the preceding chapter.

11. Although this chapter does not specifically include the illness surrounding domestic violence, Bambara sees this as a major disorder in African American communities (among others). For example, Fred Holt is on the edge of violence toward his white wife, as he thinks about her while he intentionally kills a "dark and furry thing offering itself up" on the road (82); moreover, violence against women is evident in the portrait of Obie's brother Roland, whose rage and anger at society turns into a rape of a Black woman with four children (96–98).

12. Not only is Barnwell a major nuclear plant and site of numerous antinuclear protests, but in 1980, during the writing of this novel, there was a large and volatile protest in which many activists were abused and sent to jail. It was, conjointly, a protest that included groups of various ethnic/racial backgrounds and political positions.

13. Diamond and Orenstein's collection *Reweaving the World: The Emergence of EcoFeminism* generally explores the connection between various social ills and the environmental movement through both a materialist and spiritual feminism, especially the section "Reconnecting Politics and Ethics." For a specific discussion of environmental racism, see Lee Quinby's essay "EcoFeminism and the Politics of Resistance" (128–137).

14. Revealingly, during the moment of Velma's healing, Minnie receives a message, "Pentagon" (277). She is confused by the sign but relates it to the pentagram, drawn in the dirt to invoke and make manifest the spirits, but clearly that word also evokes a major site of potential destruction, the Pentagon, in Washington, D.C.

15. This notion of a utopian vision as a counterhegemonic critique comes from a workshop on Frantz Fanon, conducted by Abdul Jan Mohammed, African Literature Association Conference, Michigan State University, 17 April 1986. See also Fanon, *The Wretched of the Earth.*

3 *The Novel as Chant*

1. Thought Woman, also known as Spider Woman or Grandmother Spider, is a creator who "thought the earth, the sky, the galaxy, and all that is into being. . . . " According to tradition, her story of creation is not completed, since "as she thinks, so we are" (Allen, *Grandmothers of the Light* 28).

2. As many critics have pointed out, Silko delves freely into various North American Indian traditions, especially from her own Laguna Pueblo group and from the Navajo, a group into which Silko gained further insight while she was teaching at Navajo Community College on the Navajo Reservation in Chinle, Arizona.

3. There have been a great many critiques of Gladys Reichert's research into the Laguna Pueblo, and much of it valid in terms of Reichert's "Eurocentric" interpretation, especially in regard to her informants— one of them being Mrs. W. G[awietsa] Marmon, Leslie Marmon Silko's great-aunt. However, because of this connection and because of the voices utilized in the anthropological data, I feel that her work is useful here. For more on this ethnographic debate, see Renae Bredin, "Falling into the Wrong Hands: Laguna Women and Ethnographic Strip Tease."

4. In *Yellow Woman and a Beauty of the Spirit*, Silko refers to her father's hard time integrating into the full-blooded Laguna community because he was mixed. Like the character Tayo, Silko's father and his elder brother went to the hills, because "whatever the ambiguities of their racial heritage, my father and my uncle understood what the old folks taught them: the earth loves all of us regardless, because we are her children" (42).

5. Certain critics have also identified specific ceremonies. For example, Elisabeth Evasdaughter and Edith Swan both point to the use of specific Navajo curing rites in the novel, and they discuss the way in which these particular ceremonies in the novel function as a sing or chant. Swan states further in her discussion of Silko's use of the sunwise cycle that the "'sing' or 'chant' terminology [captures] the inherent verbal potency of words which make thought a reality" ("Healing" 314).

6. Although Sandner identifies five stages—purification, evocation, identification, transformation, and release—I discuss only the first four, since he does not talk about "release" (the person is cured and leaves)

in terms of the actual process of the chant; moreover, the sacredness of the number four in Native American culture, and its corresponding relation to the seasons, leads me to see this fifth "stage" as not a real stage in the chant, but rather a transition after the ceremony is complete. See also Swan, "Healing via the Sunwise Cycle" in Silko's *Ceremony*."

7. At least two well-known legends are incorporated in this section of identification of the Gods, the Laguna legend of Tayo as Sun Man, and the story of Yellow Woman, with whom Ts'eh is linked.

8. This trope relating back to the belief that there is ancestral link between Asians and Native Americans because of the passage through the Bering Straits is also alluded to in other novels of Native American war veterans. In *Love Medicine*, Henry Lamartine, during a chance sexual encounter, remembers a dying Vietnamese woman who looked at him and "pointed to her eyes and his eyes. The Asian, folded eyes of some Chippewas" (138).

9. For another unusual linking of Native American and Asian cultures, among the Hmong people who came to the United States after the Vietnam War, there has been a kind of ghost sickness in certain men leading to death, an illness that defies physicians. One symptom of this disorder is the feeling that a ghost in the shape of a white woman is pressing against the man's chest, stopping all breath. See Shelley Ruth Adler's dissertation, "The Role of the Nightmare in Hmong Sudden Unexpected Nocturnal Death Syndrome: A Folkloric Study of Belief and Health."

10. For a fuller discussion of the complexities as well as possibilities for the bi- (or more) racial individual, see Maria P. P. Root, "Resolving 'Other's' Status: Identity Development of Biracial Individuals."

11. See Leslie Marmon Silko's collection, *Storyteller*, for a version of "Yellow Woman" (54–62).

12. What is difficult to articulate in English in this section is my attribution to Silko of having "invented" this legend, while Silko tells us that she is relating only what Thought Woman is thinking. This would imply that this legend exists beyond Silko. This is a contradiction I am unable to unravel within the confines of the English language; however, the novel itself, as well as Silko's other blending of narrative and legend, *Storyteller*, breaks through the limitations placed on critical writings.

4 *Becoming the Instruments of Change*

1. In her attempt to adapt the richness of Maori to English, Hulme explains the complexity of the language by stating that there are twenty-one meanings for the word *tara*, "grouped under everything from gossip to rays . . . one marvelous 21-jointed word, full of diversities" (13).

2. The generalized view of the Maori in much Pakeha fiction and culture is romanticized in a similar fashion to Euro-American presentation of the Native American as noble savage. For the Pakeha, there is a stereotypic positive identification with the cultural traditions as ar-

tifact and a pride in having some creativity in an otherwise prag-
matic, unimaginative society, but in both cases, reality presents a
harsher side: the violence in Duff and Hulme's writings as prime
examples of the volatile mix of the Maori and colonial inheritances.

3. The tohunga is connected to the sacred as well as to the healing arts.
Because of the repression of the tohunga in the early 1900s, the activities of these healers were sometimes taken over by others in the
community, particularly the elders (Sachdev, "Mana" 968). In "Maori
Healers in New Zealand: The Tohunga Suppression Act 1907,"
Malcolm Voyce comments that the tohunga were accused of "stopping civilization" and "disturbing the native mind" in resisting European influence. Moreover, doctors at this time were seen by the
colonial authorities as "a vital part of their apparatus of authority
and control; Western medicine being a way to weaken native culture
and promote allegiance to European institutions and thought" (112).

4. Mark Williams constantly criticizes Hulme for distorting "objective"
history. Evidently, Williams has not realized that in a postmodern
age, identifying any notion of history, especially his own, as "objective" is questionable at the least. For another resisting critic, see
Judith Dale, "*the bone people*: (Not) Having It Both Ways."

5. Although Bleier does not address ethnicity explicitly, since her essay focuses more on gender, it is evident in the title, "Lab Coat or
Klansman's Sheet."

6. There are indications that both Kerewin and Joe could be seen as
alcoholics, adding to their dis-ease. Moreover, not only do they allow Simon to drink too much, Joe tends to be drunk when he beats
Simon. However, I have not addressed this issue in the essay, because within the context of the novel, alcohol is not specifically cri-
tiqued as part of the problem. One example is that, in the utopian
epilogue, the people are drinking as heartily as ever! Furthermore, in
attempting to revision Maori culture, there has been some discussion of how the pub functions in certain ways as the marae. See
Perminder S. Sachdev, "Psychiatric Illness in the New Zealand
Maori," especially p. 537.

7. This trope of urban destruction of Maori culture is reflected in much
Maori fiction, but it is challenged in one of Patricia Grace's novels.
In the novel *Cousins*, the one cousin who goes to the city is the one
most tied to her Maori traditions. By the end of *the bone people*,
Hulme also appears to work toward a bridging of the gap between
urban and rural.

8. Interestingly, in light of the cross-cultural potentials for healing and
this book, the Tarot is derived primarily on a book of Jewish tradition, the Kabbalah.

9. For further discussion on violence inscribed in Western culture, see
René Girard, *Violence and the Sacred*.

10. Caribbean author Caryl Phillips examines the basis of Christian European society in much the same way as anthropologists explored
what they saw as "savage" cultures. In his 1996 novel *The Nature of
Blood*, Phillips takes three unrelated narratives—of a Holocaust sur-
vivor, Othello, from his own point of view, and of three Jews killed

in the Middle Ages for supposedly mixing the blood of a Christian boy in their matzoh—to expose a pattern of violence and domination linked to this "tribe."

11. In "Myth, Omen, Ghost and Dream," Hulme recounts the Maori belief that moths signify those ancestors who, for some reason, are communicating with the material world (32).

12. In *Bridges of the Bodymind*, Achterberg and Lawlis examine the role of internalizing anger in relation to cancer; furthermore, they note the importance of finding "an acceptable outlet for repressed negative emotions" as a way to fight the disease (120).

13. Much of the balancing act that we see in Kerewin's understanding of her cultural heritage connects with Hulme's personal vision and experience. In both Hulme's own critical writings and in interviews with her, she refers to her privileged and painful position as a bicultural/ethnic person. Hulme comments: "Now I'll throw again and again to my Maori side, but there is no way I will totally ignore or exclude, or even want to exclude, all the joys and benefits of the Pakeha side of things" (Peek 3).

14. Ranginui Walker, in his discussion of the need to form urban marae, notes that the marae can serve as a way to "help breach the social separatism of the Pakeha and integrate him [sic] into Maori society" (33). However, he warns, this cannot be done if the Pakeha maintains a sense of cultural superiority.

5 *When the Psychiatrist Is Part of the Cure*

1. This definition of Jewish identity solely on the basis of religion is implicitly challenged in reference to genetic diseases or criminal acts. For example, CBS News, in uncovering information concerning the campaign funds of Congresswoman Enid Waldholtz, exposed (as explanation?) the fact that her embezzling Presbyterian husband was really a Pittsburgh Jew. CBS referred to the husband's ethnic identity in relation to his illegally using funds to support his wife's campaign, totally disregarding the fact that he had converted to Christianity.

2. One problem in Brodkin's intriguing look into the complexities of race and ethnicity in relation to Jewish identity is that she bases her argument that the Jews became nonwhite when Eastern European Jews entered the United States, along with other so-called inferior European tribes. However, the book does not link this view of Jews to the earlier notions of a Jewish race, which was clearly within the structure of European thinking. For both a contemporary critical look and a fictionalized version of this conflict, see Caryl Phillips's *The European Tribe* and his incredible novel, *The Nature of Blood*.

3. One aspect of Jewish history, which has not been studied in any depth, is its African antecedents. Much of the work on Jewish societies has been Eurocentric, and often African-based studies deny European Jews as being "real" Jews. However, my own personal experiences in Nigeria, witnessing similar burial practices for Igbos, including tearing of the cloth and shaving the head, and reading the work of Martin Bernal, have convinced me that this area needs much more study.

4. In addition to Klein, and Rothman and Isenberg, see also Peter Gay, *A Godless Jew*. Gay's book is intriguing because, although he rejects this notion of the Jewish antecedents of psychoanalysis mostly on the grounds that Freud did not see it like that (where is the subconscious in all of this?), Gay actually makes a strong argument for the connection. See especially the chapter "The Question of a Jewish Science: 'A Title of Honor'" (115–154).

5. Howe, while promoting Jewish writers, also encouraged them to make sure their writings were universal, which we now understand to mean for the dominant group, and it is evident that assimilative writings by Jews were more likely to be read and taught in classes than those the reference group found hard to understand.

6. Although many of the women involved in what we call alternative medicine are Jewish women, there has been little study presently or in the past concerning the role of Jewish women as healers. One short but good essay that raises these questions is "On Health and Being Jewish," by Judy Freespirit. On another note, scientific research has documented that chicken soup has the same healing attributes as cold medicine, a product of the enzymes formulated by the cooking of the chicken with the parley/parsnip/celery leaves.

7. Jewish passing, although often not an explicit act, still involves the rejection of family and community, as this novel exemplifies. In a interview by George Stambolian, Eric Bentley notes that homosexual passing is similar to Jewish passing, and cites a Columbia professor's comment about Lionel Trilling, who was "able to do well on the Columbia faculty because nobody could tell he was Jewish even though everyone knew he was" (127).

8. Although there is nothing in Seid's own writing to identify that the relationship with Helen Buchman ever went beyond woman-identified bonding, Helen's brother-in-law, Philip Sharnoff, in a note to Alan Wald states that he always got along with Helen until Seid became her "consort."

9. The hidden markers in the relationship of Seid to Buchman are complex indeed. Although Helen Buchman was Jewish, she was assimilated and, as her daughter Barbara Snoek notes, the family never celebrated the Jewish holidays, but always celebrated Christmas. For Ruth-turned-Jo, the powerful memories of these Christmases with the Buchmans were part of her entrance into mainstream (read Christian) society. Seid's own exploration of her transition led scholars and even a Feminist Press catalogue of Sinclair's autobiography, *The Seasons*, to identify Buchman as "Gentile"; however, the complicated position of Jewish identity in the United States described here is clearly inscribed in the work.

10. One may conjecture that this move toward assimilation, linked to the rejection of the mother, is based in nineteenth-century concepts of the Jew as feminized. In "Jews as a Metaphysical Species," Yuval Lurie cites Otto Weininger, a converted Jew who becomes a rabid anti-Semite and eventually kills himself (due to his inability to function in a world that still perceives him as a Jew). For Weininger, "femininity and Jewishness were extricably linked. . . . He viewed Jews

and their ways of living as a manifestation of a feminine culture" (328). Therefore, we can extrapolate that for Jewish men who internalized this judgment, the only way to manhood was to reject this denigrated, "feminized" culture.

11. See Abraham Cahan's *Yekl* for a fictionalized version of this name change.

12. Despite the ideology of America as a secular environment, the hegemonic values of our national culture are Christian. Note, for example, the insistence on Sunday as the "Day of Rest" as well as Christmas and New Year's Day as holidays sanctioned by the U.S. government.

13. Lurie, in discussion of Wittgenstein, also a self-hating Jew, makes mention of a popular European anti-Semitic metaphor, equating Jews with a malignant tumor growing in the healthy national body" (326). The image of the Jew as a disease has serious implications for Jews perceiving themselves as diseased, and these kinds of European views were often passed on to the Euro-Americans with whom the Jews came in contact within this "promised land."

14. Mark Zborowski, in *Cultural Components in Responses to Pain*, identifies Jews as different from what he calls "Old Americans" and Americanized doctors in that "patients of Jewish origin focused mainly on . . . the significance of pain in relation to their health, welfare, and eventually, the welfare of their families" (286). He states further that the Jews' responses to pain and the Jewish desire to have their families constantly present in the healing process often "provoke distrust in American culture rather than provoking sympathy" (287).

15. John Efron, in *Defenders of the Race: Jewish Doctors and Race Science* , also comments that anti-Semitic "scientific" conceptions of a Jewish type inevitably contain clear elements of perceiving "Jews as a whole as an effeminate race" (7), as I noted above. For a literary discussion of this Jewish stereotype, see Wilentz, "(Re)Teaching Hemingway: Anti-Semitism as a Thematic Device in *the Sun Also Rises*."

16. I am using Robert Farris Thompson's term "cultural preparedness," which reflects the transmission of culture throughout the African Diaspora. This concept is relevant in relation to the perhaps intangible but palpable presence of the concept of *tikkun olam* within Jewish culture.

References

Aal, Kathryn Machan. "Writing as an Indian Woman: An Interview with Paula Gunn Allen." *North Dakota Quarterly* 57. 2 (spring 1989): 148–162.

Achterberg, Jeanne. *Woman as Healer.* Boston: Shambhala, 1990.

———, and G. Frank Lawlis. *Bridges of the Bodymind: Behavioral Approaches to Health Care.* Champaign, Ill.: Institute of Personality and Ability Testing, 1980.

Adedeji, J. A. "The Egungun in the Religious Concept of the Yoruba." Adegbola, 117–136.

Adegbola, E. A. Ade, ed. *Traditional Religion in West Africa.* Ibadan: Daystar Press, 1983.

Adler, Shelley Ruth. "The Role of the Nightmare in Hmong Sudden Unexpected Nocturnal Death Syndrome: A Folkloristic Study of Belief and Health." Dissertation. University of California, Los Angeles, 1991.

Alcalá, Kathleen. *Sprits of the Ordinary.* New York: Harcourt & Brace, 1997.

Allen, Paula Gunn. "The Feminine Landscape of Leslie Marmon Silko's *Ceremony*." *Studies in American Indian Literature: Critical Essays and Course Designs.* Ed. Paula Gunn Allen. New York: MLA Publications, 1983. 127–133.

———. *Grandmothers of the Light: A Medicine Woman's Sourcebook.* Boston: Beacon Press, 1991.

———. *The Sacred Hoop: Recovering the Feminine in American Indian Traditions.* Boston: Beacon Press, 1986.

———. *The Woman Who Owned the Shadows.* San Francisco: Aunt Lute Books, 1984.

Alleyne, Mervyn. *Roots of Jamaican Culture.* London: Pluto Press, 1988.

Anaya, Rudolfo A. *Bless Me, Ultima.* New York: Warner Books, 1995.

Antler, Joyce. *The Journey Home: How Jewish Women Shaped Modern America.* New York: Schocken Books, 1998.

Appiah, Kwame Anthony. "Is the Post- in Postmodernism the Post- in Postcolonial." *Critical Inquiry* 17 (winter 1991): 336–357.

Baird, Keith E. "Guy B. Johnson Revisited." *Journal of Black Studies* 10.4 (1980): (425–435).

Bambara, Toni Cade. *Deep Sightings and Rescue Missions: Fiction, Essays, and Conversations.* New York: Pantheon Books, 1996.

———. *The Salt Eaters.* New York: Vintage, 1981.

———. "Salvation Is the Issue." Mari Evans, 41–47.

Beatson, Peter. *The Healing Tongue*. Palmerston: Studies in New Zealand Art and Society 1, 1989. (Massey University, Palmerston North)

Beck, Evelyn Torton, ed. *Nice Jewish Girls: A Lesbian Anthology*. Trumansburg, N.Y.: Crossing Press, 1982.

Belenky, Mary Field, Blythe McVicker Clinchy, Nancy Rule Goldberger, and Jill Mattuck Tarule. *Women's Ways of Knowing*. New York: Basic Books, 1986.

Bell, Robert C. "Circular Design in *Ceremony*." *American Indian Quarterly* 5.1 (1979): 47–62.

Benediktsson, Thomas E. "Reawakening of the Gods: Realism and the Supernatural in Silko and Hulme." *Critique* 33,2 (1992): 121–131.

Benjamin, Walter. *Illuminations*. Ed. Hannah Arendt. New York: Schocken Books, 1985.

Benor, Daniel. "Psychic Healing." *Alternative Medicine*. Ed. J. Warren Salmon. New York: Tavistock, 1984, 165–190.

Berman, Joan R. Saks. "A View from Rainbow Bridge: Feminist Therapist Meeting Changing Woman." *Women and Therapy* 8,4 (1989): 65–78.

Bernal, Martin. *Black Athena: The Afro-Asiatic Roots of Classical Civilization*. New Brunswick, N.J.: Rutgers University Press, 1989.

Bird, Gloria. "Towards a Decolonization of the Mind and Text 1: Leslie Marmon Silko's *Ceremony*. *Wicazo Sa Review* 9.2 (fall 1993): 1–8.

Bleier, Ruth. "Lab Coat or Klansman's Sheet." *Feminist Studies/Critical Studies*. Ed. Teresa de Lauretis. Bloomington: Indiana University Press, 1986.

Braxton, Joanne, and Andreé Nicola McLaughlin, eds. *Wild Women of the Whirlwind*. New Brunswick, N.J.: Rutgers University Press, 1990.

Bredin, Renae. "Falling into the Wrong Hands: Laguna Women and Ethnographic Striptease." *Readerly/Writerly Texts: Essays on Literature, Literary/Textual Criticism, and Pedagogy* 2,1 (fall–winter 1994): 51–68.

Brodber, Erna. "Fiction in the Scientific Procedure." Cudjoe 164–168.

———. *Jane and Louisa Will Soon Come Home*. London: New Beacon Books, 1980.

———. *Louisiana*. London: New Beacon Books, 1994.

———. *Myal*. London: New Beacon Books, 1988.

———. "Oral Sources and the Creation of a Social History of the Caribbean." *Jamaica Journal* 16,4 (1983): 2–11.

Brodkin, Karen. *How Jews Became White Folks and What That Says About Race in America*. New Brunswick, N.J.: Rutgers University Press, 1998.

Buber, Martin. *Der Jude und sein Judentum*. Joseph Meltzer Verlag, 1963.

Byerman, Keith E. "Healing Arts: Folklore and the Female Self in Toni Cade Bambara's *The Salt Eaters*." *Postscript* 5 (1988): 37–43.

Cahan, Abraham. *Yekl and the Imported Bridegroom* (1898). New York: Dover Press, 1970.

Chametzky, Jules. "Immigrant Fiction as Cultural Mediation." *Our Decentralized Literature*. Amherst: University of Massachusetts Press, 1986, 58–67.

Chandler, Zala. "Voices Beyond the Veil: An Interview of Toni Cade Bambara and Sonia Sanchez." In Braxton and McLaughlin, 342–362.

Chevannes, A. Barrington. "The Repairer of the Breach: Reverend Claudius Henry and Jamaican Society." *Ethnicity in the Americas*. Ed. Francis Henry. The Hague: Mouton, 1976. 263–289.

Clarke, John Henrik. "Foreword." Twining v–vi.

Cliff, Michelle. *Abeng*. Trumansberg, N.Y.: Crossing Press, 1984.

———. *No Telephone to Heaven*. New York: Vintage Books, 1989.

Cobham, Rhonda. "Getting Out of the Kumbla." *Race Today* 14 (December 1981/January 1982): 33–34.

Coltelli, Laura. "Leslie Marmon Silko." *Winged Words: American Indian Writers Speak*. Lincoln: University of Nebraska Press, 1990. 139–154.

———. "Re-enacting Myths and Stories, Tradition and Renewal in *Ceremony*." *Native American Literatures*. Ed. Laura Coltelli. Sioux Falls, Iowa: Forum 1 (1989): 173–183.

Cooper, Carolyn. "Afro-Jamaican Folk Elements in Brodber's *Jane and Louisa Will Soon Come Home*." In Davies 279–288.

Cosentino, Donald. "Who Is That Fellow in the Many-Colored Cap? Transformations of Eshu in Old and New World Mythologies." *Journal of American Folklore* 100, 397 (1987): 261–275.

Cudjoe, Selvyn R., ed. *Caribbean Women Writers*. Wellesley, Mass.: Calaloux, 1990.

Dale, Judith. "*the bone people*: (Not) Having It Both Ways." *Landfall* 156 39,4 (1985): 413–430.

Dangaremgba, Tsitsi. *Nervous Conditions*. London: Women's Press, 1988.

Dansey, Harry. *Maori Custom Today*. Auckland: Shortland Publications, 1971.

Dash, Julie, dir. *Daughters of the Dust*. Feature film, 1991.

Davies, Carole Boyce, and Elaine Savory Fido. *Out of the Kumbla: Caribbean Women and Literature*. Trenton, N.J.: Africa World Press, 1990.

Dever, Maryanne. "Violence as *lingua Franca*: Keri Hulme's *The Bone People*:" *World Literature Written in English* 29,2 (1989): 23–35.

Diamond, Irene, and Gloria Orenstein, eds. *Reweaving the World: The Emergence of EcoFeminism*. San Francisco: Sierra Club Books, 1990.

Dorris, Michael. *Yellow Raft on Blue Water*. New York: Warner Books, 1988.

Duff, Alan. *Once Were Warriors*. New York: Vintage Books, 1995.

Durie, M. H. "A Maori Perspective on Health." *Social Science and Medicine*. 20,5 (1985): 483–486.

Eagleton, Terry. *Literary Theory: An Introduction*. Oxford, U.K.: Basil Blackwell, 1983.

Edgell, Zee. *Beka Lamb*. Portsmouth, N.H: Heinemann, 1987.

Efron, John. *Defenders of the Race: Jewish Doctors and Race Science*. New Haven: Yale University Press, 1994.

Ellison, Ralph. *Invisible Man*. New York: Signet, 1952.

Emecheta, Buchi. *Our Own Freedom*. London: Sheba Feminist Publishers, 1981.

Erdrich, Louise. *Love Medicine*. New York: Bantam Books, 1984.

Evans, Mari, ed. *Black Women Writers (1950–1980)*. New York: Anchor Books, 1984.

Evans, Miriama. "The Politics of Maori Literature." *Meanjin* 44.3 (September 1985): 358–363.

Evasdaughter, Elizabeth N. "Leslie Marmon Silko's *Ceremony*: Healing Ethnic Hatred by Mixed Breed Laughter." *MELUS* 15.1 (spring 1988): 83–95.

Eysturoy, Annie O. "Interview with Paula Gunn Allen." *This Is About Vision: Interviews with Southwestern Writers*. Ed. William Balassi, John F. Crawford, and Annie O. Eysturoy. Albuquerque: New Mexico University Press, 1990, 95–107.

Fanon, Frantz. *Black Skin, White Masks*. Trans. Charles Lamb Markmann. New York: Grove Press, 1967.

———. *The Wretched of the Earth*. Trans. Connie Farrington. New York: Grove Press, 1968.

Fisher, Dexter, ed. "Stories and Their Tellers: A Conversation with Leslie Marmon Silko." *The Third Woman: Minority Women Writers of the US*. Ed. Dexter Fisher. Boston: Houghton, 1980.

Foster, Byron. *Heart Drum: Spirit Possession in the Garifuna Communities of Belize*. Benque Viejo, Belize: Cubola Productions, 1986.

Freespirit, Judy. "On Health and Being Jewish." *The Tribe of Dina: A Jewish Woman's Anthology*. Montpelier, Vt.: Sinister Wisdom Books, 1986.

Freud, Sigmund. *Sigmund Freud: Collected Papers IV*. Trans. Joan Riviere. New York: Basic Books, 1959.

Gabbin, Joanne. "A Laying On of Hands: Black Women Writers Exploring the Roots of Their Folk and Cultural Tradition." In Braxton, 246–263.

Gadamer, Hans-Georg. *Philosophical Hermeneutics*. Trans. David E. Linge. Los Angeles: California University Press, 1976.

Gaffney, Carmel. "Making the Net Whole: Design in Keri Hulme's *The Bone People*." *Southerly* 3 (September 1986): 293–302.

Garcia, Cristina. *Dreaming in Cuban*. New York: Ballantine Books, 1992.

Garner, Shirley Nelson, Claire Kahane, and Madelon Sprengnether, eds. *The (M)other Tongue: Essays in Feminist Psychoanalytic Interpretation*. Ithaca, N.Y.: Cornell University Press, 1985.

Gates, Henry Louis, Jr. *The Signifying Monkey: A Theory of African-American Literary Criticism*. New York: Oxford University Press, 1989.

Gay, Peter. *A Godless Jew: Freud, Atheism, and the Making of Psychoanalysis*. New Haven, Conn.: Yale University Press, 1987.

Gerulskis-Estes, Susan. *The Book of Tarot*. Dobbs Ferry, N.Y.: Morgan & Morgan, 1981.

Gilman, Charlotte Perkins. "The Yellow Wallpaper." *The Heath Anthology of American Literature*, vol. 2. Ed. Lanter et al. Lexington, Mass: D. C. Heath, 1990. 761–773.

Gilman, Sander. *Jewish Self-Hatred: Anti-Semitism and the Language of the Jews*. Baltimore: Johns Hopkins University Press, 1986.

Girard, René. *Violence and the Sacred*. Trans. Patrick Gregory. Johns Hopkins University Press, 1977, 1989.

Glick, Leonard. "Types Distinct from Our Own: Franz Boas on Jewish Identity and Assimilation." *American Anthropologist* 84 (1982): 545–565.

Goldberg, David Theo, and Michael Krausz. *Jewish Identity*. Philadelphia: Temple University Press, 1993.

Goldsmith, Peter. "Healing and Denominationalism on the Georgia Coast." *Southern Quarterly* 23,3 (1985): 83–102.

Gogel, Edward L., and James S. Terry. "Medicine as Interpretation: The Uses of Literary Metaphors and Methods." *Journal of Medicine and Philosophy* 12 (1987): 205–217.

Gornick, Vivian. Introduction. Sinclair, *Wasteland* xii–xiii.

Grace, Patricia. *Baby No-Eyes*. Honolulu: University of Hawaii Press, 1998.

———. *Cousins*. Honolulu: University of Hawaii Press, 1998.

Grossinger, Richard. *Planet Medicine: From Stone Age Shamanism to Post-Industrial Healing*. Berkeley, Calif.: New Atlantic Books, 1980.

Hall, Gwendolyn M. *Africans in Colonial Louisiana*. Baton Rouge: Louisiana State University Press, 1992.

Harding, Sandra. "The Curious Coincidence of Feminine and African Moralities." *Women and Moral Theory*. Ed. Eva Kittay and Diane Meyers. Totowa, N.J.: Rowman, 1986. 299–305.

———, ed. *The "Racial" Economy of Science: Toward a Democratic Future*. Bloomington: Indiana University Press, 1993.

———. "Science and Black People." Editorial in *The Black Scholar*. Harding 456–457.

Harris, Wilson. "The Complexity of Freedom." *Explorations: A Selection of Talks and Articles 1966–1981*. Mundelstrup, Denmark: Dangaroo, 1988, 57–67.

———*Palace of the Peacock*. London: Faber & Faber, 1960.

Helman, Cecil G. *Culture, Health and Illness*. London: Wright, 1990.

Herskovits, Melville J. *The Myth of the Negro Past*. (1941). Boston: Beacon Press, 1958.

Hodge, Merle. "Challenges of the Struggle for Sovereignty: Changing the World versus Writing Stories." In Cudjoe 202–208.

———. *Crick Crack Monkey*. Portsmouth, N.H.: Heinemann, 1970.

———. *For the Love of Laetitia*. New York: Farrar Strauss & Giroux, 1993.

Hogan, Linda. *Solar Storms*. New York: Scribner, 1995.

Holloway, Joseph E. *Africanisms in American Culture*. Bloomington: Indiana University Press, 1990.

Holman, C. Hugh. *A Handbook to Literature*, 3rd ed. Indianapolis: Bobbs-Merrill, 1973.

Howe, Irving. *World of Our Fathers: The Journey of the East European Jews to America and the Life They Found and Made*. New York: Budget Book Service, 1994.

Hull, Gloria. "What It Is I Think She's Doing Anyhow." *Conjuring*. Ed. Marjorie Pryse and Hortense Spillers. Bloomington: Indiana University Press, 1985, 216–232.

Hulme, Keri. *the bone people*. New York: Viking Penguin, 1983.

———. "Mauri: An Introduction to Bicultural Poetry in New Zealand." *Only Connect: Literary Perspectives East and West*. Ed. Guy Amirthanayagam and S. C. Harrex. Adelaide and Honolulu: CRNLE, 1981. 290–310.

———. "Myth, Omen, Ghost and Dream. *Poetry of the Pacific Region: Proceedings of the CRNLE/SPACLALS Conference.* Adelaide, Australia: CRNLE, 1984.

———. *Te Kaihau: The Windeater.* Wellington, New Zealand: Victoria Press, 1986, 193–206.

Humphrey, Leslie. "A Myriad of Circles: The Kumbla Image in Erna Brodber's *Jane and Louisa Will Soon Come Home.*" *ACLALS Bulletin* 8,1 (1989): 29–38.

Hurston, Zora Neale. *Their Eyes Were Watching God* (1937). Urbana-Champaign: University of Illinois Press, 1982.

Ihimaera, Witi. *The Matriarch.* Portsmouth, N.H.: Heinemann, 1986.

———. *Whanau.* Portsmouth, N.H.: Heinemann, 1974.

———, and D. S. Long. "Introduction: Contemporary Maori Writing." *Into the World of Light: An Anthology of Maori Writings.* Auckland, New Zealand: Heinemann, 1982.

Jay, Gregory S. "The End of American Literature: Towards MultiCultural Practice." *College English* 53,3 (1991): 264–281.

Jones, David E. *Sanapia: Comanche Medicine Woman.* New York: Holt, Rinehart & Winston, 1972.

Jones, Gayl. *Eva's Man.* Boston: Beacon Press, 1987.

———. *The Healing.* Boston: Beacon Press, 1998.

Katon, Wayne, Arthur Kleinman, and Gary Rosen. "Depression and Somatization: A Review, Part 1." *American Journal of Medicine* 72 (January 1982): 127–135.

Kemp, Yakemi. "Woman and Womanchild: Bonding and Selfhood in Three West Indian Novels." *Sage* 2,1 (1985): 24–27.

Kincaid, Jamaica. *Annie John.* New York: Farrar Strauss & Giroux, 1985.

King, Michael, ed. *Te Ao Hurihuri: The World Moves On.* Wellington, New Zealand: Hicks, Smith and Sons, 1975.

Klein, Dennis B. *Jewish Origins of the Psychoanalytic Movement.* Chicago: University of Chicago Press, 1981.

Kleinman, Arthur. *The Illness Narratives: Suffering, Healing, and the Human Condition.* New York: Basic Books, 1988.

Krieger, Nancy, and Mary Bassett. "The Health of Black Folk: Disease, Class, and Ideology in Science." In Harding, 161–169.

Lacan, Jacques. *Écrits: A Selection.* Trans. Alan Sheridan. New York: W. W. Norton, 1977.

Lamming, George. *The Pleasures of Exile.* 1960. London: Allison & Busby, 1984.

Lee, Valerie. *Granny Midwives and Black Women Writers.* New York: Routledge, 1996.

Lichstein, Peter R. "Rootwork from a Clinician's Perspective." *Herbal and Medical Medicine: Traditional Healing Today.* Ed. James Kirkland, Holly F. Mathews, C. W. Sullivan III, and Karen Baldwin. Durham, N.C.: Duke University Press, 1992.

Lincoln, Kenneth. *Native American Renaissance.* Sacramento: University of California Press, 1985.

Littlefield, Daniel C. *Rice and Slaves: Ethnicity and the Slave Trade in Colonial South Carolina.* Baton Rouge: Louisiana State University Press, 1981.

Lorde, Audre. *Zami: A New Spelling of My Name.* New York: Crossing Press, 1982.

Lurie, Yuval. "Jews as a Metaphysical Species" *Philosophy* 64 (1989): 323–347.

MacCannell, Juliet Flower. *Figuring Lacan.* Lincoln: University of Nebraska Press, 1986.

Magubane, Bernard Makhosezwe. *The Ties That Bind: African-American Consciousness of Africa.* Trenton, N.J.: Africa World Press, 1987.

Mais, Roger. *Black Lightning.* Portsmouth, N.H: Heinemann, 1955.

———. *Brother Man.* Portsmouth, N.H.: Heinemann, 1954.

Makinde, M. Akin. *African Philosophy, Culture, and Traditional Medicine.* Athens: Ohio University Monographs in International Studies, African Series 53, 1988.

Malamud, Bernard. *The Tenants.* New York: Farrar Strauss & Giroux, 1971.

Maracle, Lee. *Ravensong.* Vancouver: Press Gang Publishers, 1993.

Marcus, Jane. "Still Practice/Wrested Alphabet: Toward a Feminist Aesthetic," *Tulsa Studies in Women's Literature* 3,1–2 (1984): 79–97.

Marsden, Maori. "God, Man, and Universe: A Maori View." In King, 191–218.

Marshall, Paule. *Brown Girl, Brownstones.* 1959. Old Westbury, N.Y.: Feminist Press, 1981.

———. "From the Poets in the Kitchen." *Reena.* Old Westbury, N.Y.: Feminist Press, 1983.

———. *Praisesong for the Widow.* New York: Putnam, 1983.

McBride, James. *Color of Water: A Black Man's Tribute to His White Mother.* New York: Riverhead Books, 1996.

Mehta, Brinda. "The Shaman Woman, Resistance, and the Politics of Transformation: A Tribute to Ma Cia in Simone Schwarz-Bart's *The Bridge of Beyond.*" *Sacred Possessions: Vodou, Santería, Obeah, and the Caribbean.* Ed. Margarite Fernandez Olmos and Lizabeth Paravisini-Gebert. New Brunswick, N.J.: Rutgers University Press, 1997. 231–247.

Memmi, Albert. *Pillar of Salt.* Boston, Mass: Beacon Press, 1992.

Metzger, Deena. "Healing the Planet/Healing Ourselves." *World Futures* 31 (1991): 197–204.

Miller, Arthur. *Broken Glass.* New York: Penguin USA, 1995.

Mitchell, Carol. "*Ceremony* as Ritual." *American Indian Quarterly* 5,1 (1979): 27–35.

Mitchell, Faith. *Hoodoo Medicine: Sea Island Herbal Remedies.* Berkeley, Calif.: Reed, Canon & Johnson, 1978.

Momaday, N. Scott. *House Made of Dawn.* New York: Harper & Row, 1968.

———. *The Man Made of Words.* New York: St. Martin's Press, 1997.

Morgan, Sally. *My Place.* South Fremantle, Australia: Fremantle Arts Centre Press, 1987.

Morrison, Toni. *Beloved.* New York: Knopf, 1987.

———. "Rootedness: The Ancestor as Foundation." Mari Evans, 339–345.

———. *Song of Solomon.* New York: NAL, 1977.

———. *Sula.* New York, Bantam, 1973.

Naylor, Gloria. *Mama Day.* New York: Vintage Books, 1989.

Nelson-McDermott, Catherine. "Myal-ing Criticism: Beyond Colonizing Dialectics." *ARIEL* 24,4 (1993): 53–67.

Nwapa, Flora. *The Lake Goddess*. Unpublished manuscript.

O'Callaghan, Evelyn. "Interior Schisms Dramatized: The Treatment of the 'Mad' Woman in the Works of Some Female Caribbean Novelists." Davies and Fido, 89–110.

Paley, Grace. *Enormous Changes at the Last Minute*. New York: Noonday Press, 1979.

Parsons, Clare D. F. "Notes on Maori Sickness Knowledge and Healing Practices." *Healing Practices in the South Pacific*. Ed. Clare D. F. Parsons. Honolulu: Institute of Polynesian Studies, 1985, 213–234.

Peek, Andrew. "An Interview with Keri Hulme." *New Literatures Review* 20 (winter 1990): 1–11.

Perrone, Bobette, H. Henrietta Stockel, and Victoria Krueger. *Medicine Women, Curanderas, and Women Doctors*. Norman: Oklahoma University Press, 1989.

Philip, Marlene Nourbese. "Earth and Sound: The Place of Poetry." First International Conference on Women Writers from the Caribbean, Wellesley, Mass., April 9, 1988.

Phillips, Caryl. *The European Tribe*. New York: Vintage Books, 1993.

———. *The Nature of Blood*. New York: Vintage Books, 1997.

Plant, Richard. "The Ghetto Within." *New Republic* 10 June 1946: 84.

Quinby, Lee. "EcoFeminism and the Politics of Resistance." Diamond and Orenstein, 122–127.

Reed, Ishmael. *Mumbo Jumbo*. New York: Scribner's, 1970.

Reichert, Gladys A. "Distinctive Features of Navaho Religion." *Southwestern Journal of Anthropology* 1 (1945): 199–220.

———. *Navaho Religion: A Study in Symbolism*. New York: Pantheon Books, 1950.

Reik, Theodore. *Jewish Wit*. New York: Camut Press, 1962.

Remen, Rachel Naomi. *Kitchen Table Wisdom: Stories That Heal*. New York: Riverhead Books, 1997.

Rhys, Jean. *Wide Sargasso Sea*. New York: W. W. Norton, 1966.

Rich, Adrienne. "Yom Kippur 1984." *Your Native Land, Your Life*. New York: W. W. Norton, 1986. 75–78.

Robinson, Beverly J. "Africanisms and the Study of Folklore." *Africanisms in American Culture*. Ed. Joseph E. Holloway. Bloomington: Indiana University Press, 1990, 211–224.

Root, Maria P. P. "Resolving 'Other' Status: Identity Development of Biracial Individuals." *Women and Therapy* 9,1/2 (1990): 185–205.

Roth, Philip. *Portnoy's Complaint*. New York: Vintage Books, 1994.

Rothman, Stanley, and Phillip Isenberg. "Freud and Jewish Marginality." *Encounter* 43 (December 1974): 46–54.

Ruppert, James. "The Reader's Lessons in *Ceremony*." *The Arizona Quarterly* (1988): 78–85.

Sachdev, Perminder S. "*Mana, Tapu, Noa*: Maori Cultural Constructs with Medical and Psycho-social Relevance." *Psychological Medicine* 19,4 (1989): 959–969.

———. "Psychiatric Illness in the New Zealand Maori." *Australian and New Zealand Journal of Psychiatry* 23,4 (1989): 529–541.

Salaam, Kalamu ya. "Searching for the Mother Tongue: An Interview with Toni Cade Bambara." *First World* 2,4 (1980): 48–53.

Sandberg, Elisabeth. *Jo Sinclair: A Critical Biography*. Dissertation. University of Massachusetts, 1985. Ann Arbor, Mich.: University Microfilm (UMI), 1985.

Sandner, Donald F. "Navaho Medicine." *Human Nature* (July 1978): 54–62.

Scarberry-Garcia, Susan. *Landmarks of Healing: A Study of House Made of Dawn*. Alburquerque: University of New Mexico Press, 1990.

———. "Memory as Medicine: The Power of Recollection in *Ceremony*." *American Indian Quarterly* 5,1 (1979): 19–26.

Schwarz-Bart, Simone. *The Bridge of Beyond*. Trans. Barbara Bray. Portsmouth, N.H.: Heinemann, 1982.

Secundy, Marion Gray, ed. *Trials, Tribulations, and Celebrations: African American Perspectives on Health, Illness, Aging and Loss*. Yarmouth, Maine: Intercultural Press, 1992.

Segal, Lore. *Her First American: A Novel*. New York: New Press, 1994.

Sewell, Elizabeth. "Preliminary Reflections on Magic and Medicine." Trautmann, 80–94.

Silko, Leslie Marmon. *Almanac of the Dead*. New York: Penguin, 1992.

———. *Ceremony*. New York: Viking Press, 1977.

———. *Gardens in the Dunes*. New York: Simon & Schuster, 1998.

———. "Grandmother Storyteller: Leslie Silko." Lincoln, 222–250.

———. "Landscape, History and the Pueblo Imagination." *Antaeus* 57 (1986): 83–94.

———. "Language and Literature from a Pueblo Indian Perspective." *English Literature: Opening Up the Canon*. Ed. Leslie Fiedler and Houston A. Bake, Jr. Baltimore: Johns Hopkins University Press. 1981, 54–72.

———. "Tony's Story." *Storyteller*. New York: Arcade, 1981, 123–129.

———. *Yellow Woman and a Beauty of the Spirit: Essays on Native American Life Today*. New York: Simon & Schuster, 1996.

Simmons, D. R. *Whakairo: Maori Tribal Art*. Auckland, New Zealand: Oxford University Press, 1985.

Sims, Barbara B. "Facts in the Life of a Black Mississippi-Louisiana Healer." *Mississippi Folklore Register* 15,2 (1981): 63–70.

Sinclair, Jo. *Anna Teller*. New York: Feminist Press, 1992.

———. *The Changelings* (1955). New York: Feminist Press, 1983.

———. *The Seasons: Death and Transfiguration*. New York: Feminist Press, 1992.

———. *Wasteland* (1946). Philadelphia: Jewish Publication Society, 1987.

Sow, I. *Anthropological Structures of Madness in Black Africa*. Trans. Joyce Diamanti. New York: International Universities Press, 1980.

St. Andrews, B. A. "Healing the Witchery: Medicine in Silko's *Ceremony*." *Arizona Quarterly* (1988): 86–94.

Stambolian, George. "Interview with Eric Bentley." *Homosesexualities and French Literatures: Cultural Contexts/Critical Texts*. Ed. Elaine Marks and George Stambolian. Ithaca, N.Y.: Cornell University Press, 1990, 122–140.

Stanford, Ann Folwell. "Mechanisms of Disease: African American Women, Social Pathologies, and the Limits of Medicine." *NWSA Journal* 6,1 (spring 1994): 28–47.

Stein, Diane. *The Woman's Book of Healing*. St. Paul, Minn.: Llewellyn Publications, 1991.

Stepan, Nancy Leys, and Sander L. Gilman. "Appropriating the Idioms of Science: The Rejection of Scientific Racism." In Harding, 170–193.

Swan, Edith. "Healing via the Sunwise Cycle in Silko's *Ceremony*." *American Indian Quarterly* 12,4 (1988): 313–328.

———. "Laguna Symbolic Geography and Silko's *Ceremony*." *American Indian Quarterly* 12,2 (1988): 229–249.

Tamahori, Lee, dir. *Once Were Warriors*. Feature film, 1995.

Tate, Claudia. "Toni Cade Bambara." *Black Women Writers at Work*. New York: Continuum, 1983, 12–38.

Taylor, Apirana. *He Rau Aroha: A Hundred Leaves of Love*. New York: Penguin, 1985.

Thompson, Robert Farris. *The Flash of the Spirit*. New York: Random House, 1983.

Tiffin, Helen. "The Metaphor of Anancy in Caribbean Literature." *Myth and Metaphor*. Ed. Robert Selleck. Adelaide, Australia: Center for Research in the New Literatures in English, 1982, 15–52.

Trautmann, Joanne, ed. *Healing Arts in Dialogue: Medicine and Literature*. Carbondale: Southern Illinois University Press, 1981.

Traylor, Eleanor. "Music as Theme: The Jazz Mode in the Works of Toni Cade Bambara." Mari Evans, 58–70.

Tseng, Wen-Shing, and Jing Hsu. "Suggestions for Intercultural Psychotherapy." *Health and the Human Condition: Perspectives in Medical Anthropology*. Ed. Michael H. Logan and Edward E. Hunt. North Scituate, Mass.: Doxbury Press, 1978, 294–298.

Turner, Lorenzo Dow. *Africanisms in the Gullah Dialect* (1949). Ann Arbor: University of Michigan Press, 1974.

Twining, Mary A., and Keith E. Baird, eds. *Sea Island Roots: African Presence in the Carolinas and Georgia*. Trenton, N.J.: Africa World Press, 1991.

Uffen, Ellen Serlen. "John Brown (né Jake Braunowitz) of *Wasteland* of Jo Sinclair (née Ruth Seid)." *Midwestern Miscellany XVI*. Ed. David D. Anderson. East Lansing, Mich.: Midwestern, 1988.

Voyce, Malcolm. "Maori Healers in New Zealand: The Tohunga Suppression Act 1907." *Oceania* 60 (December 1989): 99–123.

Vrettos, Athena. "Curative Domains: Women, Healing, and History in Black Women's Narratives." *Women's Studies* 16 (1989): 455–473.

Walker, Alice. *The Color Purple*. New York: Harcourt, 1982.

———. *In Search of Our Mothers' Gardens*. New York: Harcourt, 1983.

———. *Meridian*. New York: Harcourt, 1976.

———. *The Third Life of Grange Copeland*. New York: Harcourt, 1970.

Walker, Margaret. *Jubilee*. New York: Mariner Books, 1999.

Walker-Johnson, Joyce. "Autobiography, History, and the Novel: Erna Brodber's *Jane and Louisa Will Soon Come Home*." *Journal of West Indian Literature* 3,1 (January 1989): 47–59.

Walker, Ranginui. "Marae: A Place to Stand." King, 21–34.

Walters, Ronald W. *Pan Africanism in the African Diaspora*. Detroit: Wayne State University Press, 1993.

Wambutda, Daniel. "Ancestors—The Living Dead." *Adegbola*, 129–136.

Warner Lewis, Maureen. "The Nkoyu: Spirit Messengers of the Kumina." *Savacou: A Journal of the Caribbean Artists Movement*, 1977: 57–78.

Washington, Margaret. "Cultural Transmission and Female Diviners in Gullah Slave Society." Unpublished paper, Cornell University.

———. *"A Peculiar People": Slave Religion and Community-Culture Among the Gullahs*. New York: New York University Press, 1988.

Wedenoja, William. "Mothering and the Practice of Balm in Jamaica." *Woman as Healer: Cross-Cultural Perspectives*. Ed. Carol Shepherd McClain. New Brunswick, N. J.: Rutgers University Press, 1989.

Weinberg, Sydney Stahn. *The World of Our Mothers: The Lives of Jewish Immigrant Women*. Chapel Hill: University of North Carolina Press, 1988.

Welch, James. *Winter in the Blood*. New York: Penguin, 1992.

Wideman, John Edgar. *Damballah*. New York: Avon, 1981.

Wilentz, Gay. *Binding Cultures*. Bloomington: Indiana University Press, 1992.

———. "Civilizations Underneath": African Heritage as Cultural Discourse in Toni Morrison's *Song of Solomon*." *African American Review* 26,1 (1992): 61–76.

———. "Cultural Mediation and the Immigrant's Daughter: Anzia Yezierska's *Bread Givers*." *MELUS* 17,3 (1991–92): 33–41.

———. "English is a Foreign Anguish: Caribbean Writers and the Disruption of the Colonial Canon." *Decolonizing Tradition: New Approaches to Twentieth Century British Literary Canons*. Ed. Karen Lawrence. Urbana-Champaign: Illinois University Press, 1992, 261–278.

———. "If You Surrender to the Air: Legends of Flight and Resistance in African American Literature." *MELUS* 16,1 (spring 1989–90): 21–32.

———. "(Re)Teaching Hemingway: Anti-Semitism as a Thematic Device in *The Sun Also Rises*." *College English* 52,2 (1990): 186–193.

Williams, Mark. *Leaving the Highway: Six Contemporary New Zealand Novelists*. Auckland, New Zealand: Auckland University Press, 1990.

Williams, Raymond. *Marxism and Literature*. New York: Oxford University Press, 1977.

———. *Problems in Materialism and Culture*. London: NLB, 1980.

Yezierska, Anzia. *Bread Givers* (1925). New York: Persea, 1975.

———. *Salome of the Tenements* (1923). Urbana-Champaign: Illinois University Press, 1996.

Ywahoo, Dhyani. "Dhyani Ywahoo: Priestcraft Holder of the Ani Gadoah Clan, Tsalagi (Cherokee) Nation." In Perrone, et al., 57–82.

Zanger, Jules. "On Not Making It in America." *Midcontinent American Studies* (spring 1976): 39–48.

Zborowski, Mark. *Cultural Components in Responses to Pain*. New York: Irvington Publishers, 1993.

Zimra, Clarissa. "W/Righting His/tory: Versions of Things Past in Contemporary Caribbean Women Writers." *Explorations: Essays in Comparative Literature*. Ed. Mafoto Veda. Lankam, Md.: University Press of America, 1984, 227–252.

Index

Note: *n* refers to information in a note.

"A Drift in a Dream" (Hulme), 131
"A Maori Perspective on Health" (Durie), 113
abeng, defined, 175
Abeng (Cliff), 34, 46
Achterberg, Jeanne, 12–14, 19, 61, 87, 114
African American women writers, 59, 71
African Diaspora, role of traditional healing in, 30–31
African Philosophy, Culture, and Traditional Medicine (Makinde), 9–10, 18
African-based culture, role of grandmother in, 114
African-based healing practices, 9–10, 58; ancestor presence in, 59–60; basic tenets of, 70; divination in, 70–71; oral medicines, use of, 18–19, 84. *See also Jane and Louisa Will Soon Come Home; Salt Eaters*
Africanisms in the Gullah Dialect (Turner), 56
"Afro-Jamaican Folk Elements in Brodber's *Jane and Louisa*" (Cooper), 34
"alienated self," 150–151
Allen, Paula Gunn, 85, 87, 98, 99

Alleyne, Mervyn C., 19, 31, 32, 51
Almanac of the Dead (Silko), 94, 96, 105
Amerindian healing practices: health and illness, inclusive concept of, 83–84; power of words in, 84–85; storytelling, use of, 20
Anancy (West African Akan trickster), 37–38
"Ancestors—The Living Dead" (Wambutda), 59
Anna Teller (Sinclair), 150, 155
Annie John (Kincaid), 34
Anthropological Structures of Madness in Black Africa (Sow), 30, 59
Antler, Joyce, 147
Aotearoa, 111
ascent/descent, concept of, 6, 131

Baby No-Eyes (Grace), 132
Baird, Keith E., 58
Balm healers, 43, 44, 61, 174n4
Bambara, Toni Cade, 3, 73. *See also Salt Eaters*
Barnwell, 177n12
Beatson, Peter, 109–110, 114, 135
Beck, Evelyn Torton, 159
Becker, Rafael, 161
Beka Lamb (Edgell), 30
Belenky, Mary Field, 4–5

Bell, Robert, 85
Beloved (Morrison), 61
Benediktsson, Thomas E., 129–130
Benor, Daniel, 70
Berman, Joan R. Saks, 95
binary oppositions, 4, 5, 7
Binding Cultures (Wilentz), 176nn2,5
Bird, Gloria, 99
Black Lightning (Mais), 125
Black women writers, 27–28, 54, 57
Bleier, Ruth, 118
Bless Me, Ultima (Anaya), 96
Boas, Franz, 99
bone people (Hulme), 40, 48, 66, 70, 88, 91, 93, 95, 97, 107, 170; ascent/descent in, 131; assimilation in, 118, 122; biracial heritage in, 134; creative art in, 126–127, 164; cultural identity, and biology in, 122; grandmother, role of, 120, 121, 128, 130; inclusiveness of, 130; kaumatua (male healer) in, 10; mauriora, concept of, 130; metonym, use of, 127, 134; prophecy in, 127–128, 129, 134; self-hate in, 119, 120; sexual identity in, 134; tapu in, 110–111, 116, 125–126, 130; tumors, as cultural disease in, 40, 123, 133; violence in, 119, 120, 121, 124–125, 130–131, 132; whanau, concept of, 113–114, 116, 120, 122, 130, 131, 134, 136
Book of Lights (Potok), 101
Book of Tarot (Gerulskis-Estes), 125
Brathwaite, Edward, 33, 36
Bread Givers (Yezierska), 147
Bridge of Beyond (Schwarz-Bart), 29

Bridges of the Bodymind (Achterberg and Lawlis), 16, 19
Brodber, Erna, 3, 75, 83. *See also Jane and Louisa Will Soon Come Home*
Brodkin, Karen, 143
Broken Glass (Miller), 149
Brother Man (Mais), 43
Buber, Martin, 148
bulimia, 39
Byerman, Keith, 74

Cahan, Abraham, 143
Caribbean women writers, 59
Caribbean writers, and English language, 32–33, 35
Carpentier, Alejo, 117
"Carver" (Taylor), 109
Ceremony (Silko), 39, 47, 63, 66, 74, 113, 114, 118, 120–121, 122, 135, 136, 170; assimilation in, 91, 92, 103, 107; atom bomb metaphor in, 10, 104, 106; biracial identity in, 96; conventional healing in, 89–90, 91; diseased storytelling in, 93–94; evocation stage of healing in, 89; focus of, 82; ghost sickness in, 90–91; identification stage of healing in, 89, 97–98; inclusiveness of, 10, 87–88; legends, reformulation of, 105; liquor, as medicine, 93; maternal, reconnection with, 104; purification stage of healing in, 88–89, 92–93; grandmother, role of, 128; self-hate in, 91, 92; traditional healing chants in, 89; transformation stage of healing in, 89, 100–102; witchery as metaphor in, 83
Chametzky, Jules, 150

Changelings (Sinclair), 150, 155, 158–159
Chicano/a writers, 96
circular narratives, 50
Civil Rights Movement, 176n3
Clarke, John Hendrik, 56
classical narrative pattern, 15
Cliff, Michele, 28
Color of Water (McBride), 157
Color Purple (Walker), 82
Coltelli, Laura, 93, 99
"Complexity of Freedom" (Harris), 51–52
constructed knowledge, 4–5, 11
conventional medicine model, 11
Cooper, Carolyn, 34, 41, 43
Cosentino, Donald, 60
Crick Crack Monkey (Hodge), 34, 36, 46
cultural identity, 6
cultural illness, 1, 2, 141, 171
"Cultural Mediation and the Immigrant's Daughter" (Wilentz), 150
cultural self-loathing, 2, 136
"Cultural Transmission and Female Diviners in Gullah Slave Society" (Washington), 61, 70
culture, defining, 5–6
Culture, Health, and Illness (Helman), 8
curendaras, 173n4

Dandicat, Edwidge, 28
Dangaremgba, Tsitsi, 90, 105
Dash, Julie, 57, 58
Daughters of the Dust (Dash), 58, 59
depressive disorders, 42
Dever, Maryanne, 121, 124
divination, 61–62, 70–71
domestic violence, 177n11
Dreaming in Cuban (Garcia), 28

Du Bois, W.E.B., 152
dual heritage, 111
Durie, M. H., 113, 119

Eagleton, Terry, 3, 15, 17, 152
Emecheta, Buchi, 51
"End of American Literature" (Jay), 142
English language, limitations of, 32–33, 35, 55–56
Esu-Elegba, 176n4
ethnicity, 6, 143
European Tribe (Phillips), 131
Evans, Miriama, 112
Eva's Man (Jones, Gayl), 71
Eysturoy, Annie, 87

Fanon, Frantz, 43
feminism, and women's culture, 14
fiction, as tool for political protest, 34
"Fiction in the Scientific Procedure" (Brodber), 28–29
Freud, Sigmund, 1, 15, 19, 141, 145–146, 166, 170, 171
"Freud and Jewish Marginality" (Rothman and Isenberg), 145
"From the Poets in the Kitchen," 32

Gadamer, George, 7
Gaffney, Carmel, 117
Garden in the Dunes (Silko), 96, 105
Gay, Peter, 148
Geechie. *See* Gullah
Geller, Ruth, 159
Georgia, slavery in, 56–57
Gilman, Sander, 146, 148, 153, 164, 167
"God, Man and Universe" (Marsden), 115
Gogel, Edward L., 20
Goldberg, David T., 142

Goldsmith, Peter, 60–61
Gornick, Vivian, 166
Grace, Patricia, 109, 112
Grandmother Spider (Native
   American), 38, 178n1
Grossinger, Richard, 9, 16, 19–
   20, 21, 31, 142, 169
Gullah, 56–57

Harding, Sandra, 65
Harris, Denise, 28
Harris, Wilson, 33, 51
healing, cultural dimensions of:
   biomedical model of healing,
   7–8; biopsychosocial model
   of healing, 7–8; biotechnical
   model of healing, 8–9; Laguna
   Pueblo and Navajo healing,
   10; Maori healing, 10, 85,
   111, 113, 114, 115. *See also*
   African-based healing
   practices
Healing Arts in Dialogue
   (Trautmann), 18
Healing, The (Jones), 71
"Healing the Planet/Healing
   Ourselves" (Metzger), 2, 136
"Healing the Witchery," 83, 106
Healing Tongue (Beatson), 109–
   110, 114
Heller, Joseph, 152
Helman, Cecil G., 8
historical scientificism, bias of,
   11, 12
Hmong people, ghost sickness
   and, 179n9
Hodge, Merle, 28, 34, 37
*Hoodoo Medicine: Sea Island
   Herbal Remedies* (Mitchell),
   58
"Hooks and Feelers" (Hulme),
   125
House Made of Dawn
   (Momaday), 22, 82, 87, 89,
   93, 119

*How the Jews Became White
   Folks* (Brodkin), 143
Howe, Irving, 145
Hsu, Jing, 156, 157
Hulme, Keri, 3, 66, 75, 88, 105.
   See also bone people
humor, in healing, 72
Humphrey, Leslie, 44
Hurston, Zora Neale, 54

identity: African concepts of, 30;
   Native American concepts of,
   92; Jewish concepts of, 142–
   143
Igbo, 57
Ihimaera, Witi, 109, 110, 112
Ilness Narratives (Kleinman), 7–
   8, 16
"Immigrant Fiction as Cultural
   Mediation" (Chametzky), 150
"Interior Schisms Dramatized"
   (O'Callaghan), 29–30
Into the World of Light
   (Ihimaera and Long), 110
Invisible Man (Ellison), 90, 118
Isenberg, Philip, 145

Jackson-Opoku, Sandra, 27–28
*Jane and Louisa Will Soon
   Come Home* (Brodber), 64,
   95, 133–134, 154, 170;
   Anancy figure in, 38, 43, 44;
   ancestors/relatives, role in
   healing, 36–37, 44–48, 49–50,
   120, 135; becoming, notion
   of, 51, 52; community effects
   of the healing, 50; kumbla, as
   metaphor, 35, 37–38, 39, 44–
   46, 50, 78; language conflict
   in, 36–37; metaphor, use of,
   35–36; metonymy, use of, 40;
   naming/calling out in, 48;
   racism in, 39–40; Rastafarian
   culture in, 32, 43; reconcilia-
   tion in, 48–49; ring-game

song, as metaphor, 49;
sexuality/sexual identity in,
38–39; vomiting, as meta-
phor, 39–40
Jane Eyre (Brontë), 29
Jay, Gregory, 142
Jew (Buber), 148
Jewish culture: as "other," 142;
psychoanalytic movement,
effect on, 145–146; role of
men/women in, 146, 147
Jewish identity, 142–143
Jewish Identity (Goldberg and
Krausz), 6, 142
Jewish language, 146
*Jewish Origins of the Psycho-
analytic Movement* (Klein),
145
Jewish passing, 182n7
Jewish self-hate, 112
Jewish Self-Hatred (Gilman),
146
Jewish Wit (Reik), 141
Jews: African antecedents of
history of, 181n3; marginal-
ity of, 174n7; stereotypes of,
183n13. *See also Wasteland*
Jones, Gayl, 71
*Journey Home: Jewish Women
and the American Century*
(Antler), 147
Judaism, intellectual, 147–148
Jubilee (Walker), 54

"Keresan Texts" (Boas), 99
Kincaid, Jamaica, 33
Kitchen Table Wisdom (Remen),
144–145
Klein, Dennis, 145
Kleinman, Arthur, 7–8, 9, 10,
17, 21
Krueger, Victoria, 11, 20
Kumina, 175n7

"Lab Coat or Klansman's Sheet"
(Bleier), 118

Lacan, Jacques, 150, 152
Laguna Pueblo healing practices,
10
Lake Goddess (Nwapa), 71
Lamming, George, 33
Landmarks of Healing
(Scarberry-Garcia), 82
"Landscape, History, and Pueblo
Imagination" (Silko), 105
"Language and Literature from a
Pueblo Indian Perspective"
(Silko), 107–108
Lawlis, G. Frank, 19
Lee, Valerie, 71
Lerner, Gerda, 13
Lewis, Maureen Warner, 36–37
Lewisohn, Ludwig, 146
Lichstein, Peter, 8, 9
Lincoln, Kenneth, 88
literature, as a healing art, 15–
21; literary tools, 16–18; oral
medicines, 18–20;
storytelling, uses of, 20;
sustained narrative, 15–16
Literary Theory (Eagleton), 15
Long, D. S., 110
Lorde, Audre, 72
Louisiana (Brodber), 28, 40, 51, 63
Love Medicine (Erdrich), 89
Love of Laetitia (Hodge), 34

magical realism, 117
Makinde, M. Akin, 9–10, 15, 18–
19, 21, 32, 84
"Making the Net Whole"
(Gaffney), 117
male healers, 12, 70, 95
Mama Day (Naylor), 58, 69, 70
Man Made of Words (Momaday),
84
"Mana, Tapu, Noa" (Sachdev), 115
Maori authors, 110
Maori healing practices, 10, 85,
111, 113, 114, 115. *See also
bone people*

Maori health, components of, 10
Maori language, richness of, 110, 179n1
Maoritanga, 110, 114
Marsden, Maori, 115
Marshall, Paule, 32, 57, 64, 89
Marx, Karl, 63
Matriarch (Ihimaera), 129
"Mauri" (Hulme), 111
"Mechanisms of Disease" (Stanford), 62
medical anthropology, 3, 8, 9
"Medicine as Interpretation" (Gogel and Terry), 20
Medicine Women, Curanderas, and Women Doctors (Perrone, Stockel, and Krueger), 11, 20, 83
"Memory as Medicine" (Scarberry-Garcia), 90
mental illness, female, 29–30
Meridian (Walker), 63
"Metaphor of Anancy in Caribbean Literature" (Tiffin), 33
Metzger, Deena, 2, 3, 23, 81, 136
mind/body split, in Western medicine, 1–2, 8, 19, 84
Mitchell, Carol, 88
Mitchell, Faith, 58
Mohammed, Abdul Jan, 76, 136
Momaday, N. Scott, 22, 84
Morgan, Sally, 118
Morrison, Toni, 3, 27–28, 57, 59
"Mothering and the Practice of Balm in Jamaica" (Wedenoja), 44
Mumbo Jumbo (Reed), 60
My First American (Segal), 158
My Place (Morgan), 118, 121
Myal (Brodber), 28, 41, 44, 51
myalists, 28, 44
"Myth, Omen, Ghost and Dream" (Hulme), 115

Nagel, Fannie Brandeis, 147
nation language, 36
Native American culture: Asian culture, link to, 90; grandmother, role in, 114; women, role in, 87. *See also* Amerindian healing practices; *Ceremony*
Native American literature, post-World War II, 89–90
Native American Renaissance (Lincoln), 92
Nature of Blood (Phillips), 131
Navajo chantways, 88
Navajo healing practices, 10
Navajo religion, 84–85
Naylor, Gloria, 27–28, 57, 58, 69
Nervous Conditions (Dangarembga), 27, 39, 90, 105
Nice Jewish Girls (Beck), 159
No Telephone to Heaven (Cliff), 40
novel, as sustained narrative, 15–16

obeah, 174n4
O'Callaghan, Evelyn, 29–30, 35–36
"On Not Making It in America" (Zanger), 154
Once Were Warriors (Duff), 110, 119
oral medicines, 15, 18–19, 32, 84
"Oral Sources and the Creation of a Social History of the Caribbean" (Brodber), 41
orature, 18
Ozaeta, René, 1, 141

Pakeha, 109
patriarchal medicine, 11–12
Penn Center, 60, 69
Perrone, Bobette, 11, 20
Philip, Marlene Nourbese, 33, 110

Phillips, Caryl, 131
Philosophical Hermeneutics
    (Gadamer), 7
physiological metaphor, 17
Pillar of Salt (Memmi), 147
Plant Medicine (Grossinger), 9,
    16, 169
Plant, Richard, 149
Pleasure Principle (Freud), 15
"Politics of Maori Literature"
    (Evans), 112
Portnoy's Complaint (Roth),
    148
Praisesong for the Widow
    (Marshall), 28, 39, 47, 57, 58,
    64, 75, 97
"Preliminary Reflections on
    Magic and Music" (Sewell),
    18
"Psychic Healing" (Benor), 70
psychoanalytic movement:
    Jewish culture and, 144–145
Pueblo Scalp Ceremony, 90–91,
    92, 95, 97

"Racial" Economy of Science
    (Harding), 65
Rank, Otto, 145
Rastafarian culture, 32, 55, 85
Rastafarian healing practices,
    19, 43. *See also bone people*
Ravensong (Maracle), 82
Red Antway ceremony, 85
Reed, Ishmael, 60
Reichert, Gladys A., 84–85
Remen, Rachel Naomi, 144–145
Rich, Adrienne, 144, 159
Robinson, Beverly J., 58
"Rootedness: The Ancestor as
    Foundation" (Morrison), 59
Roots of Jamaican Culture
    (Alleyne), 19, 31
"Rootwork from a Clinician's
    Perspective" (Lichstein), 8
Roth, Philip, 146, 152, 166

Rothman, Stanley, 145
Ruppert, James, 86

Sachdev, Perminder S., 115
*Sacred Hoop: Recovering the
    Feminine in American
    Indian Tradition* (Gunn), 85,
    87
Salome of the Tenements
    (Yezierska), 143
salt, metaphorical/biological
    duality of, 176n6
Salt Eaters (Bambara), 28, 90, 95,
    100, 101, 107, 117, 123, 132,
    135, 158, 170; allusions, use
    of, 55; black doctors and the
    establishment in, 65–68;
    community effects of the
    healing, 76–77; complexity
    of, 55; conventional healing
    in, 65, 66; cultures as ill,
    concept of, 73; environmen-
    tal racism, 74–75; intimacy,
    horror of, 124; loa in, 62, 64,
    66–67, 69, 70, 72, 76; male
    healers in, 70; nuclear power/
    destruction in, 106; setting
    of, 56–57; socially con-
    structed diseases in, 73;
    suicide in, 62, 65, 75; title,
    significance of, 62, 65
Sandberg, Elisabeth, 149, 158
Sandner, Donald, 88
Scarberry-Garcia, Susan, 90
Schwarz-Bart, Simone, 28
Sea Island Roots (Twining and
    Baird), 56, 58
Sea Islands, slavery in, 56–57, 58
*Seasons: Death and Transfigura-
    tion* (Sinclair), 150, 160
Seid, Ruth. *See* Sinclair, Jo
selective tradition, 7
self-hate, 91, 170
Senior, Olive, 27–28
Sewell, Elizabeth, 18, 19, 21

Silko, Leslie Marmon, 3, 66, 111. *See also Ceremony*
Sinclair, Jo, 3. *See also Wasteland*
slavery, 56–57, 58
Solar Storms (Hogan), 82
somatic illness, Navajo view of, 95
"Some Character Types Met with in Psychoanalytic Work" (Freud), 1
Song of Solomon (Morrison), 57, 66, 70, 103
South Carolina, slavery in, 56–57
Sow, I., 30, 31, 32, 41, 51, 59, 61, 65, 69, 83, 120
Spider Woman, 178n1
spiritual, defined, 173n3
St. Andrews, B. A., 83, 84, 106
Stanford, Anne Folwell, 62
Stein, Diane, 11–12, 13, 14–15
stereotypes, 179n2, 183n13
Stockel, H. Henrietta, 11, 20
Sula (Morrison), 54
sustained narratives, 15–16
Swan, Edith, 99–100, 102–103

"talking cure," 19, 144
tapu, 110, 115
Taylor, Apirana, 129
Te Kaihau/The Windeater (Hulme), 110
Tempest, 44
Tenants (Malamud), 158
Terry, James S., 20
"The Reader's Lessons in *Ceremony*" (Ruppert), 86
"The Reawakening of the Gods" (Benediktsson), 129–130
Their Eyes Were Watching God (Hurston), 54
Third Life of Grange Copeland (Walker), 63, 119
Thought Woman, 82, 178n1

Tiffin, Helen, 32, 33
tohunga, 180n3
"Tony's Story" (Silko), 96
traditional healing, defined, 173n1
Trautmann, Joanne, 18
Traylor, Eleanor, 72
Tseng, Wen-Shing, 156, 157
Turner, Lorenzo, 56
Twining, Mary A., 58

Uffen, Ellen Serlen, 155, 166

"Violence as *Lingua Franca*" (Dever), 121

Walcott, Derek, 33
Walker, Alice, 27–28, 82
Walker-Johnson, Joyce, 50
Wambutda, Daniel, 59
Washington, Margaret, 61, 70–71
Wasteland (Sinclair [Seid]), 87, 117–118, 121–122, 135, 171, 193; ambiguities of, 149–150, 167–168; autobiographical elements in, 158, 166, 182n8–n9; community effects of the healing, 165–166; creative art in, 163–164, 165–166; descent/assent in, 142; double consciousness in, 152–153; feminized male, concept of, 162–163; historical period of writing of, 151; identity in, 126, 142–143, 163, 166; intercultural analysis in, 156–158; irony in, 154; isolation in, 154, 162; lesbianism in, 159–160, 163; "passing" in, 153, 157, 161; psychoanalysis as healing discourse in, 144; racism in, 160; self-hatred in, 153; structure of, 152

Wedenoja, William, 44
Weinberg, Sydney Stahn, 147
Welch, James, 101
Western concept of healing, 31
Western medicine, 11, 12, 14, 17; culture, role of, 8–9; defined, 173n1; mind/body split in, 1–2, 8, 19, 84; traditional healing, dismissal of, 9–10, 11
Whanau (Ihimaera), 113
Wide Sargasso Sea (Rhys), 29, 71
William, Raymond, 5, 9
Williams, Mark, 111, 117, 134
Winter in the Blood (Welch), 93, 101
witchery, 90, 93
Woman as Healer (Achterberg), 12–14, 61, 114
Woman Who Owned the Shadows (Allen), 82
women healers, 3; challenge to medical establishment, 14–15; holistic approach of, 12–13; role shift in con-temporary health care, 13–14
Women's Book of Healing (Stein), 11–12
Women's Ways of Knowing (Belenky), 4–5
World of Our Fathers (Howe), 147
World of Our Mothers (Weinberg), 147

Yellow Raft on Blue Water (Dorris), 82, 103
"Yellow Wallpaper, The" (Gilman), 17, 71
Yellow Woman, 179n7
Yezierska, Anzia, 143
"Yom Kippur 1984" (Rich), 144
Yoruba, 9, 57, 59, 72
Ywahoo, Dhyani, 83–84

Zami (Lorde), 72
Zanger, Jules, 154, 155
Zimmerman, Bonnie, 159
Zimra, Clarissa, 45

About the Author

Gay Wilentz is director of ethnic studies and professor of English at East Carolina University and visiting professor at the University of Belize. Her first critical work, *Binding Cultures: Black Women Writers in Africa and the Diaspora*, examines women's role in the transmission of culture on both sides of the Atlantic. Wilentz is the coeditor of Africa World Press' *Emerging Perspectives on Ama Ata Aidoo*, and she is the book editor of the reprinting of Jewish immigrant writer Anzia Yezierska's 1923 novel, *Salome of the Tenements*. She has also published in *College English*, *African American Review*, *Research in African Literatures*, *Twentieth Century Literature*, and *MELUS*, among others. She is presently working on a cultural study on blacks and Jews in the 1920s through an exploration of the friendship of Zora Neale Hurston and Fannie Hurst, as well as an anthology of Belizean women writers.